Java™ 2
Weekend Crash Course™

Java™ 2
Weekend Crash Course™

Julio Sanchez and Maria P. Canton

IDG
BOOKS
WORLDWIDE

IDG Books Worldwide, Inc.
An International Data Group Company
Foster City, CA • Chicago, IL • Indianapolis, IN • New York, NY

Java™ 2 Weekend Crash Course™
Published by
IDG Books Worldwide, Inc.
An International Data Group Company
919 E. Hillsdale Blvd., Suite 400
Foster City, CA 94404
www.idgbooks.com (IDG Books Worldwide Web site)

ISBN: 0-7645-4768-2
Printed in the United States of America
10 9 8 7 6 5 4 3 2 1
10/QX/RS/QQ/FC
Distributed in the United States by IDG Books Worldwide, Inc.
Distributed by CDG Books Canada Inc. for Canada; by Transworld Publishers Limited in the United Kingdom; by IDG Norge Books for Norway; by IDG Sweden Books for Sweden; by IDG Books Australia Publishing Corporation Pty. Ltd. for Australia and New Zealand; by TransQuest Publishers Pte Ltd. for Singapore, Malaysia, Thailand, Indonesia, and Hong Kong; by Gotop Information Inc. for Taiwan; by ICG Muse, Inc. for Japan; by Intersoft for South Africa; by Eyrolles for France; by International Thomson Publishing for Germany, Austria, and Switzerland; by Distribuidora Cuspide for Argentina; by LR International for Brazil; by Galileo Libros for Chile; by Ediciones ZETA S.C.R. Ltda. for Peru; by WS Computer Publishing Corporation, Inc., for the Philippines; by Contemporanea de Ediciones for Venezuela; by Express Computer Distributors for the Caribbean and West Indies; by Micronesia Media Distributor, Inc. for Micronesia; by Chips Computadoras S.A. de C.V. for Mexico; by Editorial Norma de Panama S.A. for Panama; by American Bookshops for Finland.

For general information on IDG Books Worldwide's books in the U.S., please call our Consumer Customer Service department at 800-762-2974. For reseller information, including discounts and premium sales, please call our Reseller Customer Service department at 800-434-3422.
For information on where to purchase IDG Books Worldwide's books outside the U.S., please contact our International Sales department at 317-572-3993 or fax 317-572-4002.
For consumer information on foreign language translations, please contact our Customer Service department at 800-434-3422, fax 317-572-4002, or e-mail rights@idgbooks.com.
For information on licensing foreign or domestic rights, please phone +1-650-653-7098.
For sales inquiries and special prices for bulk quantities, please contact our Order Services department at 800-434-3422 or write to the address above.
For information on using IDG Books Worldwide's books in the classroom or for ordering examination copies, please contact our Educational Sales department at 800-434-2086 or fax 317-572-4005.
For press review copies, author interviews, or other publicity information, please contact our Public Relations department at 650-653-7000 or fax 650-653-7500.
For authorization to photocopy items for corporate, personal, or educational use, please contact Copyright Clearance Center, 222 Rosewood Drive, Danvers, MA 01923, or fax 978-750-4470.

Library of Congress Cataloging-in-Publication Data
Canton, Maria P.
    Java 2 weekend crash course / Maria P. Canton, Julio Sanchez.
        p. cm.
    Includes index.
    ISBN 0-7645-4768-2 (alk. paper)
    1. Java (Computer program language)
I. Sánchez, Julio. II. Title.
QA76.73.J38 C367   2000
005.13'3--dc21   00-047150

ABOUT IDG BOOKS WORLDWIDE

Welcome to the world of IDG Books Worldwide.

IDG Books Worldwide, Inc., is a subsidiary of International Data Group, the world's largest publisher of computer-related information and the leading global provider of information services on information technology. IDG was founded more than 30 years ago by Patrick J. McGovern and now employs more than 9,000 people worldwide. IDG publishes more than 290 computer publications in over 75 countries. More than 90 million people read one or more IDG publications each month.

Launched in 1990, IDG Books Worldwide is today the #1 publisher of best-selling computer books in the United States. We are proud to have received eight awards from the Computer Press Association in recognition of editorial excellence and three from Computer Currents' First Annual Readers' Choice Awards. Our best-selling ...*For Dummies®* series has more than 50 million copies in print with translations in 31 languages. IDG Books Worldwide, through a joint venture with IDG's Hi-Tech Beijing, became the first U.S. publisher to publish a computer book in the People's Republic of China. In record time, IDG Books Worldwide has become the first choice for millions of readers around the world who want to learn how to better manage their businesses.

Our mission is simple: Every one of our books is designed to bring extra value and skill-building instructions to the reader. Our books are written by experts who understand and care about our readers. The knowledge base of our editorial staff comes from years of experience in publishing, education, and journalism — experience we use to produce books to carry us into the new millennium. In short, we care about books, so we attract the best people. We devote special attention to details such as audience, interior design, use of icons, and illustrations. And because we use an efficient process of authoring, editing, and desktop publishing our books electronically, we can spend more time ensuring superior content and less time on the technicalities of making books.

You can count on our commitment to deliver high-quality books at competitive prices on topics you want to read about. At IDG Books Worldwide, we continue in the IDG tradition of delivering quality for more than 30 years. You'll find no better book on a subject than one from IDG Books Worldwide.

John Kilcullen
Chairman and CEO
IDG Books Worldwide, Inc.

Eighth Annual Computer Press Awards ➤1992

Ninth Annual Computer Press Awards ➤1993

Tenth Annual Computer Press Awards ➤1994

Eleventh Annual Computer Press Awards ➤1995

Credits

Acquisitions Editor
Greg Croy

Project Editors
Andy Marinkovich
Neil Romanosky

Technical Editor
David M. Williams

Copy Editors
Richard H. Adin
Chris Jones

Project Coordinators
Joe Shines
Danette Nurse

Quality Control Technician
Dina F Quan

Graphics and Production Specialists
Robert Bihlmayer
Jude Levinson
Michael Lewis
Victor Pérez-Varela
Ramses Ramirez

Permissions Editor
Laura Moss

Media Development Specialist
Angela Denny

Media Development Coordinator
Marisa Pearman

Book Designer
Evan Deerfield

Illustrators
Gabriele McCann
Shelley Norris

Proofreading and Indexing
York Production Services

About the Authors

Julio Sanchez is an associate professor of computer science at Minnesota State University, Mankato. Julio is the author of 18 books in the field of computer programming, six of which have been translated into foreign languages. He teaches courses and seminars in Java programming, C++, and Windows.

Maria P. Canton is an assistant professor of computer science at Minnesota State University, Mankato. Maria is the president of Skipanon Software Company, a programming and consulting company in business since 1983. She is the principal author of one book and the coauthor of 14 other titles in the field of computer programming.

Preface

This book is for people who want to learn to program in Java. No experience in Java or in any other programming language is required, although you should have basic familiarity with the PC and the Windows operating system, as well as keyboarding skills. The book's focus is Java as a full-featured programming language used in application development. It is not about developing Java applets for the World Wide Web. The book supports Java 2 and Java 2D. It includes a CD-ROM with shareware programs and sample code mentioned in the text.

Who Should Read this Book

This book is for you if you wish to learn Java programming on a PC and have some experience using Microsoft Windows. It is also for you if you have learned Java but need to review or refresh your skills.

Java™ 2 Weekend Crash Course™ is designed to teach you the fundamentals of Java programming in a series of short lessons you can cover in one weekend. The first session starts Friday evening, and the last session ends Sunday afternoon. There are 30 sessions, each requiring approximately one-half hour.

About Programming

Mastering programming starts with learning to communicate with the alien being we call a computer. The task is not a difficult one, but giving orders to a machine requires some psychological adjustments.

We are used to dealing with human beings. In communicating with people, we assume a considerable amount of worldly knowledge, some common sense, and a few social skills. Our instructions to a fellow human often lack details we consider unnecessary. Computers, on the other hand, have no knowledge of the world, no common sense, and no social skills. If you omit a detail in a set of instructions to a human being, you can often assume that the human knows what you mean and will perform the task anyway. With a computer program, on the other hand, you must be totally explicit and must cover every detail of execution. Machines never *know* what you mean — they have to be told in no uncertain terms.

In *Java 2 Weekend Crash Course*, we start from the assumption that learning programming means learning to think like a computer. Often, the most important task in developing a program is coming up with logic that solves each problem.

What's in the Book

The book begins by introducing the Java programming language and explaining the keywords and fundamental constructs. At first, we rely on your intuition. We postpone the details and complications of the language. Applied to programming, the Paretto principle states that 20 percent of a language solves 80 percent of the problems. In this part of the book, we present the 20 percent of Java that does 80 percent of the work.

Once we cover the fundamentals of the language, we shift the focus to object-orientation. Java is a pure, object-oriented language. This means that a Java program statement resides within a structure of classes and objects. We use class diagrams and object-oriented analysis to acquaint you with the style of object-oriented programming. At this stage, our emphasis is to force you to "think objects" and to avoid the conventional crutches of structured programming. Inheritance, encapsulation, polymorphism, and dynamic binding are concepts that underlie the discussion. We stress the use of the this operator so that object references are always clear to the programmer. Object composition techniques, including arrays of objects and objects as parameters, are among the most powerful constructs of object-oriented programming. We introduce these elements early and revisit them often.

Java is a small language. We achieve most of the functionality required in a commercial application by means of the Java Libraries. However, learning to use these libraries is no menial task. The number of available libraries, classes, and methods can be intimidating. In addition, the libraries are based on sophisticated inheritance and object-composition constructs, which make them both powerful and complex. The book is designed to make sure you acquire all the background knowledge and programming maturity necessary to understand and use the Java libraries.

Operating systems with graphical user interfaces (GUIs) have gained predominance in recent years, making text-based programs a rarity. However, we continue to teach programming languages as we did in the days when DOS was king. One reason we do this is that graphics programming has always been considered difficult and complicated. However, Java has changed this. To make code portable, the Java language designers were forced to simplify the graphical interface and hide many programming complications. The result is that it is easier for us to master graphics in Java and to develop GUI applications. The final part of the book covers graphics programming in Java and the development of full-featured GUI applications for Windows.

Organization and Presentation

We organize the book into 30 sessions, each requiring approximately 30 minutes. We divide the sessions as follows:

- Friday evening. Sessions 1 through 4. Reading time: 2 hours.
- Saturday morning. Sessions 5 through 10. Reading time: 3 hours
- Saturday afternoon. Sessions 11 through 16. Reading time: 3 hours.
- Saturday evening. Sessions 17 through 20. Reading time: 2 hours.
- Sunday morning. Sessions 21 through 26. Reading time: 3 hours.
- Sunday afternoon. Sessions 27 through 30. Reading time: 2 hours.

At the end of each session, we present questions designed to check your progress.

The text is sprinkled with icons designed to catch your attention.

The "minutes to go" icons mark your progress in the session.

**30 Min.
To Go**

The Tip icons offer suggestions on style and mention shortcuts that can save programming effort.

The Note icons highlight incidental or technical information that clarifies and expands the discussion.

The CD-ROM icon refers to material furnished on the book's CD. Use it to find electronic versions of programs and software elements mentioned in the text.

Contacting the Authors

We can't guarantee we will solve all your Java-programming problems in this book, but we promise to take a look at your questions and see if we can help. If you get stuck, you can contact us at the following e-mail addresses:

    julio.sanchez@mankato.msus.edu
    cantom@mail.mankato.msus.edu

Acknowledgments

In this project, we have been very lucky to have the collaboration of many talented professionals. First, we would like to thank Greg Croy, the acquisitions editor, who made the book possible. The project editors, Neil Romanosky and Andy Marinkovich, directed and supervised the editorial and production processes and furnished many useful comments and suggestions. David Williams, the technical editor, detected several inconsistencies and pointed out better ways to approach some of the most difficult topics. Chris Jones and Richard Adin, copy editors, provided corrections and suggestions that made the book more consistent and readable. We also thank Colleen Totz, editorial manager; Joe Shines, the project coordinator; and Laura Carpenter in Media Development. We could not have wished for a more capable team.

Contents at a Glance

Contents

Java™ 2
Weekend Crash Course™

☑ **Friday**

☐ Saturday

☐ Sunday

Part I — Friday Evening

PART

I

Friday
Evening

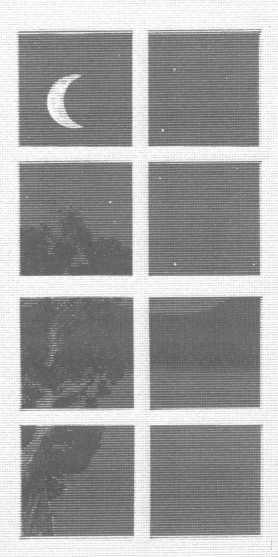

Introducing Java

Session Checklist

✔ The Java language

✔ Portability: A key to Java's instant success

✔ Java's fundamental characteristics

✔ The Java libraries

✔ Using flowcharts to develop your programs

**30 Min.
To Go**

The first version of the Java programming language was released in late 1995, and it was successful instantly. In a few months, Java became the preferred programming language of the World Wide Web and, a few years later, one of the most commonly used general-purpose programming languages ever developed.

Java's success is due to many factors. Perhaps the most important factor is its timeliness. The Java language was first released when the World Wide Web was rapidly gaining popularity. The Web is an international network of basically incompatible computers. Using scores of operating systems and software environments, dozens of manufacturers make the machines, each with unique hardware characteristics. To this world of variation and irreconcilable differences, Java brings a promise of uniformity and compatibility. Java's promise is that a program written in this language will execute on any Java-compatible machine. This means that a programmer can code a small application in a Java applet. This applet, typically contained in a Web page, runs on any browser that supports Java and on any machine. Thus, Java provides a way of extending the functionality of Web browsers in a way that is hardware-independent.

 The language used to create Web pages and other Internet documents is called HTML (Hypertext Markup Language). Java code can be embedded in HTML documents in a capsule called a Java applet.

With Java you can create a Web page that performs processing operations that exceed HTML's capabilities. This processing is contained in a Java applet that runs on any Java-enabled browser, such as Mosaic, Netscape Navigator, or Internet Explorer. The applet executes correctly on a PC running Windows, on a Macintosh, on a UNIX machine, or on an IBM mainframe. The result is the same if you are connected to the Internet through a high-speed network or a slow-speed modem. This platform-independence makes Java unique.

The Portability Issue

Initially, Java's portability related to applets intended for the Web. Soon it became evident that a full-featured Java programming language would make it possible to develop complete applications that would be portable to any Java-supporting platform. Not only could a Java programmer develop a routine to embed in HTML code but also could use the language to create a full-featured application that would be machine- and platform-independent.

The benefits of this machine-independence extend beyond the obvious problems related to hardware incompatibility. In the rapidly-evolving world of personal computers, operating systems are changing at a rate often faster than hardware. In the late 1990's the same machine could run a half dozen versions of MS DOS, Windows 3.0/3.1, Windows 95, Windows 98, Windows 2000, NT 3.1, 3.5, 4.0, or Windows CE, and Linux. Applications have to be constructed taking into account many variations in the system software to make them compatible with a given subset of software and hardware environments. Restricting an application to a specific hardware and software configuration may lose potential customers. The resulting task is often a programming nightmare in which the code has to take into account many software and hardware variations.

Java promises a simplification of the programming task and a solution to incompatibility problems. No longer does the programmer have to deal with a "moving target" of hardware and operating software incompatibilities. Instead, Java proposes a new model for software development, based on the principle: "Code Once, Run Anywhere." Furthermore, Java serves to "future proof" your code by ensuring that it will continue to run in the machines and operating systems of the future.

The following section is a description of Java as a programming language. If you are anxious to get on to more practical topics, you can skip it or read it lightly.

The Language of Java

Another reason for Java's success is that it is syntactically similar to C and C++. This makes it easy for C and C++ programmers to learn Java. In addition, someone who learns Java as a first language can pick up C and C++ later without much effort.

As a language, Java is *strongly-typed*. This means that all data types are statically bound; in other words, each variable name is associated with a single data type and this data type is known at compile time. In a strongly-typed language, type errors are always and promptly detected. This prevents the misuse of variables and makes the code more reliable. C and C++ are not as strongly typed as Java because these languages have looser type checking.

The designers of Java proposed to solve several problems that had plagued C and C++ and to eliminate features that were considered non-essential. Java differs from C and C++ in the following ways:

- In Java, memory address operations, sometimes called pointer arithmetic, are handled internally by the language.
- Java has no language preprocessor; therefore, there are no preprocessor directives.
- Java does not perform automatic type conversions. This is one of the reasons why Java is more strongly typed than C and C++.
- Java has no global functions or variables. Every Java program element must exist inside a class.
- Java does not support type definitions by means of the `typedef` operator.
- Java does not support templates.

- Java does not allow explicit operator overloading.
- Java does not support multiple inheritance.

What this all means is that Java is a smaller and simpler language than C and C++. It is easier to learn and to use and is more reliable.

In comparing Java and C++ we have used terms with which you may not be familiar. The same is true with other statements in this Section. You can safely ignore these terms now, since we will later cover these topics.

One interesting feature of the Java language, which is mandated by its portability objective, is that the size of the data types is the same for all platforms. For example, an `int` primitive data type must be encoded in 32-bit signed 2's complement representation in every platform to which Java is ported. The same applies to all other built-in data types.

In contrast with C and C++, Java performs automatic garbage collection at run time. The language, not the programmer, takes care of reclaiming storage that is no longer in use. This simplifies the coding and program design.

Java also supports multithreading. A thread can be loosely defined as an individual program task. Multithreading allows an application to perform several tasks simultaneously. By supporting thread synchronization and scheduling, as well as the handling of deadlocks, Java makes it possible to develop code that makes better use of system resources and enhances performance.

Java allows the programmer to deal with error conditions by means of exceptions. This simplifies the code and reduces clutter by offloading the error processing operations.

Finally, Java is free. Sun Microsystems provides Java compilers, run-time, and standard libraries free of charge. You can download software from the Sun Web sites at no cost, and you do not have to pay royalties to use it.

You can sell the programs you build using Java software without displaying acknowledgements, disclaimers, or other statements of acceptance or recognition.

Java Libraries

The Java language is quite small. Two types of libraries extend its functionality: the core libraries that are part of the Java Development Kit (JDK) and the optional library additions. The core libraries must be present in every implementation of Java, although the optional libraries can be present or not. However, if a feature in

**20 Min.
To Go**

an optional library is supported in a particular implementation, it must be fully supported in the standard way.

The number and complexity of the Java libraries is impressive and can intimidate a beginning programmer. Version 1.2 of the JDK has 12 core libraries with a total of 1391 classes. Table 1-1 lists the core Java libraries.

Table 1-1
Core Java Libraries in JDK 1.2

Name	classes	Description
java.lang	93	Basic runtime support for the Java language. Threads, reflection, and exceptions.
java.applet	4	Applets support
java.awt	298	Windowing and GUI support
javax.swing	500	Supplements java.awt and improves GUI support
java.io	75	Supports input and output
java.util	77	Utility data structures
java.rmi	65	Remote method calls
java.sql	26	Supports Java Database Connectivity
java.security	106	Supports secure data coding and decoding
java.net	38	TCP/IP, UDP, IP, and other network support
java.beans	43	Component software support to promote rapid application development by reuse of existing code fragments
java.text	50	Support for localized text elements such as dates, times, and currency
java.math	2	Support for the DECIMAL and NUMERIC types in the SQL database. Do not confuse with java.lang.Math class
javax.accessibility	14	Supports large text sizes for the visually impaired

**10 Min.
To Go**

The Elements of a Java Program

Java is an interpreted language. An application called the Java interpreter executes a Java program. The Java interpreter must be installed in the host system. The Java interpreter is named *Java*. The interpreter reads the code contained in a file produced by the Java compiler, called *Javac*. The compiler, in turn, reads a source file written in the Java programming language. The result of the compilation step is a file usually called the Java byte code. The Java source file, which serves as input to the compiler, has the extension **.java**. The Java byte code file generated by the Javac compiler has the extension **.class**. The Java interpreter executes the file with the **.class** extension.

Programming Logic

A program, in general terms, is a sequential set of instructions designed to perform a specific task. In this sense, the instructions you would follow to start up a particular automobile model could be described as the start-up program for that vehicle. A computer program, on the other hand, consists of logical instructions that make the computer perform a specific function. A computer program that calculates the interest that accrues when you invest a given amount of money at a certain rate for a specific period of time is an example. In both cases, the concept of a program requires instructions that follow a sequential order and a predictable result. Haphazard instructions that lead to no predictable end do not make a program.

The Flowchart

Computer scientists have come up with logical aids that help develop computer programs. A *flowchart* is one of the simplest and most useful of these aids. A flowchart is a graphical representation of the options and actions that form a program. It is a diagram with graphic symbols that represent and describe different types of program operations. Figure 1-1 shows the more common flowchart symbols.

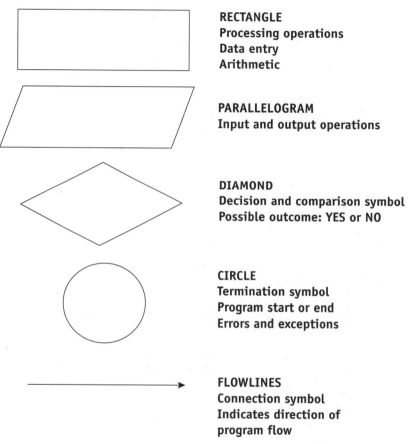

RECTANGLE
Processing operations
Data entry
Arithmetic

PARALLELOGRAM
Input and output operations

DIAMOND
Decision and comparison symbol
Possible outcome: YES or NO

CIRCLE
Termination symbol
Program start or end
Errors and exceptions

FLOWLINES
Connection symbol
Indicates direction of
program flow

Figure 1-1
Flowcharting symbols

The use of a flowchart is best shown with an example. Consider a program for turning on a computer in which you can connect the components to the power line in three possible ways:

1. All components are connected to a power strip, which is connected to the wall outlet.

2. All components are connected directly to the wall outlet.

3. Some components are connected to a power strip and some are connected directly to wall outlets.

The logic for turning on this system first requires investigating if all components are connected to a power strip. In this case, switching on the power strip turns on the system. The second possibility is that all components are connected individually to wall outlets. In this case, we must individually switch on each component. The third possibility is that some components are connected to a power strip and some are connected directly to wall outlets. In this case, we must switch on the individual components as well as the power strip to turn on the system. A flowchart can express this logic, as shown in Figure 1-2.

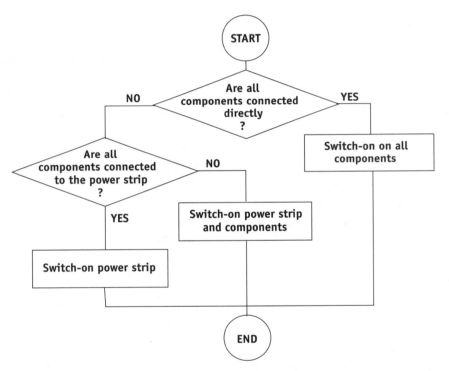

Figure 1-2
Flowchart for starting-up a computer system

Note that the diamond symbols represent program decisions in Figure 1-2. These decisions are based on elementary logic, which requires two choices but not more than two. These possible answers are usually labeled YES and NO in the flowchart. Decisions are the crucial points in the logic. A program that requires no decisions or comparisons consists of such simple logic that a flowchart is probably unnecessary.

For instance, a flowchart that consists of three processing steps (start, solve problem, and end) is not very useful.

Done!

Computing machines do not have human-like intelligence. For this reason, obvious assumptions when dealing with human beings may be invalid regarding computers. Computer programs can leave no loose ends and can make no presumption of reasonable behavior. You cannot tell a computer "well...you know what I mean!" or assume that a certain operation is so obvious that you do not need to state it explicitly. You can use a flowchart to make certain that each processing step is clearly defined and that the operations are performed in the required sequence.

REVIEW

Java originated as a Web tool, and it evolved into a full-fledged, portable programming language. Java is related to the languages C and C++ and has considerable similarities, as well as some differences, with them. Java achieves the functionality of its languages through its libraries. The Java libraries are free of charge and easy to use. Sun Microsystems, the developer of the Java language, provides interactive documentation on their functions. Flowcharts are development tools that help you define and describe the logical steps necessary in a program.

QUIZ YOURSELF

1. Why was the Java language an unprecedented success? (See "About Java.")
2. What is Java's greatest promise? (See "The Portability Issue.")
3. List two similarities and two differences between Java and C++. (See "Java, the Language.")

Loading and Installing Java

Session Checklist

✔ The Java Software Development Kit (JDK)

✔ System Requirements

✔ Downloading the JDK from the Java Website

✔ Installing the JDK in Windows

✔ Setting the PATH variable

✔ Setting the CLASSPATH

I n this chapter, we discuss loading and installing the Java Software Development Kit, which Sun Microsystems provides free of charge. You need to install Java in your system before you can start programming in Java.

**30 Min.
To Go**

The instructions in this session refer to installing Java in a PC running Windows 95, 98, 2000, or Windows NT. Instructions for loading and installing Java in other platforms are available at the Sun Microsystems Web site.

Java Software

The Java Software Development Kit, called the JDK, is available for download at the Sun Microsystems Java software Web site at:

```
http://java.sun.com
```

The Web site provides useful Java programming information, JDK documentation, demos, and answers to frequently asked questions (FAQ). The current version of the Java Development Kit is 1.3.

Also notice that the development tools available for the Windows platform are designed for use from the MS DOS command line. The appleviewer utility is the only tool that provides a graphical user interface. Appleviewer is part of the JDK package.

System Requirements

The Java 2 JDK is available for the following platforms:

- Win32 Version for Windows 95, Windows 98, Windows 2000, and Windows NT 4.0 on Intel hardware. This version requires a 486/DX or faster processor and a minimum of 32 megabytes RAM minimum.
- Solaris/SPARC Version. Versions 2.5.1, 2.6 and 7 are supported. Requires 32 megabytes of RAM minimum.
- Solaris/Intel Version. Versions 2.5.1, 2.6 and 7 are supported. Requires a 486/DX or faster processor and 32 megabytes RAM.

 In this book we primarily consider the Win32 version of the JDK.

The installation requires 65 megabytes of disk space on all systems. The documentation takes up an additional 90 megabytes of free disk space.

**20 Min.
To Go**

Downloading the Software

The Software Development Kit requires you to download three different components:

- The Java JDK software
- The JDK installation instructions
- The JDK documentation

The installation instructions are available at a different Web site, and you must download them separately. The Web addresses are:

Win32 Installation Instructions:

```
http://java.sun.com/products/jdk/1.2/install-windows.html
```

Solaris Installation Instructions:

```
http://java.sun.com/products/jdk/1.2/install-solaris.html
```

The Java 2 JDK Documentation is available online. It contains API specifications, developer guides, tool references, demos, and links to other related information. You can download the documentation from the following Web site:

```
http://java.sun.com/products/jdk/1.2/docs/
```

Table 2-1 lists other useful Web pages at the Sun Microsystems Java software Web site.

Table 2-1
Useful Java Web Pages

Address	Contents
java.sun.com/products/jdk/1.2/	JDK and documentation.
java.sun.com/	The Java Software Web site. Has the latest information on Java technology, products, and development news.
java.sun.com/products/jdk/1.2/index.html	Java 2 JDK products and download page.

Continued

Table 2-1 *Continued*

Address	Contents
java.sun.com/docs	Java platform documentation. Access to white papers, tutorials, and other documents.
developer.java.sun.com/	The Java Developer Connection Web site. (Free registration required.) Contains additional technical information, news, and features.
java.sun.com/products/	Java Technology Products & API.
www.sun.com/solaris/java/	Java Development Kit for Solaris.

You can download the Java software development kit from the Java Web site as a single file or as a set of fifteen individual files that you must later link (concatenate) to form a single unit. The reason for the multiple-files option is that the entire package takes up approximately 20MB. Some users that connect to the Java Web site with a modem may prefer to download several small packages rather than a single large one. Loading several small chunks makes transmission errors less costly. However, if you have a reliable Web connection, it is easier to download the JDK as a single file.

When you download the JDK in individual chunk files, you have the following individual files in the download directory:

```
jdk1_2_2-001-win-a.exe
jdk1_2_2-001-win-b.exe
jdk1_2_2-001-win-c.exe

...
jdk1_2_2-001-win-o.exe
```

In order to concatenate the fifteen individual files into a single file, you must execute the following MS DOS command:

```
C:\> copy /b jdk1_2_2-001-win-a.exe +
     jdk1_2_2-001-win-b.exe + jdk1_2_2-001-win-c.exe +
     jdk1_2_2-001-win-d.exe + jdk1_2_2-001-win-e.exe +
     jdk1_2_2-001-win-f.exe + jdk1_2_2-001-win-g.exe +
     jdk1_2_2-001-win-h.exe + jdk1_2_2-001-win-i.exe +
     jdk1_2_2-001-win-j.exe + jdk1_2_2-001-win-k.exe +
     jdk1_2_2-001-win-l.exe + jdk1_2_2-001-win-m.exe +
```

```
jdk1_2_2-001-win-n.exe + jdk1_2_2-001-win-o.exe
jdk1_2_2-001-win.exe
```

The resulting file is a self-extracting archive that decompresses all the JDK components and installs them in your system.

**10 Min.
To Go**

Installing Java in Windows

Installing the Java development software is a simple matter of running the self-extracting archive mentioned in the previous section. You may run the Java 2 JDK installer from the MS DOS command line, or you may double-click the icon for **jdk1_2_2-001-win.exe** in Windows Explorer.

After the Java 2 JDK software installer unpacks the installation files, it displays a screen with a license agreement. When you accept the agreement, the installation program displays a destination location selector for the software, as shown in Figure 2-1.

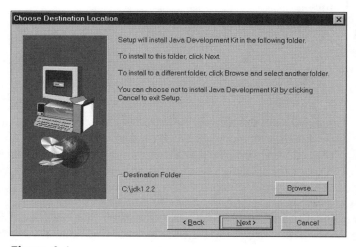

Figure 2-1
Java JDK destination location selector

You can accept the default location or click on the Browse button to select a different one. If your system has sufficient space on the default drive, it is a good idea to use the default path. Changing to another drive or directory may create installation problems in some versions of Windows.

The installer program decompresses the JDK files, creates the necessary directories, and copies the files to these directories. Figure 2-2 shows the first three levels of the directory tree that results from installation.

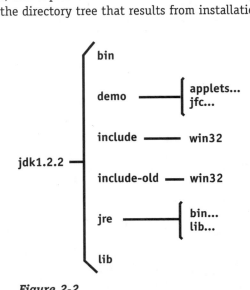

Figure 2-2
Java JDK directory tree

Setting the PATH Variable

When the MS DOS program loader executes, it automatically searches the current directory for the target file. If the program or batch file is not in the current directory, the loader searches all other drives and directories in the system path variable. Use the MS DOS PATH command to specify these additional drives and directories.

You do not need the path variable to use the Java development tools as long as all the necessary software is in the current directory, nor do you need the path variable when you type the entire pathname in the command line. However, it is convenient to set the path variable so that the system searches automatically for the development software. The path, in this case, is the drive and directory address where **java.exe**, **javac.exe**, **javadoc.exe**, and other development applications are located. If you perform the installation in the default drive and directory, the path to the development software is the following:

```
C:\jdk1.2.2\bin
```

Otherwise, the path is the drive and directories you select at installation time.

The MS DOS system PATH command is usually in the **autoexec.bat** file, which is executed during system startup and permanently sets the path variable. Alternatively, you can enter the PATH command from the MS DOS command line. The syntax of the path command is as follows:

```
PATH=[drive:][path];[drive:][path]...]
```

For example, if you install the Java software in the default directory, the path command is:

```
PATH=C:\jdk1.2.2\bin
```

More than one drive:\directory specifications can be in a single path command. In this case, semi-colons separate the individual subpaths, as follows:

```
PATH=C:\jdk1.2.2\bin;D:\Corel8\data;
```

In Windows 95, 98, and 2000, setting a permanent path consists of editing the autoexec.bat file so that it contains the required PATH command. You can accomplish this in several ways. One way is to start the system editor by choosing "Start," "Run," typing, and "sysedit" in the edit box and by clicking OK. When the system editor starts, several windows appear on the screen. Select the Window that contains the **autoexec.bat** file, and look for an existing PATH command. If one is available, add the path to the Java development software. Make sure the new path is preceded by a semi-colon, for example:

```
PATH=C:\Windows;C:\Windows\Command;C:\jdk1.2.2\bin
```

Figure 2-3 shows the PATH command in the corresponding system editor window.

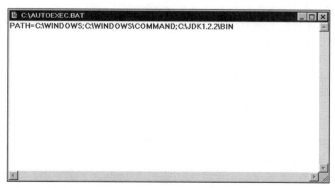

Figure 2-3
Setting the PATH variable (Windows 95/98/2000)

To set the new path effect without restarting the system, you can execute the **autoexec.bat** file from the MS DOS command prompt, as follows:

```
C:> c:\autoexec.bat
```

To make sure the new path is installed, type the PATH command at the MS DOS command prompt, as follows:

```
C:> path
```

MS DOS now displays the current path, which should include the drive:\ directory where the Java development software is located.

In Windows NT, you must set the path differently. First, start the Control Panel, select System, then Environment, and look for "Path" in the User Variables and System Variables. You can add the path to the Java development software at the right end of the "Path" in the User Variables. Here again, the system ignores capitalization. After you enter the path, click "Set," "OK," or "Apply." In Windows NT, the new path takes effect when you open the MS DOS Command Prompt window.

Setting the CLASSPATH

At compile time a Java program must usually have access to other Java classes. The classpath variable tells the Java compiler where the class files are. More exactly, the classpath variable signals the location of a special file named **tools.jar**, which contains the paths to the Java system classes. The classpath variable contains the location of the **tools.jar** file.

In the current version of the Java JDK, assuming that you use default installation, **tools.jar** is located in the following path:

```
C:\jdk1.2.2\lib\tools.jar
```

If this is not the case, you can locate the **tools.jar** file by using the Find command in the Tools menu of the Windows Explorer utility. When you determine the location of the **tools.jar** file, you must enter its address in the **autoexec.bat** file using the CLASSPATH command. For example:

```
SET CLASSPATH=.;C:\jdk1.2.2\lib\tools.jar;
```

Notice that the CLASSPATH command starts with the . ; symbols. This ensures that the system searches for class files in the current directory.

Edit the **autoexec.bat** file so that it includes the CLASSPATH command by following the instructions previously listed for the PATH command. Figure 2-4 shows

CLASSPATH commands in a system in which the Java software is installed in the default location.

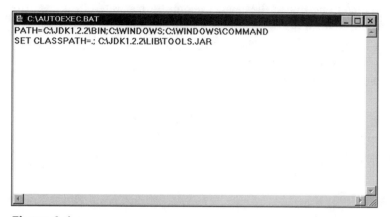

Figure 2-4
Setting the CLASSPATH variable (Windows 95/98/2000)

Here again, you can set classpath without restarting the system by executing the **autoexec.bat** file from the MS DOS command prompt, as follows:

```
C:> c:\autoexec.bat
```

To make sure the new classpath is installed, type the following command at the MS DOS command prompt:

```
C:> echo %classpath%
```

Done!

MS DOS now displays the current classpath, which should refer to the drive:\directory where the **tools.jar** file is located.

REVIEW

Programming in Java requires you to have the Java development software available. This package, usually called the JDK, is provided free of charge by Sun Microsystems and is available at their Web site. In this session, you have learned how to download and install the JDK in a Windows computer; also, you have learned how to set the path and classpath variables so that the development software operates correctly.

QUIZ YOURSELF

1. Are you able to download the Java development software (JDK) from the Sun Microsystems Web site? (See "Downloading the Software.")

2. Are you able to install the JDK in your Windows system? (See "Installing Java in Windows.")

3. Have you set the `path` variable for your system (See "Setting the PATH Variable.")

4. Have you set the `classpath` (See "Setting the CLASSPATH.")

Creating a Java Program

Session Checklist

✔ Selecting an editor program

✔ Developing the HelloJava program

✔ Basic rules of the Java language

✔ Program analysis

✔ Compiling and running the sample program

**30 Min.
To Go**

In this session, we develop a simple Java program called "HelloJava." The program does nothing more than display a message on the screen. The idea is to get you programming in Java as quickly as possible, but even the simplest computer program requires understanding many new concepts. At this point, we have relied on your intuition and have left many language details partially, or even totally, unexplained. In the sessions that follow, we look at program elements in increasing levels of detail.

Selecting an Editor Program

We assume that you have installed the Java development software, also called the JDK, and that you have set the PATH and CLASSPATH command as described in Session 2. To create a Java program, you need one additional software tool: a text editor for creating the Java source file.

Several text editors are available for a PC. *Edit* is the MS DOS editor, and *Notepad* and *Wordpad* work in Windows. Although any of these programs can serve in a pinch, all three have drawbacks. Edit, the MS DOS editor, mangles filenames that contain more than 8 characters. This makes it difficult to navigate through typical Windows folders, which usually have long names. To use Edit, you may consider placing all your source files in a first-level directory with a short name.

Notepad and Wordpad are Microsoft editors that run in Windows. Wordpad is the more powerful of the two. The main objection to using these editors for Java programming is that they do not save a file with the extension **.java**. Instead, Wordpad and Notepad add the extension of the selected text type. For example, if you attempt to save a file under the name **Demo.java**, either editor appends the extension of the selected text type. In this case, if the selected file type is a text document, the editor names the resulting file **Demo.java.txt**. The result is that you need to edit the filename before you run the compiler. Some versions of Microsoft Word have the same problem.

Note that when you use Save As and select All files (*.*), neither Notepad nor Wordpad adds an extension, so you can use .java without having to edit the filename later.

The HelloJava Program

In the first edition of their now-classic book, *The C Programming Language*, authors Kernighan and Ritchie introduce the language with a simple program that displays a screen message with the text "Hello World." Many programming books follow suit. Our Java version of the Hello World program is as follows:

```
//   Java version of the Hello World program
//   Developed for the book "Java 2 Weekend Crash Course"
//   by IDG Books Worldwide
public class HelloJava
{
  public static void main(String[] args)
```

```
    {
       System.out.println("Hello World from Java");
    }
  }
```

The Basic Rules

20 Min. To Go

Before we attempt to analyze the code in the HelloJava program, we should note some general rules of syntax the Java language uses:

- Java is case-sensitive. When you type Java code, you must be careful to use the correct upper- and lower-case letters. In Java programming, the words *Main* and *main* are different.

- In general, Java ignores white space. White space consists of characters that do not appear on the screen, such as blanks, tabs, returns, and others used in formatting text. Use white space to make the code more pleasant and more readable.

- Braces {} are grouping symbols in Java. They mark the beginning and end of a program section. A Java program has an equal number of left and right braces. A *block* is the section of a Java program between braces. Because Java ignores white space, you can choose among several styles of braces. For example:

```
    {  public.static void main (...
```

  or

```
    {
       public.static void main(...
```

- Every Java statement ends in the ; symbol. A statement is a program element (expression) that generates a processing action. Not every Java expression is a statement.

- Computer programs contain *comments,* text that clarifies or explains the code. A special symbol must precede comments so that the compiler ignores the text. Java offers two ways to insert comments:

  The // symbol creates a comment that extends to the end of the line. For example:

```
    // This is a single-line comment
```

  The // symbol can appear anywhere in a program line.

/* and */ symbols delimit a comment that can span more than one line, for example:

```
/* This is a
   multiple line
   comment  */
```

Program Headers

Most programs begin with several commented lines, sometimes called the program header. Usually, these lines contain the following elements:

- The program name
- The name of the author or authors
- A copyright notice, if one is appropriate
- The date of program creation
- A description of the program's purpose and basic functionality
- A history of program changes and updates
- A list of the tools used in developing the program
- A description of the software and hardware environment required to run the program

Most programmers create their own standard program headers, which they paste into all their sources. The following is a general-purpose program header that you can adapt to suit your needs.

```
//**********************************************************
//**********************************************************
//  Program name
//  Copyright (c) 200? by
//  ALL RIGHTS RESERVED
//**********************************************************
//**********************************************************
// Date:                      Coded by:
// Filename:                  Module name:
//                            Source file:
// Program description:
//
//**********************************************************
```

```
// Libraries and software support:
//
//****************************************************************
// Development environment:
//
//****************************************************************
// System requirements:
//
//****************************************************************
// Start date:
// Update history:
//              DATE           MODIFICATION
//
//****************************************************************
// Test history:
//  TEST PROTOCOL              DATE        TEST RESULTS
//
//****************************************************************
// Programmer comments:
//
//
//****************************************************************
//****************************************************************
```

The preceding sample header is in the Session 3 directory on this book's CD-ROM. The name of the file is HeaderTemplate.java

Program Analysis

We now examine the **HelloJava** program line-by-line. The entire program is re-listed for your convenience:

```
//    Java version of the Hello World program
//    Developed for the book "Java 2 Weekend Crash Course"
//    by IDG Books Worldwide
public class HelloJava
{
  public static void main(String[] args)
```

```
  {
    System.out.println("Hello World from Java");
  }
}
```

The first three program lines are as follows:

```
//   Java version of the Hello World program
//   Developed for the book "Java 2 Weekend Crash Course"
//   by IDG Books Worldwide
```

These three program lines are a comment. The compiler ignores them, and their only purpose is to document and explain the code. We have used the // symbol to comment the lines individually; however, we can code these lines as follows:

```
/*   Java version of the Hello World program
     Developed for the book "Java 2 Weekend Crash Course"
     by IDG Books Worldwide */
```

The first non-comment line of the **HelloJava** program is as follows:

```
public class HelloJava
{
```

Programming languages use special language elements called *keywords*, which are reserved and cannot be used in regular expressions. The keyword public, called an access modifier, determines if other parts of the program can use this code. The keyword class is necessary because everything in a Java program exists in a class.

The first class in a Java program, called the *driving class*, must have the same name as the file in which it is stored. The source file must have the extension **.java**. In this example, the source file has the filename **HelloJava.java**. The Java compiler names the byte code **HelloWorld.class**.

In the program HelloJava, listed at the beginning of this section, the left-hand roster symbol indicates the beginning of the class named **HelloJava**. At the end of the program listing, there is a right-hand roster symbol that terminates the **HelloJava** class.

The next statement in the **HelloJava** program is as follows:

```
public static void main(String[] args)
  {
```

This line creates the first method of the program. A method is a program unit that performs a specific action.

We discuss Java methods in Session 10.

Every Java program must have a method named `main()`. The `main()` method is public static and is void. Void indicates that it returns nothing to the operating system. The element inside parentheses indicates that `main()` can receive a string the user types (sometimes called the *command tail*). Command tails are seldom used in Java programming. Each class can have a `main()` method; however, execution always starts with the main method of the Java class that drives the application, that is, the class that has the same name as the application's source file.

We use parentheses following the name of methods to make them easier to identify. For example, we type the method named main as `main()`**. This is a common style that many programming books follow.**

The left-hand roster indicates the beginning of the `main()` method. Later in the listing, you can see a right-hand roster that marks the end of `main()`. The following statement is in `main()`:

```
System.out.println("Hello World from Java");
```

This program line displays the message "Hello World" on the screen. `System` is a built-in class that is part of the standard Java libraries while `out` is an object of this class. The word `println()`, pronounced print line, refers to a method of the `System.out` stream. It displays a single text line on the console device (usually the video display). The text to be displayed is in double quotes. This is called a *string literal*. Visualize a stream as a sequence of characters between a source (reader) and a destination (writer). The `print()` method is similar to `println()`, but it does not force the end of a screen line.

The elements of the program line are listed below:

```
System.out                =        stream
Hello World from Java      =        println() parameter list
System                     =        class
```

out	=	object
println	=	method
(	=	start of parameters
"	=	start of string
Hello World from Java	=	string
"	=	end of string
)	=	end of parameters
;	=	terminator

At the end of the program listing, we see two right-hand rosters. The first marks the end of the main() method. The second marks the end of the class HelloJava, which in this case is the end of the program.

**10 Min.
To Go**

Compiling and Running the Sample Program

Make sure your development system is working correctly by compiling and running the HelloJava program that appears earlier in this chapter. Begin by starting the editor of your choice and typing the code. Since Java is case-sensitive, use the same capitalization as in the listing. Figure 3-1 shows the program as it appears in the Textpad editor screen.

When you type the program into the editor, you must save it with the name you used in the driving class: in this case, **HelloJava**. The source file is the text file that contains the program code. In Java, the source file must have the extension **.java**. Therefore, save the program as:

```
HelloJava.java
```

Here again, make sure the capitalization is the same in the name of the source file and in the name of the driving class. Also note that Java ignores white space in text formatting but that it does not ignore spaces inside a name. In this case, Hello Java and HelloJava are different names.

In Windows, you must run the Java development software that comes with the JDK from the MS DOS command line. If you correctly enter the PATH and CLASSPATH commands in your **autoexec.bat** file, as we describe in Session 2, the system can locate the development software without having to type the path specification. However, this does not ensure that the development tools can find the source files to compile the program. For this reason, it is a good idea to execute the Java compiler from the directory that contains the source files.

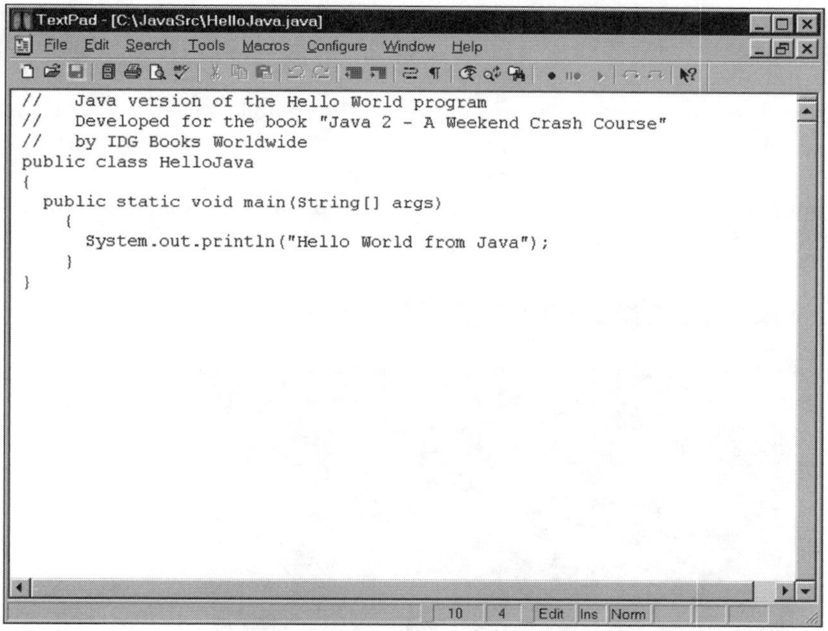
TextPad - [C:\JavaSrc\HelloJava.java]
File Edit Search Tools Macros Configure Window Help
//   Java version of the Hello World program
//   Developed for the book "Java 2 - A Weekend Crash Course"
//   by IDG Books Worldwide
public class HelloJava
{
public static void main(String[] args)
{
System.out.println("Hello World from Java");
}
}
10 4 Edit Ins Norm

Figure 3-1
Typing the HelloJava program

To execute the Java compiler, proceed as follows:

- Open a window with the MS DOS command prompt. If there is no MS DOS icon on your Windows desktop, you can find the MS DOS command prompt in the Programs command of the Start menu.
- Log-on to the directory that contains the source file you intend to compile.
- Execute the java compiler from the MS DOS command prompt.

The command for the HelloJava program is:

```
javac HelloJava.java
```

Javac is the name of the Java compiler. If compiled correctly, the system displays no error message, and the MS DOS command prompt returns to the screen. If the system reports a compiler error, you must locate the error in the source code and correct it before you attempt to re-compile. At this stage of Java programming, most errors result from typing mistakes.

When the program compiles without error, the compiler generates a file with the extension **.class**. This class file is the executable that the Java interpreter can run. The name of the java interpreter is java.exe.

Figure 3-2 shows the MS-DOS prompt window during the compilation and execution of the HelloJava program.

Figure 3-2
Compiling and executing the HelloJava program

Because developing a Java application requires you to go back and forth between the editor and the compiler, it is a good idea to place the editor in a desktop window and the MS DOS command prompt in a different window. Then you can use both windows while you develop the application or make corrections in the source. Figure 3-3 shows the Windows desktop with both windows open.

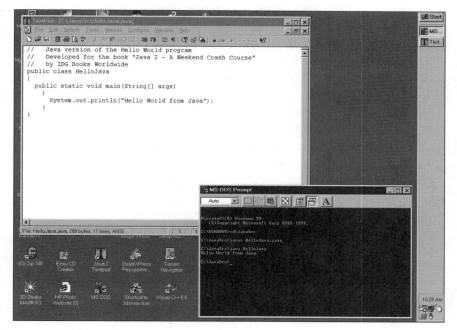

Figure 3-3
Windows desktop for Java development

Done!

REVIEW

In this session, we have developed a simple Java program, which we call **HelloJava**. The purpose of the program is to get you programming in Java as quickly as possible. In the process, we have cut a few corners and have left some concepts unexplained. In the sections that follow, we review these fundamentals, covering all points at a greater level of detail.

At this point, you have selected an editor program to create your Java source code. Also, you have some familiarity with the appearance of a Java program, the purpose of some of its fundamental elements, and the basic rules of syntax of the Java language. In addition, you have typed, compiled, and executed the sample program successfully, thereby learning to use Java's development tools.

QUIZ YOURSELF

1. Have you selected an editor program to use in developing your Java programs and become familiar with its operation? (See "Selecting an Editor Program.")

2. Are you familiar with the structure of a simple Java program? (See "The HelloJava Program.")

3. Is Java a case-sensitive language? (See "The Basic Rules.")

4. How does Java handle white space characters? (See "The Basic Rules.")

5. What are the Java grouping, comment, and statement terminator symbols? (See "The Basic Rules.")

6. Are you able to type, compile, and run the sample program named **HelloJava** in this session? (See "Compiling and Running the Sample Program.")

Session Checklist

✔ Computer number systems

✔ Binary and hexadecimal numbers

✔ Data in computer memory

✔ Representing characters and numbers

**30 Min.
To Go**

A programmer's work consists mostly of storing, manipulating, and processing data. In this session, we look at how to store information in a computer system. We begin by explaining the number systems used in computer work. A working knowledge of binary and hexadecimal numbers is indispensable to the computer programmer. Then we look at how to store numeric and character data in computer memory and how to use the various character data encodings in Java programming.

Number Systems

A number system is a collection of rules and symbols used in counting and in performing arithmetic. One number system, called the Hindu-Arabic or decimal system, has worldwide acceptance. We are all familiar with the Hindu-Arabic symbols:

```
0  1  2  3  4  5  6  7  8  9
```

Often, theorists say that the decimal system of numbers results from the practice of counting with our fingers and that if we had six fingers instead of 10, our number system would have six symbols.

Counting is the fundamental use of numbers, and tallying is the simplest form of counting. The tally system, to which we all resort occasionally, consists of drawing a vertical line that corresponds with each counted element. We refine the tally system when we make groups of five elements by drawing a diagonal line for each fifth unit we count. The tally system does not require numerical symbols. We probably derive Roman numerals from the tally system because we can detect the vertical and diagonal traces used in tallying in some Roman numerals. The limitations of the system of Roman numerals are the uncertainty in the positional value of the digits, the absence of a symbol for zero, and the fact that some digits require more than one symbol. These limitations complicate the rules of counting and arithmetic when we use Roman numerals.

The Hindu-Arabic system of numbers uses a counting scheme in which the column position of each digit determines the digit's value, as follows:

```
4 5 7 3
| | | |_____ units
| | |_____ ten units
| |_____ hundred units
|_____ thousand units
```

We obtain the total value by adding the column weights of each unit.

```
      4000 ---- 4 thousand units
       500 ---- 5 hundred units
  +     70 ---- 7 ten units
        3 ---- 3 units
      ------
      4573
```

Binary Numbers

Computers built in the United States during the early 1940s used decimal numbers to store data used in arithmetic operations. In 1946, John von Neumann observed that computing machinery is easier to build and performs more reliably if the electronic circuits are based on two states, usually labeled ON and OFF, which the digits 1 and 0 can represent. The *Binary System* is the system of numbers consisting of only two digits. With binary numbers, the two states of an electronic cell correspond to the digits 0 and 1.

The binary system of numbers is the simplest possible set of symbols we can use to count and to perform positional arithmetic. Hexadecimal numbers, appearing later in this session, are a convenient shorthand for representing groups of four binary digits. Figure 4-1 shows the relations among a group of four electronic cells and various number systems.

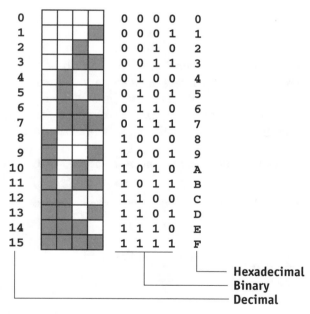

Figure 4-1
Decimal, binary, and hexadecimal number systems

If we think of each cell as a miniature light bulb, we can use the binary number 1 to represent the state of a charged cell (light bulb ON) and the binary number 0 to represent the state of an uncharged cell (light bulb OFF). In this sense, we can say that a bit is set if its binary value is 1 and that a bit is reset, or clear, if its binary value is 0.

Hexadecimal Numbers

The column to the right of the binary numbers in Figure 4-1 contains the hexa-decimal, or hex, numbers. These groups of four electronic cells are the building blocks of computer systems. In most modern computers, memory cells, registers, and data paths are designed in multiples of four binary digits. In Figure 4-1, we see that we can encode all possible combinations of four binary digits in a single hexadecimal digit.

20 Min. To Go

Computer Memory

In today's computer hardware, memory is usually in the form of a silicon wafer housed in a rectangular, integrated circuit package. Each memory cell is a transistor circuit capable of storing two stable states. The binary symbol 1 represents one state, and the binary symbol 0 represents the other. Usually, memory cells are arranged in groups of 8 bits, called a byte. In most machines, the byte is the smallest addressable storage element.

Table 4-1 lists the most common units of measurement associated with computer memory.

Table 4-1
Units of Memory Storage

Unit	Equals to	Numerical Range
bit		0 and 1
nibble	4 bits	0 to 15
byte	8 bits	0 to 255
	2 nibbles	

Unit	Equals to	Numerical Range
word	16 bits	0 to 65535
	4 nibbles	
	2 bytes	
kilobyte	1024 bytes	
megabyte	1024 kilobytes	
gigabyte	1024 megabytes	

Computer memory is linear. The *memory address* is the sequential number assigned to each unit. The maximum number of memory units in a particular system depends on its internal architecture. Each memory cell in a typical computer consists of one byte (8 bits) of data. Figure 4-2 shows the conventional numbering of the individual bits within a byte.

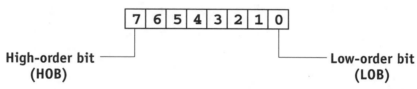

**High-order bit
(HOB)**   **Low-order bit
(LOB)**

Figure 4-2
Conventional bit numbering scheme

Representing Character Data

We use groups of electrical cells to store computer data, each of which can hold binary 1 or 0. Because patterns of 1's and 0's provide the most convenient way to represent computer information, we store character data in this manner as well. To store letters of the alphabet or other symbols, we must develop a correspondence scheme among these symbols and the numeric values that represent them. For example, if we agree to represent the upper-case letter A with the number 1, the letter B with the number 2, and so forth, we represent the upper-case letter Z with the number 26. When we accept this scheme for representing letters with numbers, we can encode text messages using numbers instead of letters. In this manner, the numbers 1, 3, 26 represent the letters ACZ.

Programmers have used several methods to encode character data in computer technology. The Hollerith code and the Extended Binary Coded Decimal Interchange Code (EBCDIC) were popular some time ago. More recently, the American Standard Code for Information Interchange, or ASCII (pronounced as-key), has gained considerable acceptance. Although Java recognizes several character sets, including ASCII, it prefers Unicode. ASCII characters are stored in 8-bits, but Unicode is based on 16-bit values. This wider format allows you to support non-English and multilingual environments. Figure 4-3 shows the symbols in the ASCII character set, as well as their decimal and hexadecimal values.

Decimal →		0	16	32	48	64	80	96	112
↓	HEX	0	10	20	30	40	50	60	70
0	0			(space)	0	@	P	`	p
1	1			!	1	A	Q	a	q
2	2			"	2	B	R	b	r
3	3			#	3	C	S	c	s
4	4			$	4	D	T	d	t
5	5			%	5	E	U	e	u
6	6			&	6	F	V	f	v
7	7			'	7	G	W	g	w
8	8			(	8	H	X	h	x
9	9			)	9	I	Y	i	y
10	A			*	:	J	Z	j	z
11	B			+	;	K	[	k	{
12	C			,	<	L	\	l		
13	D			–	=	M	]	m	}
14	E			.	>	M	^	n	~
15	F			/	?	O	_	o	

Figure 4-3
The ASCII character set, as well as their decimal and hexadecimal values

The ASCII Character Set

We can use Figure 4-3 to determine the decimal and hex value of any ASCII symbol. First, we determine the column value of the symbol and then add the row value. For example, the decimal ASCII code for the letter c is 96 plus 3 or 99. By the same token, the value of the ASCII symbol for the number 6 is 36 hexadecimal or 54 decimal.

We store characters in computer memory according to their numeric values in the adopted representation. For example, in ASCII, encoding the name "Jim" appears in computer memory as the decimal values 74, 105, and 109 because these are the ASCII decimal values for the letters J, i, and m. In Hex, the values are 4A, 69, and 6D. In binary, the three byte-size computer cells storing the name "Jim" are as follows:

```
01001010-01101001-01101101
```

You may want to use the table in Figure 4-1 to check these values.

**10 Min.
To Go**

Representing Numeric Data

One way to represent numbers in a computer system is to use the corresponding characters in the adopted character set. For example, you can store the number 128 in three bytes that hold the decimal values 49, 50, and 56. In this case, the values 49, 50, and 56 correspond to the ASCII encoding for the digits 123, as you can confirm in Figure 4-3. Although often we store numeric data in character form, computers are binary machines and perform arithmetic operations only on binary numbers. Therefore, to multiply the number 128 (encoded in ASCII digits) by the number 2 (also in ASCII digits), the computer must convert these text-like representations into binary.

A more reasonable approach is to store numbers directly in binary. For example, you can store the number 128 in binary as follows:

```
1000000
```

You save considerable space when you store the value in a single byte; the ASCII representation requires three bytes. Furthermore, you can perform binary arithmetic directly on the encoding.

Although you can represent unsigned integer numbers directly in binary, the representation of negative and positive numbers requires additional consideration.

One common scheme is to use one bit to represent the sign of the number. Conventionally, we use a 0 binary digit to represent a positive number and a 1 to represent a negative number. Usually, the leftmost bit, called the high-order bit, encodes the sign. This scheme for representing signed numbers is a *sign-magnitude representation*. For example, the decimal numbers 93 and -93 are represented as follows:

```
|<---------------------------- sign bit
|
01011101 binary = +93 decimal
11011101 binary = -93 decimal
```

Sign-magnitude representation, although simple and straightforward, has drawbacks. One drawback is that there are two encodings for 0, one negative and one positive. Usually, a -0 is wasteful and unnecessary. But perhaps the greatest limitation of the sign-magnitude scheme is that it complicates machine arithmetic. For example, to add two signed numbers, first we have to investigate whether they have the same sign. If they have the same sign, we add the numbers and give the sum the common sign. If the numbers have different signs, we subtract the smaller number from the larger number and give the difference the sign of the larger number. If either number is 0 or -0, the result is the other operand. If both numbers are -0, the sum is 0.

Radix-complement representations eliminate the -0 and simplify machine arithmetic. In binary systems, the radix-complement representation is the *two's complement*. You can obtain the two's complement of a signed number by calculating the difference between the number and the next integer power of 2 that is greater than the number. Usually, the machine hardware contains instructions that calculate the two's complement. The great advantage of two's complement representations is that addition and subtraction become a single operation and that arithmetic rules and manipulations become simpler and more effective.

Encoding Fractions

The binary encoding of fractions poses some additional problems. Because there is no way to represent a decimal point in binary, we must adopt some scheme to define the location of the decimal point. Several approaches are feasible. In one of them, called a *fixed-point representation*, a previously determined number of binary digits is used to encode the integer part and another number is used to encode the fractional part. Although the fixed-point approach was used in earlier computers, it is wasteful and ineffective.

An alternative encoding for fractional numbers uses a scheme similar to scientific notation. In scientific notation, or exponential form, we write the number 310.25 as follows:

```
3.1025 x 10²
------   ---
    |      |_____ exponent
    |_____ base
```

As 10^2 equals 100, the result is 310.25. We can write numbers smaller than 1 using a negative exponent. For example, we represent the number .0004256 as follows:

```
4.256 x 10⁻⁴
```

To avoid superscripts, computer notation uses the letter E for the exponent part. For example:

```
3.1025 E2
4.256 E-4
```

Done!

Because the radix point *floats* according to the value of the exponent, these are *floating-point representations*. Since their invention, computers have used floating-point binary representations to encode decimal numbers. For many years, computer manufacturers came up with their own encoding schemes to represent decimal numbers in floating-point binary. In 1985, the American National Standards Institute (ANSI) approved a binary floating-point standard based on the work of the Computer Society of the Institute for Electric and Electronic Engineers (IEEE). Generally, manufacturers follow this standard, designated as ANSI-IEEE 754. Java uses the ANSI-IEEE 754 formats to store decimal numbers encoded in binary.

REVIEW

A number system is a set of rules and symbols used to count and to perform arithmetic. All number systems in use today are positional. The binary system is the simplest possible number system and consists of two symbols, 0 and 1. The hexadecimal system is a convenient shorthand for binary numbers. Computer memory uses several binary-based storage units, including the bit, nibble, byte, word, kilobyte, megabyte, and gigabyte. Computers represent character data by means of numeric encodings.

Java uses the ASCII, ISO Latin 1, and Unicode character sets. Binary numbers represent integer numeric values. Signed integers are represented in sign-magnitude or two's complement form. Decimal numbers are represented in floating-point format according to the ANSI-IEEE 754 standard.

Quiz Yourself

1. Describe the fundamentals of a positional number system.
   (See "Number Systems.")
2. Using the table in Figure 4-1, convert the following binary numbers to hexadecimal:

   ```
   11001111
   00111100
   00001101
   ```

   (See "Binary Numbers.")
3. Answer the following questions:

   How many bits are in a byte?

   How many nibbles are in a byte?

   How many kilobytes are in a megabyte?

   (See "Computer Memory.")
4. What are the limitations of the sign-magnitude representation?
   (See "Representing Numeric Data.")
5. Convert the following numbers to floating-point in scientific notation:

   ```
   12.3344
   .0000456
   12345
   ```

   (See " Representing Numeric Data.")

PART

I

Friday Evening
Part Review

1. Why was the Java language an unprecedented success?
2. What is Java's greatest promise?
3. List two similarities and two differences between Java and C++.
4. Are you able to download the Java development software (JDK) from the Sun Microsystems Web site?
5. Are you able to install the JDK in your Windows system?
6. Have you set the PATH variable for your system?
7. Have you set the CLASSPATH?
8. Have you selected an editor program to use in developing your Java programs and become familiar with its operation?
9. Are you familiar with the structure of a simple Java program?
10. Is Java a case-sensitive language?
11. How does Java handle white space characters?
12. What are Java's grouping and comment symbols?
13. Are you able to type, compile, and run the sample program named **HelloJava** in Session 3?
14. Describe the fundamentals of a positional number system.
15. Using the table in Figure 4-1, convert the following binary numbers to hexadecimal:

    11001111

    00111100

    00001101

16. Answer the following questions:

    How many bits are in a byte?

    How many nibbles are in a byte?

    How many kilobytes are in a megabyte?

17. What are the limitations of the sign-magnitude representation?

18. Convert the following numbers to floating-point in scientific notation:

    12.3344

    .0000456

    12345

19. What is Java's statement-terminator symbol?

20. List three elements that should appear in the program header.

☑ Friday

☑ **Saturday**

☐ Sunday

PART

II

Saturday Morning

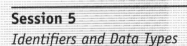

Identifiers and Data Types

Session Checklist

✔ Variables and constants

✔ Java Strings

✔ Identifiers

✔ Primitive data types

✔ Typecasting

✔ Literals

**30 Min.
To Go**

We have described computers as general-purpose machines that process data according to rules. A program is a set of concrete instructions based on these rules and is designed to perform a specific task. Usually, a program's main purpose is to transform data. One of the main functions of a programming language such as Java is to classify, manipulate, and store computer data. In this session, we look at how you can store data in a Java program.

Computer Data

Data is a generic designation that applies to many types of objects. Computer science refers to scalar data types, such as those that encode individual objects, and to structured data types to describe collections of individual objects. More commonly, we speak of *numeric data, alphanumeric,* or *character data, date data*, and *logical data*. We can use numeric data to perform mathematical operations such as arithmetic, exponentiation, or the calculation of transcendental functions. Alphanumeric or character data are letters and numbers that serve as language symbols. In Session 4, we learn how to store numeric and character data. Date data represents conventional dates, such as November 7, 1942. Logical data, discussed later, define trueness or falseness.

Programming languages such as Java allow you to store and manipulate several types of data objects. When you assign a data item to a particular type, it processes according to the rules for that type. For example, you cannot manipulate data objects assigned to character types arithmetically, and you cannot separate numeric data into its individual symbols. The programmer assigns each data object to the data type that corresponds to the object's intended use rather than to the object's appearance. For instance, a telephone number is an alphanumeric data type because usually we have no need to perform arithmetic operations on the digits of a telephone number.

Variables and Constants

Using mathematical terminology, sometimes we classify numeric computer data as *variables* and *constants*. In Java, we assign names to variables and store them in a memory structure that the variable type determines. You can change the contents of a variable anywhere in the program. Visualize a variable as a labeled container, which you define, for storing a data object.

Constants, on the other hand, represent values that do not change in the course of program execution. For example, a mathematical program can define a constant to store the value of Pi. When the program defines this value, it can recall the value whenever it needs it.

Java Variable Types

We have said that Java is a strongly typed language. This means that every variable must have a declared type and that the language enforces strict type checking. The Java language contains eight primitive types: four integral (or integer) types (`byte`, `short`, `int`, and `long`); two float types (`float` and `double`); one character type (`char`); and one boolean type (`boolean`). Table 5-1 lists the Java primitive data types.

Table 5-1
Java Primitive Data Types

Groups	Variable Type	Storage	Approximate Range
integrals	`int`	4 bytes	+/- 2 billion
	`short`	2 bytes	+/- 32,767
	`long`	8 bytes	+/- 9.2 x 1018
	`byte`	1 byte	-129 to 127
floating-point	`float`	4 bytes	7-8 digits
	`double`	8 bytes	16-17 digits
character	`char`	2 bytes	65,536
boolean	`boolean`	---	true and false

Declaring Variables

You must declare every variable in a Java program by specifying its name and type. The variable name must be a legal Java identifier, and the variable type must be one of the primitive data types in Table 5-1. The variable declaration informs the compiler of a variable's name and type so that the compiler reserves a memory space to store data and associates it with the assigned identifier. The following is the declaration of a variable of type `int`:

```
int num1;
```

Java allows you to declare several variables of the same type by separating the variable names with commas, for example:

```
int num2, num3, num4;
```

A variable declaration can include its initialization. In this case, the equal sign precedes the value assigned to the variable, for example:

```
float radius = 1.22;
```

You can declare several variables and can choose the ones you want to initialize, for example:

```
int valA = 1, val2, val3, val4 = 77;
```

The Java String Class

Frequently, Java programs use groups of characters called *strings*. A Java string is a class, not a primitive type. The Java String class is part of the java.lang library that you can access through any Java program. Therefore, an application can create objects of the Java String class as if they are variables of a primitive data type. However, because String is a class, it begins with an upper-case letter, although all other primitive data types in Table 5-1 begin with lower-case letters.

 We use the Java String class so often in programming that we tend to think of it as another primitive data type. The fact that "String" starts with a capital "S" indicates that it is a class.

A String object represents a sequence of characters. In contrast to your options with primitive data types, you cannot change a string once you create it. You declare and initialize a String object similarly to any of the primitive types. Double quotation marks delimit the string. For example:

```
String uName = "Minnesota State University";
String ssn = "263-98-2233";
```

The Java String class contains methods that allow you to manipulate and convert strings; we discuss these methods later.

Identifiers

Identifiers are the names of program elements. In Java, you use identifiers to name variables, constants, classes, and methods. Legal characters for identifiers are the letters and digits of the Unicode character set, as well as the symbols $ and _. The space is not a legal character in identifiers because Java uses the space to mark the end of the name. Because Java is case-sensitive, the names aVar and Avar represent different identifiers. An identifier cannot start with a digit. The length of an identifier is virtually unlimited, although it is a good idea to keep identifiers to fewer than 30 characters. The following are legal identifiers in Java:

```
personal_name
```

```
PI
y_121
$$128
User_address_and_zipcode
```

The following identifiers are illegal:

```
1_value
User name
%%123
```

An identifier cannot be one of the special keywords the Java language uses; usually, these keywords are called *reserved words*. As the word suggests, reserved words are intended for special use in the programming language. Table 5-2 lists Java's reserved words.

Table 5-2
Java Reserved Words

abstract	boolean	break	byte
case	catch	char	class
const	continue	default	do
double	else	extends	final
finally	float	for	future
generic	goto	if	implements
import	inner	instanceof	int
interface	long	native	new
null	operator	outer	package
private	protected	public	rest
return	short	static	super
switch	synchronized	this	throw
throws	transient	try	var
void	volatile	while	

One of your crucial jobs as a programmer is to select good identifiers. Ideally, an identifier is descriptive and easy to type. Cryptic or meaningless identifiers make the code more difficult to understand and maintain. Verbose or complicated identifiers can lead to typing errors. For example, in a program that calculates the area of a circle, we can choose identifiers named radius, area, and PI. In this program, cryptic identifiers, such as v1, v2, and v3, make the code more difficult to follow and increase the probability of error.

Scope of a Variable

When you declare a variable, it assumes certain attributes. One of these attributes is the variable's scope, the part of a program over which the variable is recognized. The closest set of roster symbols, {and}, that contains the variable determines the scope of the variable. You can use the variable only in the part of the code that is within these rosters. By strictly enforcing scope rules, Java makes it difficult to misuse variables. However, you must be careful to declare a variable so that the code can access it.

Java Constants

Java constants are variables defined with the final and static keywords. Java has strict requirements for the declaration of constants. The language does not allow you to define constants inside a particular method. Instead, you must define constants at the class level. For this reason, they are sometimes called class constants. If an application requires a local constant, it can define a variable and use it as a constant. The following statement declares a constant:

```
static final double PI = 3.141592653589793;
```

 Many programmers use upper-case letters for constant names, as in the preceding constant PI. This style makes it easy to identify variables and constants in the code listing.

Java Primitive Data Types

**20 Min.
To Go**

Java classifies primitive data types into three categories: numeric types, character types (also called alphanumeric data), and boolean types. Each of these types serves its own purpose in a Java program. Before we approach complex Java programming, we must have clear notions of the three categories of Java data and of the specific types in each.

Numeric Data

Many Java applications perform a substantial amount of number crunching. Therefore, topics related to the storage and manipulation of numeric data are important. We use numeric data to perform mathematical operations and calculations. In numeric data, the number symbols represent quantities. This notion excludes the use of numbers as designators, for example, a telephone number or social security number.

Numeric data appears in Java code in the form of variables or constants. In addition, you can enter numeric data explicitly in an operation. In Table 5-1, we see numeric data classified into integral types and floating-point types. Sometimes we call floating-point types *reals*.

Each data type corresponds to a category of numbers; for example, you can use the integer data type to represent whole numbers and the floating-point data type to represent fractions. For each data type, Java provides several *type specifiers* that determine the characteristic and range of representable values. Table 5-1 shows these.

Character Data

Character (alphanumeric) data refers to items that serve as textual designators. We do not treat these items in conventional arithmetic. We use the letters of the alphabet and other non-numeric symbols as designators. Also, pure numeric symbols are valid in alphanumeric data. So are telephone numbers, street addresses, zip codes, social security numbers, and many other designators.

In Java, alphanumeric data belongs either to the char data type or to the String class. Java treats char data as a 16-bit unsigned integer, with values in the range 0 to 65535, or as a single Unicode character. This means char you can use the data type to represent unsigned integers in the range 0 to 65,535, and that it supports basic arithmetic on these values. However, usually it is preferable to use the numeric data types for this purpose and to leave the char type for alphanumeric data.

The single quotation marks declare a char data type. Sometimes we call these "tick" marks. For example:

```
char aLet = 'f';
```

Recall that double quotation marks declare String objects:

```
String aCity = "Mankato";
```

Boolean Data

The third data type classification of the Java language is the *boolean*, which a single data type represents, also called boolean. The boolean data type owes its name to the English logician George Boole who, in the nineteenth century, addressed the relations between mathematics and logic.

A Java boolean variable takes two values: true and false. You must type these values in lower-case letters. Typically, boolean variables represent program elements that indicate the validity of a statement or proposition. You must declare and initialize them in the same manner as you declare and initialize numeric or alphanumeric types. For example:

```
boolean switchIsOn = true;
```

**10 Min.
To Go**

Type Conversions

In Java programs, situations often arise in which you must convert one data type to another. For example, an application that manipulates two integer values has to obtain their ratio. Such is the case in a program that operates a control valve with a maximum flow and a series of flow-control settings, as follows:

```
int maximumFlow = 10;
int flowSetting = 5;
```

In this case, we obtain the current gas flow ratio (0.5) by dividing the flow setting value into the maximum valve flow value. The problem is that integer arithmetic produces integer values in Java. Therefore, when we use integer division in the operation 5 / 10, the result is 0, not the value 0.5. To obtain the desired ratio, we must convert the two integer operands into floating-point types (float or double) and perform floating-point division.

Because Java is a strongly-typed language, we know every variable type at compile time. The language performs extensive type checking and contains restrictions on how we may convert variable types.

There are two forms of type conversions: *explicit* and *implicit*. In explicit conversions, code deliberately changes the data type of an operand through a process called *type- casting*. The language performs implicit conversions automatically.

Implicit Conversions

Java performs implicit conversions between numeric types only if no loss of precision or magnitude results from the conversion. In the case of unary conversions, it converts operands of type byte and short automatically to type int. Java preserves all other types. The following rules govern binary conversions:

1. For operations on integer types, if one of the operands is long, Java converts the other to long. Otherwise, it converts both operands to int.

2. The result of an expression is an int unless the value is too long for the int format. In this case, Java converts the value to long.

3. For operations on floating-point types, if one operand is a double, Java converts the other to double; the result is of type double. Otherwise, Java converts both operands to float, and the result is a float type.

Type-Casting

You can use type-casting to perform explicit conversions. To type-cast, precede the operand with the type you desire and enclose it in parentheses. In the example at the beginning of this section, we need to convert two integer variables to a floating-point type; the cast looks like this:

```
int maximumFlow = 10;
int flowSetting = 5;
double flowRate;
. . .
flowRate = (double) maximumFlow / (double) flowSetting);
```

Java type-casting must comply with the following rules:

1. You cannot cast boolean variables into any other type.

2. You can cast any of the integer data types into any other type, except boolean. Casting into a smaller type can result in loss of data.

3. You can cast floating-point types into other float types or into integer types. These casts may result in loss of data.

4. You can cast the `char` type into integer types. Because the char is 16-bits wide, casting into a `byte` type may result in loss of data or in garbled characters.

Literal Declarations

In the declaration of literal values, Java assumes that floating-point literals are of type `double`. The following statement is an example:

```
float aVal = 12.33;
```

This statement generates an error because Java assumes that the value 12.33 is in `double` format and that it loses precision when it converts the value to a `float` type. You can perform a type-cast by forcing the literal into a `float` type, as follows:

```
float aVal = 12.33f;
```

Done!

The small-case letter following the literal value performs a type-cast.

REVIEW

We store computer data in scalar and structured data types. We can store numeric data as variables or as constants. Java has several primitive data types: four integral types (`int`, `short`, `long`, and `byte`); two floating-point types (`float` and `double`); a boolean type (`boolean`); and a character type (`char`). In Java, a string is not a primitive data type but an object of the `String` class that is part of the Java libraries. Identifiers are names assigned to program elements, such as variables, constants, classes, and methods. Java identifiers are case-sensitive and must start with an alphabetic character. Spaces are illegal in Java identifiers. An identifier cannot be a Java reserved word. The part of the program that recognizes a variable is its scope. Type conversions can be implicit or explicit. We perform explicit conversions by type-casting.

QUIZ YOURSELF

1. List the Java primitive data types. (See "Java Variable Types.")
2. Describe Java's rules for identifiers. (See "Identifiers.")
3. How are Java's primitive data types classified? (See "Classification of Primitive Data Types.")
4. Write Java code to cast a floating-point variable type into an integer type. (See "Type-Casting.")

Arrays and Java I/O

Session Checklist

✔ Arrays

✔ The Length of an Array

✔ Multi-dimensional arrays

✔ Java Input and Output

✔ Escape characters

✔ A sample program

**30 Min.
To Go**

I n this session, we cover two topics: arrays and Java input and output operations. Arrays provide the programmer with a way to store several data items of the same type in a single structure. They are a necessity in practical programming. For example, a payroll program can use arrays to store the names, social security numbers, addresses, wages, deductions, and number of dependants for each employee. You can retrieve and process this information using the corresponding position in the array for each data entry.

Input and output operations provide a mechanism for communicating with the computer. We input data into a program to enter information. For example, in the previous payroll program, we perform an input operation to enter information about each employee. Output operations allow us to access and view data stored in the computer. A program communicates with its users by means of output.

Arrays

An array is an ordered group of variables of the same type. Three distinct operations are necessary in creating an array:

- Array declaration
- Array creation or allocation
- Array initialization or access

Declare an array of type int as follows:

```
int[] studentGrades;
```

To create an array, use the new keyword:

```
studentGrades = new int[14];
```

You can perform both operations in a single statement:

```
int[] studentGrades = new int[14];
```

Where:

StudentGrades	=	declaration
New int[14]	=	allocation

At this point, we have declared and allocated an array of 14 elements. The first element has the index number 0, and the last element has the index number 13. You can access these elements as follows:

```
studentGrades[0] = 78;
studentGrades[1] = 88;
   . . .
studentGrades[13] = 55;
```

There is a special array syntax that implies the new operator i and declares and initializes the array in a single statement, for example:

```
int fibNums[] = {1, 1, 2, 3, 5, 8, 13, 21, 34};
```

 In contrast to C and C++, Java checks arrays thoroughly. If you try to access a non-allocated array, Java throws a NullPointerException. If you attempt to access an array element out of the array bounds, Java throws an ArrayIndexOutOfBoundsException. We discuss exceptions in Session 19.

You can create and initialize a String array as follows:

```
String[] studentNames = {"Jim", "Jane", "Harry", "Lucy"};
```

Where:

String[]	=	type
studentNames	=	array name
{	=	roster starts init list
"Jim, "Jane", "Harry", "Lucy"	=	initialization list
}	=	closing roster

Because you can attach brackets to the array type or to the name in the array declaration, this process may seem confusing at first. For example:

```
int[] Array1 = new int[12];    // Brackets on type
int Array1[] = new int[12];    // Brackets on name
```

The Length of an Array

Once you allocate an array, you cannot change its length. You can use the length operator (which is not a method) with an array name to obtain the number of elements in the array. For example:

```
for(int x = 0; x < studentNames.length)
    System.out.println(studentName[x]);
```

The following program, **Arrays.java**, demonstrates how you can declare and initialize arrays simultaneously and how you can use the length operator.

The source file for the program Arrays.java is in the Session 6 directory on the book's CD-ROM.

```java
//    File name: Arrays.java
//    Reference: Session 6
//
//    Java program to demonstrate arrays
//    Topics:
//        1. Simultaneous Array declaration and initialization
//        2. Use of the length operator
//
//    Note:
//        This program contains Java output statements
//        described later in this session

public class Arrays
{
   public static void main(String[] args)
   {

      int[] fibs = {1, 1, 2, 3, 5, 8, 13, 21};
      char[] lets = {'t', 'h', 'i', 's', ' ', 'i', 's'};

      for(int x = 0; x < fibs.length; x++)
         System.out.println(fibs[x]);

      for(int x = 0; x < lets.length; x++)
         System.out.print(lets[x]);

      System.out.flush();
   }
}
```

**20 Min.
To Go**

Multidimensional Arrays

An array can have more than one dimension. We can create a two-dimensional array to represent the entries in a table. In this case, the array has subscripts for the table rows and the table columns. Visualize the result as a rectangular grid in which two parameters determine the position of any element.

```
// Declare and allocate an array of bytes
byte[][] screenPix = new byte[10][5];
```

Java fakes multidimensional arrays because they are actually "arrays of arrays." For this reason, a two-dimensional array can be rectangular or ragged, although rectangular arrays are more common. Picture a ragged array as follows:

```
              COLUMNS
              - - - - - -
          |   x x
          |   x x x
   ROWS   |   x x x x
          |   x x x x x
          |   x x x x x x
```

To create a ragged array of 5 rows, with 2, 3, 4, 5, and 6 elements in each row, proceed as follows:

```
// First allocate the five rows
byte[][] raggedArray = new byte[5][];

// Now allocate each column
for(int x = 0; x < 5; x++)
    raggedArray[x] = new byte[x + 2];
```

When you initialize or access a ragged array, be careful not to overstep the bounds of each array row.

We have used the length operator to obtain the size of a one-dimensional array, for example:

```
byte[] anArray = new byte[25];
. . .
System.out.println("Length is: " + anArray.length);
```

Because a multidimensional array can be a ragged array, you can define the size of a multidimensional array only for the number of rows. However, if you use a constant to declare a multidimensional rectangular array, you can obtain the number of allocated columns, as follows:

```
// Declare array constants
int ROWS = 10;
int COLS = 5;
// Allocate array
byte[][] screenPix = new byte[ROWS][COLS];

// Obtain and store array dimensions
rowCount = screenPix.length;          // Number of rows
colCount = screenPix[COLS].length;    // Number of columns
totalSize = rowCount * colCount;      // Calculate total elements
```

The following expressions generate errors:

```
screenPix[ROWS].length
screenPix[ROWS][COLS].length
```

You can initialize multidimensional arrays in the same manner as one-dimensional arrays. For example:

```
byte[][] smallArray = {
                       {10, 11, 12, 13},
                       {20, 21, 22, 23},
                       {30, 31, 32, 33},
                       {40, 41, 42, 43}
                      };
```

Notice that each array row is initialized separately; also, notice that a comma must be at the end of each row. As with multidimensional arrays, you can initialize a ragged array at the time it is declared, as follows:

```
byte[][] raggedSmall = {
                        {10, 11, 12, 13},
                        {20, 21, 22},
                        {30, 31},
                        {40}
                       };
```

The sample program, **MultiArrays.java**, demonstrates how you can create and manipulate multidimensional arrays.

The source file for the program MultiArray.java is in the Session 6 directory on the book's CD-ROM.

```java
//    File name: MultiArray.java
//    Reference: Session 6
//
//    Java program to demonstrate multidimensional arrays
//    Topics:
//        1. Simultaneous declaration and initialization
//        2. Use of the length operator to obtain the size
//            of multidimensional arrays
//
//    Note:
//          This program uses output statements
//          described later in this chapter

public class MultiArray
{
    // Declare constants
    final static int ROWS = 10;
    final static int COLS = 5;

    public static void main(String[] args)
    {

    // Local variables
    int rowCount;
    int colCount;
    int totalSize;

    // Declare and allocate an array of bytes
    byte[][] screenPix = new byte[ROWS][COLS];

    // Obtain and store array dimensions
    rowCount = screenPix.length;
```

```
colCount = screenPix[COLS].length;
totalSize = rowCount * colCount;
// The following expressions generate an error:
// screenPix[ROWS].length
// screenPix[ROWS][COLS].length

// To obtain the total number of elements of a
// two-dimensional array, you need to get the size of
// each array dimension separately, as shownin the
// preceeding example.

// Display array dimensions
System.out.println("Array row size:    " + rowCount);
System.out.println("Array column size: " + colCount);
System.out.println("Total size:        " + totalSize);

//*************************
//      ragged arrays
//*************************
// First allocate the rows of an array
byte[][] raggedArray = new byte[5][];

// Now allocate the columns
for(int x = 0; x < 5; x++)
   raggedArray[x] = new byte[x+2];

//***********************************
//      static array initialization
//***********************************
byte[][] smallArray = {
                    {10, 11, 12, 13},
                    {20, 21, 22, 23},
                    {30, 31, 32, 33},
                    {40, 41, 42, 43},
                    };

// Display array elements
int i, j;
for(i = 0; i < 4; i++)
   {
```

```
        for(j = 0; j < 4; j++)
            System.out.println(smallArray[i][j]);
        }
    }
}
```

**10 Min.
To Go**

Java Input and Output

You can classify, store, and initialize data with relative independence from a machine's hardware. The designers of a programming language create data types and data-manipulation instructions in a way that ensures that you can implement these constructs with relative ease in any modern computer. However, this is not the case with data input and output operations, which relate intimately with hardware devices such as keyboards, mice, video display, and printers. Because I/O is device-dependant, it is very difficult to define and implement in Java architecture, where the fundamental goal is to achieve a high degree of device-independence. This explains why Java input and output operations seem sometimes difficult and complicated.

Data Input

The Java language contains no instructions for keyboard input. Although this is the case in other popular programming languages such as C and C++, these languages contain input functions in their standard libraries. However, The Java's input functions take place at the data stream level. To input an integer, a string, or a floating-point number, we have to develop a rather complicated routine based on the methods and subclasses of the Java InputStream class, which is part of the java.io library. Alternatively, you can develop an input routine using the methods of the System class, which is part of the java.lang library.

Although the processing required to obtain keyboard input is not difficult to implement, it is beyond our present level. However, even the simplest demonstration program requires some form of data input. For this reason, we have a class that performs data input. We call this class Keyin, and it contains the following methods:

inString()	inputs a string from the keyboard
inInt()	inputs an integer number
inDouble()	inputs a float in double format

We develop the Keyin **class during the Saturday evening sessions.**

To use these methods, the code must have access to the Keyin class. Your easiest option is to copy the file **Keyin.class** from the book's CD-ROM to your current development directory. When you do this, your program can input strings, integers, and floating-point numbers.

Each of the methods in the Keyin class is capable of displaying a prompt message. The methods pass the message as a parameter to the call, as in the following code fragment:

```
int age1;
. . .
age1 = inInt("Please enter your age" );
```

When the method inInt( ) executes, the prompt message "Please enter your age" appears. When you enter a valid value and press the <Enter> key, you assign the value to the variable age1. The methods inString( ) and inDouble( ) operate similarly.

You may look at the source code of the Keyin **class by loading the file Keyin.java into your editor program. Keyin.java is on the book's CD-ROM.**

Data Output

Fortunately, data output in Java is easier to implement than data input. You can use the out object to display program data directly. This object is part of the System class, which is in the java.lang library. By means of the object, you can use the print( ) and println( ) methods of the PrintStream class in java.io. The resulting expressions are as follows:

```
System.out.println("Hello World from Java");
```

The elements of a println( ) statement line are listed below:

System.out.println	=	stream
"Hello World from Java"	=	parameter list
System	=	class

`out`	=	object
`println`	=	method
`(`	=	start of parameters
`"`	=	start of string
`Hello World from Java`	=	string
`"`	=	end of string
`)`	=	end of parameters
`;`	=	terminator

The `println()` method terminates the displayed line automatically. The result is that the current text output marker moves to the next screen line automatically. The `print()` method, on the other hand, sends data to the video display at the current position of the text output marker but does not index to the next screen line. For example, the statements:

```
System.out.print("value");
System.out.print("      number");
System.out.print("      code");
System.out.flush();
```

Produce the following output:

```
value       number       code
```

In this case, use the `flush()` method to terminate the line.

Escape Characters

The Java display statements `print` and `println` use characters to delimit and format the string or character to be displayed. Because these characters have a special purpose in the statement grammar, you must restrict their use. For example, the " symbol marks the beginning and end of the string to be displayed. If we include this symbol as a displayable character, the processing logic cannot format the output correctly. Observe the error in the following code fragment:

```
System.out.println("She said her name was "Ellen"");
```

In this case, the processing logic interprets that the second quotation mark indicates the end of the output string. It cannot decipher the rest of the statement, producing a compiler error.

Java uses the \ symbol as a special character that indicates that the character that follows is interpreted in a special way. We call the \ symbol the *escape character*. You can use the escape character to display characters used in statement formatting and also to control code. Table 6-1 shows the Java escape characters.

Table 6-1
Java Escape Characters

Literal	Value	Action
\b	0x08	backspace
\t	0x09	horizontal tab
\n	0x0a	linefeed
\f	0x0c	formfeed
\r	0x0d	carriage return
\"		double quotation mark
\'		single quotation mark
\\		backslash

By using the escape symbol, we can reformat the previous statement as follows:

```
System.out.println("She said her name was \"Ellen\"");
```

A Sample Program

The following program, **Area.java**, demonstrates some of the programming elements and constructs we have discussed.

The source file for the program Area.java is in the Session 6 directory on the book's CD-ROM.

```
//    File name: Area.java
//    Reference: Session 6
//
//    Java program to calculate the area of a circle
```

```
//    Topics:
//       1. Using numeric variables and constants
//       2. Obtaining keyboard input
//       3. Displaying program data
//       4. Performing simple numeric calculations
//
//    Requires:
//       1. Keyin class in the current directory

public class Area
{
    // Constant PI is defined at the class level
    static final double PI = 3.141592653589793;

    public static void main(String[] args)
      {
        // Local variables
        double radius, area;

        // Input radius from keyboard
        radius = Keyin.inDouble("Enter radius: ");

        // Perform calculations and display result
        area = PI * (radius * radius);
        System.out.println("The area is: " + area);
      }
}
```

Done!

REVIEW

Arrays are an essential facility in programming languages. Without arrays, it is extremely difficult, if not impossible, to develop most commercial applications. An array is an ordered group of variables of the same type. Operations related to Java arrays are the declaration, allocation, and initialization. The length operator returns the number of elements in an array. Arrays can have more than one dimension and multidimensional arrays can be ragged.

Java contains no instructions for keyboard input. We use the methods of the Keyin class, developed in Session 20, to obtain keyboard input. The Java escape symbol is \. The out method of the System class uses escape characters to display reserved symbols and to perform control functions.

QUIZ YOURSELF

1. Write a Java program to create three arrays: one of type int, one of type double, and an array of String. Display the first element in each array. (See "Arrays.")

2. Use the length operator to obtain the number of characters in each of the arrays in the previous quiz exercise. (See "The Length of an Array.")

3. Create a multidimensional array with four columns and three rows. Make sure the program compiles correctly. (See "Multidimensional Arrays.")

4. Write a Java program that performs input and output of data in int, double, and String formats. Test it to make sure it works as expected. (See "Data Input.")

5. What is the Java escape character, and why is it necessary? (See "Escape Characters.")

Session Checklist

✔ Operators and their actions

✔ The assignment operator

✔ Lvalues and Rvalues

✔ Arithmetic and logical operators

✔ Bitwise and bitwise shift operators

✔ Compound assignment operators

✔ Hierarchy of operators

**30 Min.
To Go**

An expression in a programming language consists of operators and operands. Operators are special symbols that indicate specific processing operations. In this session, we discuss the operators of the Java programming language.

Operators

Operators are the symbols and special characters we use in a programming language to change the value of an operand. For example, the + symbol is the addition operator in Java. We use this operator to perform the sum of two operands, as in the following code fragment:

```
int val1 = 7;
int val2 = 3;
int val3 = val1 + val2;
```

 We also use the + symbol in appending strings. When we use it in this manner, we call it the concatenation operator. We discuss string concatenation later in this session.

In this case, we find the value of integer variable val3 (10) by adding the values of variables val1 and val2. We can functionally classify the fundamental Java operators as follows:

- Simple assignment
- Arithmetic
- Concatenation
- Increment and decrement
- Logical
- Bitwise
- Compound assignment

We classify the Java operators according to the number of operands:

- unary
- binary
- ternary

We discuss the Java ternary operator (?:) in Session 8 in the context of decision constructs.

Operator Actions

We use Java operators in expressions that produce program actions. For example, if a, b, and c are variables, the expression

```
c = a + b;
```

uses the = and the + operators to assign to the variable c the value that results from adding the variables a and b. The operators in this expression are the = (assignment) and + (addition) symbols.

We must use Java operators as elements of expressions; they are meaningless when used by themselves. For example, the term

```
-a;
```

is a trivial expression that does not change the value of the variable, although the expression

```
b = -b;
```

assigns a negative value to the variable b. The code fragment illustrates this action.

The Assignment Operator

We use the = sign in Java as a simple assignment operator. The result of the statement

```
a = a + 2;
```

is that the variable a is "assigned" the value that results from adding 2 to its own value. In other words, a "becomes" a + 2. It is important to note that this use of the = sign in Java is limited to assigning a value to a storage location referenced by a program element. We cannot interpret an expression containing the = sign algebraically. For example, in elementary algebra, we learn to solve an equation by isolating a variable on the left-hand side of the = sign, as follows:

```
2x = y
x = y/2
```

However, in Java, the statement line

```
2 * x = y;
```

generates a compile-time error. The fact that programming languages are not designed to perform even the simplest algebraic manipulations explains this.

Lvalues and Rvalues

In the study of programming languages, we refer to lvalues (short for left values) and rvalues (short for right values). An lvalue is an expression we can use to the left of the = sign. In a Java assignment expression, the lvalue must represent a single storage location. In other words, the element to the left of the = sign must be a variable. In this manner, if x and y are variables, the expression

```
x = 2 * y;
```

is a valid one. However, the expression

```
y + 2 = x;
```

is not valid because the lvalue is not a single storage location but an expression in itself.

Arithmetic Operators

Some Java arithmetic operators coincide with the familiar mathematical symbols. Such is the case with the + and - operators for addition and subtraction. However, some conventional mathematical symbols are not available on computer keyboards because their use gives rise to ambiguities. For example, the conventional symbol for division is not a standard keyboard character. In a similar sense, using the letter x as a symbol for multiplication is impossible because the language cannot differentiate between the mathematical operator and the alphanumeric character. For this reason, Java uses the / symbol to indicate division and the * to indicate multiplication. Table 7-1 lists the Java arithmetic operators.

Table 7-1
Java Arithmetic Operators

Operator	Action
+	addition
-	subtraction
*	multiplication
/	division
%	remainder

The % operator gives the remainder of a division. This operator has been inappropriately called the modulo or modulus operator. It is limited to integer operands. The following code fragment shows its use:

```
int val1 = 14;
int result = val1 % 3;
```

In this case, the value of the variable result is 2 because 2 is the remainder of dividing 14 by 3.

Concatenation Operator

We can use the + operator, used for arithmetic addition, to concatenate strings. The term "concatenation" comes from the Latin word "catena," which means chain. Consistent with this origin, to concatenate strings is to chain them together. The following code fragment shows the action of this operator:

```
// Define strings
String str1 = "con";
String str2 = "ca";
String str3 = "ten";
String str4 = "ate";
// Form a new word using string concatenation
String result = str1 + str2 + str3 + str4;
// result = "concatenate"
```

The operation of the concatenation operator is consistent with the notion of string "addition." In Java, if we add a numeric value to a string, the numeric operand is first converted into a string of digits and then concatenated to the string operand, as in the following code fragment:

```
String str1 = "Catch ";   // Define a string
int value = 22;           // Define an int
result = str5 + value;    // Concatenate string + int
                          // result = "Catch 22"
```

Notice that concatenation requires that one of the operands be a string. If both operands are numeric values, arithmetic addition takes place.

Increment and Decrement Operators

Very often in programming, we need to tally the number of times an operation or routine takes place. To do this, it is convenient to have a simple form of adding or subtracting 1 from the value of a variable. Java contains operators that allow this manipulation. These operators, which originated in the C language, are the increment (++) and decrement (- -) operators. The following expressions add or subtract 1 from the value of the operand.

```
x = x + 1;      // add 1 to the value of x
y = y - 1;      // subtract 1 from the value of y
```

We can use the increment and decrement operators to achieve the same result in a more compact way, as follows:

```
x++;            // add 1 to the value of x
y--;            // subtract 1 from the value of y
```

We can place the ++ and - - symbols before or after an expression. When the symbols precede the operand, the operator is in prefix form. When it follows the operand, it is in postfix form. For example:

```
PREFIX FORM         POSTFIX FORM
z = ++x;            z = x++;
```

The prefix and postfix forms are equivalent in unary statements. The variable x is incremented by 1 in both of these statements:

```
x++;
++x;
```

However, when we use the increment or decrement operators in an assignment statement, the results are different in each case. In the case of the prefix form, the increment or decrement is first applied to the operand, and the result is assigned to the lvalue of the expression. In the postfix form, the operand is first assigned to the lvalue, and then the increment or decrement is applied. The following code fragment shows both cases.

```
int x = 7;
int y;
. . .
y = ++x;            // y = 8, x = 8
y = x++;            // y = 7, x = 8
```

Relational Operators

We use relational operators, as their name suggests, to evaluate whether a relationship between operands is true or false. Table 7-2 lists the Java relational operators.

Table 7-2
Java Relational Operators

Operator	Action
<	less than
>	greater than
<=	less than or equal to
>=	greater than or equal to
==	equal to
!=	not equal to

In the following examples, we set the value of a boolean variable according to a comparison between the numeric variables x and y. If x = 4 and y = 2, the variable result is true or false, as shown in the following cases:

```
Case        Java statement              Variable result
1           result = x > y;             true
2           result = x < y;             false
3           result = x == 0;            false
4           result = x != 0;            true
5           result = x <= 4;            true
```

Notice in case 3 the difference between the assignment operator and the relational operator. The assignment operator (=) in this expression assigns to the variable result the boolean value of comparing x to 0. The result is false because the value of the variable x is 4. One common programming mistake is to use the assignment operator instead of the relational operator. The error is particularly dangerous because the resulting expression is often invalid.

Logical Operators

We use the relational operators, described in the preceding section, to evaluate whether a condition relating two operands is true or false. However, conditional expressions in Java are often complex. For example, to determine if a user is a teenager, we must test whether this person is older than twelve years and younger than twenty years. The logical operators allow us to combine two or more conditional statements into a single expression.

The principal use of logical operators is in combining two or more conditional statements. Like relational expressions, expressions that contain logical operators return true or false. Table 7-3 lists the Java logical operators.

Table 7-3
Java Logical Operators

Operator	Action
&&	AND
||	OR
!	NOT

For example, if x = 4, y = 2, and z = 0, the boolean variable result evaluates to either true or false, as in the following cases:

```
CASE    EXPRESSION                              VALUE OF result
 1      result = (x > y && z == 0)              true
 2      result = (x > y && z != 0)              false
 3      result = (x == 0 || z == 0)             true
 4      result = (x < y || z != 0)              false
```

Note in case 1 that the variable result evaluates to true because both relational elements in the statement are true. On the other hand, case 4 evaluates to false because the OR connector requires that at least one of the relational elements be true, but both are false (x > y and z = 0).

We use the logical NOT operator to invert the value of the variable of a boolean variable. Therefore, !true is false and !false is true. For example:

```
boolan var = false;
boolean result = var == !true;
```

In this case, the last statement evaluates to true because `!true` is false and `var` is false. Later, we see how we can use conditional expressions to make program decisions.

Bitwise Operators

The Java bitwise operators allow us to manipulate the individual bits of an integral data type. The operators are in Table 7-4.

Table 7-4
Java Bitwise Operators

Operator	Action
&	AND
|	OR
^	XOR
~	NOT
<<	left-shift
>>	right-shift
>>>	unsigned right-shift

The first four operators in Table 7-4 perform logical functions on the bits of the operands. By adopting the convention that associates a binary 1 with the concept of logical true and a binary 0 with false, we can use binary numbers to show the results of a logical operation. In this manner we can state the following:

```
1 OR 0 = 1
1 AND 1 = 1
1 AND 0 = 0
NOT 1 = 0
```

It is sometimes useful to think of the binary numbers to the left of the equal sign as a representation of the presence or absence of an element and the binary to the right of the equal sign as a representation of true or false. A truth table is a listing of all possibilities that result from a logical operation. The truth tables for the bitwise-logical operators AND, OR, XOR, and NOT are in Table 7-5.

Table 7-5
Truth Table for Bitwise/Logical Operations

AND |		OR |		XOR |		NOT |	
0 0 |	0	0 0 |	0	0 0 |	0	0 |	1
0 1 |	0	0 1 |	1	0 1 |	1	1 |	0
1 0 |	0	1 0 |	1	1 0 |	1		
1 1 |	1	1 1 |	1	1 1 |	0		

Although the bitwise operators AND, OR, and NOT perform similar functions as their logical counterparts, it is important to recall that the logical operators return true and false but do not change the contents of the variables. The bitwise operators, on the other hand, manipulate variable data. Thus, the result of a bitwise operation is often a different value from the previous one. In the following discussions, recall that it is customary to number the bits in an operand from right-to-left, with the rightmost bit designated as bit number 0, as shown back in Figure 4-2.

10 Min. To Go

The AND Operator

The AND bitwise operator (&) performs a boolean AND of the operands. This determines that a bit in the result is set only if the corresponding bits are set in both operands. The action corresponds to the AND truth table shown in Table 7-5.

A common use of the bitwise AND is to clear one or more bits without affecting the remaining ones. This is possible because ANDing with a zero bit always clears the result bit, and ANDing with a one bit preserves the original value of the first operand. Programmers sometimes refer to one of the operands of a bitwise operation as a mask. You can picture the effect of an AND mask as a filter that passes the bits that are ANDed with a 1-bit and clears the bits that are ANDed with a 0-bit, as in the following example:

```
                    0101 0111B
bitwise AND         1111 0000B  <- MASK
                    ----------
                    0101 0000B
```

The program named **AndBit7**, available on the book's CD-ROM, inputs a byte operand from the user and ANDs this value with a binary mask. The mask (number 128) has its high bit set and all other bits clear

```
128 = 1 0 0 0 0 0 0 0 B
```

Since ANDing with a zero bit always produces zero, we know that the seven low-order bits of the result are zero. The value of the high order bit of the result depends on the value we enter. We can describe the operation as follows:

```
                  x x x x x x x x  = user input
and operator (&) 1 0 0 0 0 0 0 0  = mask
                 ----------------
                 ? 0 0 0 0 0 0 0  = result
```

The result can be either the value 0 or the value 128. A zero result indicates that bit 7 of the user's input is not set. A value of 128 indicates that bit number 7 of the user's input is set.

The source file for the program AndBit7.java is in the Session7 directory on the book's CD-ROM.

```
//    File name: AndBit7.java
//    Reference: Session 7
//
//    Java program to demonstrate the action of the bitwise
//    AND operator
//    Topics:
//       1. Using the bitwise AND to determine the state
//          of an operand bit
//    Requires:
//       1. Keyin class in the current directory

public class AndBit7
{
  public static void main(String[] args)
    {
    // Local variables
       int mask = 128;
       int userInput;
```

```
    int result = 0;

    // Processing
    userInput = Keyin.inInt("Enter value: ");
    result = userInput & mask;

    // If if bit 7 was set in the user input, then
    // result = 128. Otherwise, result = 0
    System.out.println("result = " + result);
    }
}
```

The OR Operator

The OR bitwise operator (|) performs the Boolean inclusive OR of the operands. This determines that a bit in the result is set if at least one of the corresponding bits in the operands is also set. The action of the inclusive OR corresponds to that of the truth table in Table 5-5. Because the inclusive OR sets a bit in the result if either or both bits in the operands are set, a frequent use of this operation is to selectively set bits in an operand. We can describe this action of the OR operation by stating that ORing with a 1-bit always sets the result bit, whereas ORing with a 0-bit preserves the value of the other operand. For example, to make sure that bits 5 and 6 of an operand are set, we can OR it with a mask in which these bits are 1, as follows:

```
                  0001 0111B
    BITWISE OR    0110 0000B  <- MASK
                  -----------
                  0111 0111B
```

Because bits 5 and 6 in the mask are set, the OR operation guarantees that these bits are set in the result independently of the value they have in the first operand.

The XOR Operator

The XOR bitwise operator (^) performs the Boolean exclusive OR (XOR) of the operands. This means that a bit in the result is set if the corresponding bits in the operands have opposite values. If the bits have the same value (1 or 0), the result bit is clear. The action of the XOR operation corresponds to that of the truth table of Table 7-5.

Notice that XORing a value with itself always generates a zero result because all bits necessarily have the same value. On the other hand, XORing with a 1-bit inverts the value of the other operand because 0 XOR 1 = 1 and 1 XOR 1 = 0 (see Table 7-5). By properly selecting an XOR mask, we can control which bits of the operand are inverted and which are preserved. For example, to invert the two high-order bits of an operand, you can XOR with a mask in which these bits are set. If the remaining bits are clear in the mask, the original value of these bits is preserved in the result, as in the following example:

```
                  0101 0101B
BITWISE XOR       1100 0000B  <- MASK
                  ----------
                  1001 0101B
```

The NOT Operator

The NOT bitwise operator acts on a single operand by inverting all its bits. In other words, the NOT operation converts all 1-bits to 0 and all 0-bits to 1. This action corresponds to the Boolean NOT function, as in Table 7-5. The following example shows the result of a NOT operation:

```
                  0101 0101B
BITWISE NOT       ----------
                  1010 1010B
```

Bitwise Shift Operators

We use the Java shift left (<<) and shift right (>> and >>>) operators to transpose all the bits in the operand to the left or right. The operators require a second operand that specifies the number of bits to be shifted. For example, the following expression shifts left, by 2 bit positions, all the bits in the variable `bitPattern`:

```java
int bitPattern = 127;
bitPattern = bitPattern << 2;
```

We can see a left shift by a 1-bit position in Figure 7-1.

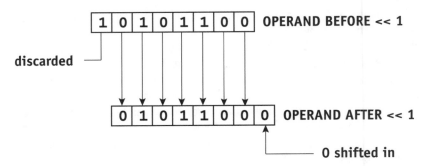

Figure 7-1
Left Shift of a byte variable by 1-bit

Notice that in the left-shift we discard the most significant operand bit i. Because in signed representations the high-order bit encodes the sign of the number, discarding this bit can effectively change positive values into negative and vice-versa. This is true in all Java integer data types, except `char`, which is an unsigned value. In the example in Figure 7-1, the original number, which is negative (high-bit set), is changed into a positive value.

The simple right-shift operator (>>) shifts the left operand based upon the number of bits in the right operand. For example:

```
int bitPattern = 127;
bitPattern = bitPattern >> 1;
```

In the right shift, the low-order bit is discarded and the high-order bit is duplicated into all the bits that are abandoned by the shift. The result is extending the sign bit into the new operand. The action of a right shift by 1 bit position is in Figure 7-2.

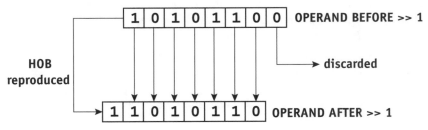

Figure 7-2
Right shift of a byte variable by 1-bit

The unsigned right shift operator (>>>) performs similarly to the conventional right shift (>>), but in this case the vacated positions on the left of the operand are zero-filled. Figure 7-3 shows an unsigned right shift by 1 bit position.

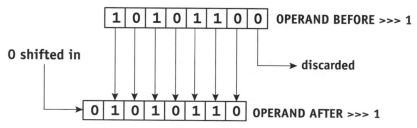

Figure 7-3
Unsigned right shift of a byte variable by 1-bit

Compound Assignment Operators

Java provides a series of compound operators that facilitate writing compact code. These compound assignment operators consist of a combination of the simple assignment operator (=) and an arithmetic or bitwise operator. For example, to add 4 to the variable x, we can code the following:

```
x = x + 4;
```

or we can combine the addition operator (+) with the simple assignment operator (=) and can code the following:

```
x += 4;
```

In both cases, the final value of x is its initial value plus 4, but the latter form reduces the size of the program. Table 7-6 lists the compound assignment operators.

Table 7-6
Java Compound Assignment Operators

Operator	Action
+=	addition assignment
-=	subtraction assignment
*=	multiplication assignment

Continued

Table 7-6 *Continued*

Operator	Action
/=	division assignment
%=	remainder assignment
&=	bitwise AND assignment
|=	bitwise OR assignment
^=	bitwise XOR assignment
<<=	left shift assignment
>>=	right shift assignment
>>>=	compound right shift assignment

Notice that the simple assignment operator always appears last in the compound assignment form. Also, notice that the compound assignment form is not available for the NOT (~) bitwise unary operator or for the unary increment (++) or decrement (- -) operators. The explanation is that unary (one element) statements do not require simple assignment; therefore, the compound assignment form is unnecessary.

Operator Hierarchy

Programming languages must establish rules of hierarchy to determine the order in which each element in an expression is evaluated. For example, the expression

```
boolean result = 5 - 4 < 3;
```

evaluates true (1) because Java arithmetic operators have higher precedence than relational operators. Therefore, in this case, the compiler first calculates 5 - 4 = 1 and then evaluates 1 < 3. Table 7-7 lists the precedence of the Java operators.

Table 7-7
Precedence of Java Operators

Operator	Precedence levels
. [] ()	highest
+ - ~ ! ++ - -	

Operator	Precedence levels
* / %	
<< >> >>>	
< <= > >= >	
== !=	
&	
^	
|	
&&	
||	
?:	
=	lowest

It is also possible that several operators in the same expression have the same precedence. In this case, the order of evaluation must agree with rules of associativity. For example, in the expression

```
z = a - b - c;
```

the rules of associativity determine which subtraction is performed first. In most programming languages, including Java, the basic rule of associativity for arithmetic operators is left-to-right. Therefore, Java performs the above subtraction as in the expression (a - b) - c. In Java, left-to-right associativity applies to all binary operators. However, unary and assignment operators have right-to-left associativity. The following code fragment shows a case in which the rules of associativity determine the value of an expression that contains the assignment operator.

```
int x = 0;
int y = 3;
. . .
x = y = 7;      // Associativity rule must be applied
```

If we evaluate the expression x = y = 7 left-to-right, the resulting value of variable x is 3. However, if we evaluate it right-to-left, the value of the variable x is 7.Because the assignment operator has right-to-left associativity, the value of x is 7.

Done!

REVIEW

The assignment operator is the = sign. An lvalue is the part of an assignment expression to the left of the = sign, and the rvalue is the part to the right. The lvalue must be a single storage location represented by a variable name. The arithmetic operators are +, -, *, /, and %. We also use the + operator in string concatenation. The increment (++) and decrement (--) operators originated in the C language. We use the logical operators (&&, ||, and !) in combining two or more conditional statements. We use the bitwise operators (&, |, ^, ~, <<, >>, and >>>) in manipulating bits of an integral data type. Compound assignment operators (+=, -=, *=, /=, %=, &=, |=, ^=, <<=, >>=, and >>>=) combine the arithmetic or bitwise operators with the assignment operator to produce compact code. The Java rules of hierarchy determine precedence in expressions that contain several operators.

QUIZ YOURSELF

1. What is the action of the assignment operator? (See "The Assignment Operator.")

2. In a Java expression, what can be to the left of the equal sign? (See "Lvalues and Rvalues.")

3. List the arithmetic operations, and describe the action of the remainder (%) operator. (See "Arithmetic Operators.")

4. Which operator performs string concatenation? (See "Concatenation Operator.")

5. Write the simplest possible Java expression that adds 1 to the value of a variable. (See "Increment and Decrement Operators.")

6. Which operator expresses less-than-or-equal-to? (See "Relational Operators.")

7. Which operator indicates a logical AND? (See "Logical Operators.")

8. Write the truth table for the XOR operation. (See "Bitwise Operators.")

9. Which operator indicates compound assignment in division? (See "Compound Assignment Operators.")

10. Use the Java rules of precedence and associativity to determine the value of the following expressions:

```
x = 6 * 2 + 3;
x = 6 * 2 / 2;
```

(See "Operator Hierarchy.")

Decision Constructs

Session Checklist

✔ The computer as a decision-making machine

✔ Decision in Java

✔ Statement blocks

✔ Decision statements: if, nested if, if-else, and switch constructs.

✔ Conditional expressions

**30 Min.
To Go**

I n this session, you learn about the elements of the Java language used in making decisions. Programs are able to process information logically because of the computer's decision-making ability. One of the programmer's most important tasks is to implement processing logic in code. We can implement logic in code by means of the language's decision constructs.

The section that follows serves as background information about decision constructs in Java. You can skip it and still follow the rest of the session.

The Computer as a Decision-Making Machine

One fundamental characteristic that sets apart the computer from a calculating machine is the computer's ability to make a simple decision and to change its course of action according to the result. Without this ability, the computer is only capable of executing programs that consist of a simple and unchanging sequence of operations. The decision-making capability of the computer requires the implementation in hardware of two basic functions:

- The possibility of comparing two operands.
- The possibility of directing program execution as a result of a comparison operation.

The comparison itself is based on examining the result of an arithmetic subtraction. The designers of the Central Processing Unit (the Pentium chip, in the case of a modern PC) provide the hardware components and the microcode. Several single-bit storage components in the CPU, called flag registers or flags, reflect the result of a comparison operation. Because the flags are single-bit registers, we use similar terms when we describe data bits. In this context, we say that a flag is set if it holds a 1-bit and cleared (or reset) if it holds a 0-bit. The following are some of the CPU flags used in decision making:

- The carry flag is set if the subtrahend is larger than the minuend. In other words, if in the operation

    ```
    x = A - B,
    ```

    B is numerically larger than A.
- The zero flag is set if the result of the operation is zero.

By examining these flags after a subtraction operation, we can effectively compare the two operands. For example, if the zero flag is set, both operands are equal. If the carry flag is set, the subtrahend (b) is larger than the minuend (a). If neither the carry nor the zero flag is set, the subtrahend is smaller than the minuend. Notice that the CPU contains a special comparison instruction that sets the flags as if a subtraction operation has taken place but does not change the value of the operands.

The second element of the decision-making machine is its ability to direct program execution according to the result of a comparison. Because the flags represent these results, we require only CPU instructions that direct execution to a particular memory location according to the state of one or more of the flags. These instructions are conditional jumps.

Equipped with a comparison instruction that sets the flags accordingly and with conditional jump instructions that direct execution according to these flags, we are able to build a simple decision-making machine. For example, we can develop a routine that calculates the absolute difference between two numbers, labeled A and B. The logic is based on comparing A and B by setting the carry and the zero flags according to the result of the following operation:

```
x = A - B
```

The code proceeds as follows:

1. If the carry flag is set, B is larger than A. In this case, jump to the routine that returns x = B - A.

2. If the zero flag is set, B is equal to A. In this case, jump to the routine that returns x = 0.

3. If neither the zero nor the carry flags is set, A is larger than B. In this case, return x = A - B.

We cannot implement the previous processing logic in a sequential processing machine that does not have decision-making capabilities. The flowchart in Figure 8-1 shows the logic we use in this case.

The previous logic, shown in Figure 8-1, is designed to show decision-making based on both the carry and the zero flag. In actual programming, the step in which we determine whether both operands are equal is unnecessary. It is common to discover flaws and possible simplifications in our initial logic. We develop most programs through consecutive refinements that eventually lead to a satisfactory result.

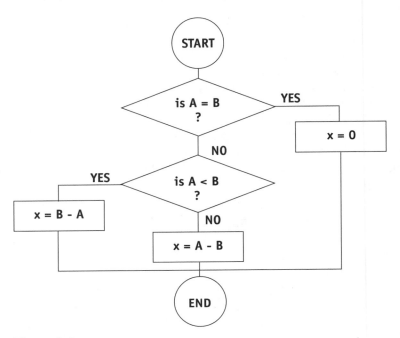

Figure 8-1
Calculating the absolute difference

Decisions in Java

Java contains several high-level decision constructs that make selection possible among several processing options. The major decision-making mechanisms are the if and the switch constructs. We also use the conditional operator (?:) in decision making, which is the only Java operator that contains three operands.

The if Construct

An if construct in the Java language consists of three elements:

1. The if keyword.
2. A test expression, also called a conditional clause, enclosed in parentheses.
3. One or more statements that execute if the test expression evaluates to logical, true.

The following program, **Beeper.java**, displays the message "BEEP-BEEP" if we enter the number 1 or 2. Otherwise, it displays no message. The code uses an if construct to test whether the typed keystroke matches the required numbers.

 The source file for the program Beeper.java is in the Session 8 directory on the book's CD-ROM.

```
//    File name: Beeper.java
//    Reference: Session 8
//
//    Java program to demonstrate simple decision
//    Topics:
//        1. Using the if construct
//
//    Requires:
//        1. Keyin class in the current directory

public class Beeper
{

  public static void main(String[] args)
    {
      int userInput;

      userInput = Keyin.inInt("Enter 1 or 2 to beep: ");
      if(userInput == 1 || userInput == 2)
          System.out.println("BEEP-BEEP");
    }
}
```

The listed code uses a simple form of the Java if construct. In this case, the compiler evaluates the expression in parentheses, following the if keyword, which is the following:

```
if(userInput == 1 || userInput == 2)
```

The expression uses the logical OR operator (discussed in Session 7) to create a compound condition. In this case, the parenthetical expression evaluates to true if the variable userInput is equal to 1 or 2. If the expression evaluates to true, the statement that follows is executed. If the expression evaluates to false, the statement associated with the if clause is skipped. Because there are no more statements in the Beeper program, execution concludes after the test.

Statement Blocks

In its simplest form, the if construct contains a single statement that executes if the conditional expression is true. This is the case in the if statement used in the Beeper program. However, a program often has to perform more than one operation associated with a decision statement. Java provides a simple way of grouping several statements so that the compiler treats them as a unit. We perform the grouping by means of curly brace ({}) symbols. We call the statements within two braces compound statements or statement blocks.

Using statement blocking, we can modify the Beeper program so that more than one statement executes when the test condition evaluates to true. For example:

```
if(userInput == 1 || userInput == 2)
{
    System.out.println("BEEP-BEEP");
    System.out.println("The value entered was " + userInput);
}
```

Here we have used the brace symbols ({ and }) to associate more than one statement with the if construct. Therefore, both println statements execute if the conditional clause evaluates to true and are skipped if it evaluates to false.

The Nested if

If statements can be nested so that the execution of one statement or statement group is conditioned to two or more conditional clauses. For example, we can modify the if construct in the Beeper program so that the code provides processing for the case that the user input is the value 2, as follows:

```
if(userInput == 1 || userInput == 2)
    {
    System.out.println("BEEP-BEEP");
        if(userInput == 2)
        System.out.println("Input = 2");
    }
```

In this code fragment, the `if` statement that tests for a value of 2 in the user input is nested inside the `if` statement that tests for a user input of either 1 or 2. In this case, we never reach the inner `if` statement if the outer one evaluates to false. Also notice the indentation that indicates that the second `if` statement is subordinate to the first. Although white space has no effect on the code, text line indentation shows the logical flow of a program routine. Figure 8-2 is a flowchart of a nested `if` construct.

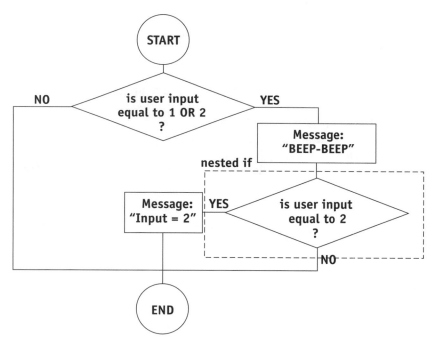

Figure 8-2
Flowchart of a nested if construct

The else Construct

**20 Min.
To Go**

The simple `if` construct executes a statement, or a statement block, if the conditional clause evaluates to true, but it takes no alternative action if the expression evaluates to false. The `if-else` construct allows Java code to provide two alternative processing options: one if the conditional clause is true and a one if it is false.

We sometimes call the `else` **construct the** `if-else` **construct.**

We can use the Java `else` construct to modify the Beeper program so that it displays a different message if we input the numbers 1 or 2 or if we enter a different value. The following code fragment shows the processing in this case:

```
if(userInput == 1 || userInput == 2)
     System.out.println("BEEP-BEEP");
else
     System.out.println("Invalid input");
```

In typing the `else` construct, it is customary to align the `if` and the `else` keywords, as in the preceding fragment. Here again, white space indents the text lines in a manner that helps visualizing the program logic.

Like the `if` clause, the `else` clause can contain a statement block that is delimited by braces. This is necessary if more than one statement executes on the `else` program branch. Figure 8-3 is a flowchart of the preceding `if-else` construct.

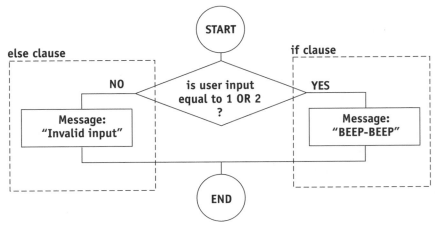

Figure 8-3
Flowchart of an if-else construct

The Dangling else Problem

Because the else statement is optional, we can have several nested if constructs, some of which without a corresponding else clause. This situation, sometimes referred to as a *dangling else*, can give rise to uncertainty about the pairing of if and else clauses. For example, the else clause in the following fragment is paired with the inner if statement:

```
if(a != 0 )
   if(a > 1)
     System.out.println("x is positive and non-zero);
   else
     System.out.println("x is zero or negative);
```

The compiler's general rule in solving the dangling else is that each else statement is paired with the closest if statement that does not have an else and that is in the same block. The indentation in the preceding code fragment serves to indicate that the else statement is linked to the statement if(a > 1).

We can use braces to force a different association between statements. For example:

```
if(a != 0 )
  {
    if(a > 1)
        System.out.println("x is positive and non-zero);
  }
else
   System.out.println("x must be zero");
```

In this case, the closest if statement without an else located in the same block is the statement if(a != 0).

Here again we have used indentation of the text lines to indicate the if-else pairing.

The else-if Clause

A common cause of program errors is the failure to recognize the relationship among two or more consecutive if statements. In the preceding section, we see how the dangling else problem can determine an incorrect if-else association. The relationship between two consecutive if statements can also cause logical flaws in the code. We have seen the case of a cascaded if construct, in which a second if statement is conditioned to the first one being true, as in the flowchart of Figure 8-2. On the other hand, if we do not nest the second if statement in the first one, its evaluation is independent of the result of the first if. The following code fragment shows this case.

```
if(userInput == 1 || userInput == 2)
    System.out.println("BEEP-BEEP");
if(userInput == 2)
    System.out.println("Input = 2");
```

In the preceding code fragment, the second if statement is unrelated to the first one and evaluated in any case.

Alternatively, the else-if construct allows subordinating the second if statement when the first one evaluates to false. All that is necessary in this case is to nest the second if within the else clause of the first one. For example:

```
int age;
. . .
if(age == 12)
  System.out.println("You are 12");
    else if(age == 13)
      System.out.println("You are 13");
        else if(age == 14)
          System.out.println("You are 14");
            else
                System.out.println("You not 12, 13, or 14");
```

Notice in the preceding code fragment that the last if statement (println) executes only if all the preceding if statements have evaluated to false. If one of the if statements evaluates to true, the rest of the construct is skipped. In some cases, several logical variations of the consecutive if statements may produce the desired results, but in other cases it may not. Drawing a flowchart is usually a simple way of determining if the logic is correct.

The switch Construct

**10 Min.
To Go**

Often, computer programs must use the value of an integer variable to direct execution to one of several processing routines. A typical scenario is a program that displays a menu of processing options, any of which we select by entering a numeric value, as in the following example:

```
********************************
|     GEOMETRICAL CALCULATIONS  |
|            PROGRAM            |
********************************
| Figure:                      |
|          1. circle           |
|          2. parallelogram    |
|          3. triangle         |
|          4. ellipse          |
********************************
| Type number desired:         |
********************************
```

In this case, we enter an integer value for selecting the desired menu option. One possible way of implementing this processing option is to use several consecutive if statements to test the value of the input variable. In addition, the Java language contains a switch construct that provides a simpler way of implementing multiple processing alternatives based on the value of an integer value. The switch construct consists of the following elements:

- The switch keyword
- A controlling expression, of integral type, enclosed in parentheses (usually a variable name). Floats and boolean types are illegal.
- One or more case statements followed by an integer or character constant (or an expression that evaluates to a constant). A colon (:) symbol terminates these statements.
- An optional break statement at the end of each case block that allows exiting the switch structure immediately.
- An optional default statement, which receives control if none of the preceding case statements have executed. A colon symbol terminates the default statement.

The switch construct provides an alternative to a complicated if, else if, else chain, also called an if ladder. The general form of the switch statement is as follows:

```
switch (expression)
{
    case value1:
```

```
      statement;
      statement;
      . . .
      [break;]
   case value2:
      statement;
      statement;
      . . .
      [break;]
   ...
   [default:]
      statement;
      statement;
      . . .
      [break;]
}
```

The preceding example is in a non-existent computer language, sometimes called pseudocode. The idea of pseudocode is to show the fundamental logic of a programming construct without having to comply with the formal requirements of any particular programming language. There are no strict rules to pseudocode; the syntax is left to the writer's imagination. In the preceding pseudocode listing, we freely combine elements of the Java language with other symbols. The ... characters (sometimes called ellipses) indicate that other program elements can follow at this point. We use the bracket symbols to signal optional components.

In the switch construct, the controlling expression, enclosed in parentheses, evaluates to an integer type. Although the control expression is usually a variable name, it is possible to have a control expression that uses more than one variable, that contains literal values, or that performs integer arithmetic.

The case keyword marks the code position where execution is directed. An integer or character constant follows it or an expression that evaluates to an integer or character constant. If the control statement is a char type, the case constant is enclosed in single quotes, as in the following code fragment:

```
char sw_var1;
. . .
switch (sw_var1)
```

```
{
    case 'A':
        System.out.println("Input was A");
        break;
    case 'B':
        System.out.println("Input was B");
        break;
. . .
}
```

Alternatively, if the control statement evaluates to an `int` type, the case constant does not require quotes, as in the following code fragment:

```
int sw_var2;
. . .
switch (sw_var2)
{
    case 1:
        System.out.println("Input was 1");
        break;
    case 2:
        System.out.println("Input was 2");
        break;
. . .
}
```

Although the `break` keyword is optional, if it is not present at the end of a case block, the following case or default blocks execute. In fact, execution in a `switch` construct continues until we encounter a `break` keyword or the end of the construct. By the same token, when we encounter a `break` keyword i, execution is immediately directed to the end of the `switch` construct. A `break` statement is not required on the last block (case or default statement) but is usually included to improve readability.

We must enclose all execution blocks within a `switch` construct in braces, but the case and the default keywords automatically block the statements that follow them. For this reason, braces are not necessary to indicate the main execution block within a case or default block.

The following program, Menu.java, contained on the book's CD-ROM in the Session 8 folder, shows the processing necessary for implementing menu selection using a Java switch **construct.**

```java
//    File name: Menu.java
//    Reference: Session 8
//
//    Java program to demonstrate menu selection
//    Topics:
//        1. Using the switch construct
//
//    Requires:
//        1. Keyin class in the current directory

public class Menu
{

   public static void main(String[] args)
     {
       // Local variable
       int userInput;

       // Display menu graphics
       System.out.println("=============================");
       System.out.println("|    MENU SELECTION DEMO     |");
       System.out.println("=============================");
       System.out.println("| Options:                   |");
       System.out.println("|           1. Draw          |");
       System.out.println("|           2. Paint         |");
       System.out.println("|           3. Exit          |");
       System.out.println("=============================");
       userInput = Keyin.inInt(" Select an option: ");

       // Switch construct
       switch(userInput)
       {
           case 1:
```

```
            System.out.println("Draw selected");
            break;
        case 2:
            System.out.println("Paint selected");
            break;
        case 3:
            System.out.println("Exit selected");
            break;
        default:
            System.out.println("Invalid selection");
            break;          // This break is not necessary
    }
  }
}
```

Conditional Expressions

Java contains a ternary operator that uses two operands as an argument. We call it the *conditional* operator, and it uses the symbols ?:. We use a conditional expression to substitute an if-else construct. Its syntax is as follows:

```
exp1 ? exp2 : exp3
```

In this case, if exp1 is true, exp2 executes. If exp1 is false, exp3 executes. Suppose we want to assign to a variable named minVal the smaller of two integer variables, named a and b. Using a conventional if-else statement, we can code as follows:

```
int a, b, minVal;
. . .
if (a < b)

    minVal = a;
else
    minVal = b;
```

Using the conditional construct, we can code as follows:

```
minVal = (a < b) ? a : b;
```

Where:

```
MinVal    =        lvalue
(a < b)   =        first expression
a    =        second expression
b    =        third expression
```

In the preceding statement, the elements to the right of the assignment opera-tor (=) form the conditional expressions. In the conditional part, we can distin-guish three elements: The first expression — in this case (a < b) — evaluates either to logical true or false. If it evaluates to true, the value of the second expression is assigned to the lvalue. If the first expression evaluates to false, the value of the third expression is assigned to the lvalue.

 Lvalues and rvalues are discussed in Session 7.

Done!

REVIEW

The most elementary decision-making construct is the if statement. We can use roster symbols to associate more than one processing operation with the result of an if clause. In the nested if, we cascade more than one statement to test for several associated conditions. The else construct provides a processing option for the case in which an associated if clause is not true. The else-if provides a way for conditioning a second if clause to a preceding one that has evaluated to false. The switch construct, often used in menu-like operations, is a shorthand for a series of cascaded if statements. The conditional expression is based on a ternary operator that allows the compact coding of a simple if-else construct.

QUIZ YOURSELF

---

1. What is the fundamental difference between a computer and a calculat-ing machine? (See "The Computer as a Decision-Making Machine.")
2. Write an if construct that tests whether a person is in the teenage years. (See "The if Construct.")

3. How can you associate two if statements so that execution takes place only if both statements are true? (See "The Nested if.")

4. Describe the purpose of the else clause. (See "The else Construct.")

5. What coding situation produces the condition known as a "dangling else" problem? (See "The Dangling else Problem.")

6. Use a code sample that contains an else-if clause. (See "The else-if Clause.")

7. Write a Java program that uses a switch construct to provide selection among several options in a menu. (See "The switch Construct.")

8. Write a Java conditional expression that sets a boolean variable named isSweet to true if the value of an int variable named sugarContents is greater than 10 and sets isSweet to false otherwise. (See "Conditional Expressions.")

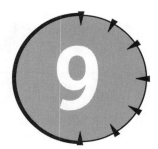

Iteration and Flow Controls

Session Checklist

✔ Java iterative statements

✔ The program loop

✔ The for loop

✔ Compound statements

✔ The while loop

✔ The do-while loop

✔ Selecting a loop

✔ Direct flow control: break and continue

**30 Min.
To Go**

Computer programs often perform repetitive tasks. For instance, a payroll program estimates wages and deductions by performing the repetitive calculations for each employee in the system. These repetitions usually take place by means of programming constructs called iteration control statements or loops. In this chapter, we discuss the three Java loop constructs: the *for loop*, the *while loop*, and the *do-while loop*. We also discuss Java instructions that produce abrupt changes in program execution: the *break* and *continue* statements.

Java Iterative Statements

A loop construct is merely a programming convenience. Its advantage is that it saves coding effort and programming time. Loops do not offer any unique functionality that is not otherwise available in the programming language. However, in many cases, explicitly coding each program operation is quite cumbersome. Imagine a payroll program for a company with one thousand employees in which the code that performs the calculation must be repeated 1,000 times.

In the context of loops and other repetitive constructs, we often use program *iteration*. To iterate, in this sense, means to do something repeatedly. Each transition through the statement or group of statements in the loop structure is an iteration. When referring to a program loop that repeats a group of statements three times, we speak of the first, the second, and the third loop iteration. But notice that the concept of program iteration is not limited to loop structures. The word "iteration" describes any form of repetitive processing, independently of the logical means by which we perform it.

Elements of a Program Loop

In any programming language, a loop involves three characteristic steps:

1. The *initialization* step primes the loop's logical elements and variables to an initial state.

2. The *processing* step performs the repetitive processing. This portion of the code is repeated during each iteration.

3. The *testing* step evaluates the variables or conditions that determine the continuation of the loop. If they are met, the loop execution continues. If not, the processing operation or operations end.

A simple loop structure can be a routine that performs the factorial calculations. The factorial is the product of all whole numbers equal to or less than the operand. For example, factorial 4 (written 4!) is the following:

```
4! = 4 * 3 * 2 * 1 = 24
```

If we create the variable facPro to hold the accumulated product and the variable curFac to hold the current factor, we can design a program loop that calculates the factorial, as follows:

1. Initialize the variables facPro to the number whose factorial we calculate and the variable curFac to this number minus 1.

2. Make `facPro` equal to `curFac` times `facPro`, and subtract 1 from `curFac`.

3. If `curFac` is greater than 1, repeat step 2; if not, terminate the loop.

Notice that testing for a factor greater than 1 eliminates the multiplication by 1, which is trivial. When the loop concludes, the factorial is in the variable `facPro`. Figure 9-1 is a flowchart of the logic used in the preceding factorial calculation.

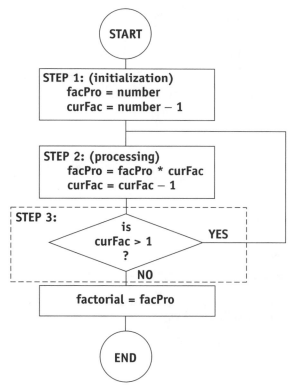

Figure 9-1
Flowchart for calculating the factorial

The for Loop

Consider the for loop as Java's simplest iterative construct. It repeats execution of a program statement, or statement block, a fixed number of times. The typical for loop consists of the same steps in the previous section for a generic program loop:

1. An initialization step that assigns a starting value to the loop variable.
2. One or more processing statements that perform the required operations and update the loop variable.
3. A test expression that determines conditions that terminate the loop.

In the case of the for loop, these steps are somewhat hidden in the loop structure. The general form of the for loop instruction is as follows:

```
for(var = 0; var < 5; var++)
    {
        // processing statements
    }
```

Where:

for	=	for keyword
var = 0	=	initializing element
var < 5	=	test element
var++	=	update element

For example, we can use the for loop in the following code fragment to calculate the factorial according to the flowchart in Figure 9-1.

```
int number = 5;        // Factorial to be calculated
int facPro, curFac;    // Local variables

// Initialization step
facPro = number;       // Initialize operational variable

// Loop processing
for (curFac = number - 1; curFac > 1; curFac--)
    facPro = curFac * fac_pro;

// Done
System.out.println("Factorial is: ", + facPro);
```

In the preceding code fragment, the expression

```
for(curFac = number - 1; curFac > 1; curFac --)
```

contains a loop expression that includes elements from steps 1, 2, and 3. The first statement inside parentheses (curFac = number - 1) sets the initial value of the factor variable, which is part of the initialization function in step 1. The second statement inside the parentheses (curFac > 1) contains the test condition that terminates the loop. This test operation is part of step 3 in the general description. The third statement in parentheses (curFac --) uses the decrement operator (--) to diminish the loop variable by 1 during each iteration. This operation is part of the processing in step number 2.

Although the for loop expression does not terminate in a semicolon, it contains embedded semicolons. In this instance, the semicolon separates the initialization element from the test element and the test element from the update element. This allows us to use multiple statements in each element of the loop expression, as in the following example:

```
unsigned int x, y;
for(x = 0, y = 5; x < 5; x++, y--)
    System.out.println("x is: " + x, " y is: " + y);
```

Where:

x = 0, y = 5	=	initialization
x < 5	=	termination
x++, y--	=	update

Notice in the preceding code fragment that the initialization element sets the variable x to an initial value of 0 and the variable y to an initial value of 5. The update element instructs the compiler to increment x and decrement y during each iteration. The comma operator isolates the components in each loop element.

The second element in the for loop construct, sometimes called the test expression, is evaluated during each loop iteration. If the result of this evaluation is false, the loop terminates immediately. Otherwise, loop execution continues. It is important to remember that for the loop to execute the first iteration, the test expression must initially evaluate to true. Notice that the test expression determines the condition under which the loop executes, not the condition under which it terminates. Notice the following code fragment:

```
for(x = 0; x == 5; x++)
    System.out.println(x);
```

The processing element of this loop does not execute because the test expression x == 5 initially evaluates to false. By the same token, the following loop executes endlessly because the terminating condition is assigned a new value during each iteration.

```java
int x;
for (x = 0; x = 5; x++)
    System.out.println(x);
```

The test element of a for loop can contain a complex logical expression. In this case, the entire expression is evaluated to determine if the condition is met. For example:

```java
int x, y;
for(x = 0, y = 5; (x < 3 || y > 1); x++, y--)
```

In this case, the test expression

```java
(x < 3 || y > 1)
```

evaluates to true if either x is less than 3 or if y is greater than 1. The end of the loop is reached when x = 4 or when y = 1.

In the previous example, we use parentheses to improve the readability of the code, but the test expression evaluates correctly without them.

20 Min. To Go

Compound Statement in Loops

In Java, we use the roster symbols ({ and }) to group several statements into a single block. We use statement blocks in loop constructs to make the code perform more than one processing operation. The following program, **Factorial.java**, uses a statement block in a for loop to display the partial product during the factorial calculation.

The source file for the program Factorial.java is in the Session 9 directory on the book's CD-ROM.

```java
//   File name: Factorial.java
//   Reference: Session 9
```

```
//
//   Java program to demonstrate looping
//   Topics:
//      1. Using the for loop
//      2. Loop with multiple processing statements
//
//   Requires:
//      1. Keyin class in the current directory

public class Factorial
{

  public static void main(String[] args)
  {

      int number;
      int facPro;
      int curFac;

      System.out.println("FACTORIAL CALCULATION PROGRAM");
      number = Keyin.inInt("Enter a positive integer: ");

      facPro = number;       // Initializing

      for(curFac = number - 1; curFac > 1; curFac--)
      {
         facPro = curFac * facPro;
           System.out.println("Partial product: " + facPro);
           System.out.println("Current factor:  " + curFac);
      }

    // Done. Display factorial
    System.out.println("\n\nFactorial is: " + facPro);
  }
}
```

The while Loop

The Java while keyword makes a second type of loop possible. As the keyword implies, the while loop repeats execution of a statement or statement block "while" a given condition evaluates to true. Like the for loop, the while loop requires initialization, processing, and testing steps. However, in the for loop, the initialization and testing steps are part of the loop itself. In the while loop, these steps are outside the loop body. The following program, called **Ascii.java**, uses a while loop to display the ASCII characters in the range 0×10 to 0×20.

The source file for the program Ascii.java is in the Session 9 directory on the book's CD ROM.

```
//    File name: Ascii.java
//    Reference: Session 9
//
//    Java program to demonstrate looping
//    Topics:
//       1. Using the while loop
//
//    Requires:
//       1. Keyin class in the current directory

public class Ascii
{

  public static void main(String[] args)
  {

     char value = 0x10;

        while(value < 0x20)
        {
           System.out.println(value);
           value++;
        }
  }
}
```

In the **Ascii.java** program, notice that the initialization of the loop variable takes place outside the while construct. The loop variable is updated inside the loop. The only loop element in the loop expression is the test element. The following are the elements of the while loop:

```
loopVar = 0;               // External initializtion

while(loopVar != 10)            // Loop continuation test
{
    System.out.println(loopVar); // Processing
    loopVar++;                 // Update
}
```

The while loop evaluates the test expression before the loop statement block executes. For this reason, the while loop displays all the integers between 0 and 9. This mode of operation is consistent with the meaning of the word while.

The do-while Loop

The third iterative construct of Java is the do-while loop. In the do-while loop, the test expression is evaluated after the loop executes. This mode of operation ensures that the loop executes at least once. This contrasts with the while loop in which the test expression is evaluated before the loop executes. For example, the while loop in the following code fragment does not execute the statement body because the variable x evaluates to 0 before the first iteration:

```
int x = 0;
while (x != 0)
    System.out.println(x);
```

We can use the do-while loop to ensure that the loop body executes at least once, as follows:

```
int x = 0;

do
    System.out.println(x);
while (x != 0);
```

In this case, the loop's first iteration always takes place because the test is not performed until the loop body executes. The following are the elements of the do-while loop:

```
loopVar = 0;                     // External initializtion

do                               // Start of loop
{
    System.out.println(loopVar); // Processing
    loopVar++;                   // Update
}
while(loopVar != 10);            // Test expression
```

In many cases the, the do-while loop's processing is identical to that of the while loop. Notice that the test expression in a do-while loop terminates in a semicolon.

10 Min.
To Go

Selecting a Loop Construct

Java offers three constructs for performing program iterations: the for loop, the while loop, and the do-while loop. The for loop provides a neat structure that contains the required three loop elements: initialization, test, and processing. This mode of operation makes the for loop useful in situations in which the we know the loop conditions in advance. For example, we can code a routine to display the ASCII characters in the range 16 to 128 using a for loop, as follows:

```
for(char ascii = 16; ascii < 129; ascii ++)
    System.out.println(ascii);
```

Notice in the preceding code fragment that the loop variable ascii is declared inside the for statement. The result is that ascii is a local variable whose scope is limited to the loop itself.

The while loop, on the other hand, creates an iteration structure that repeats while a certain test condition is met. This mode of operation makes the while loop useful in creating loop structures in which the terminating condition is unpredictable.

The do-while loop provides an alternative to the while loop in which the test condition is evaluated after the processing statements execute. This ensures that the loop executes at least once.

In many cases, a program must use several loop constructs, often nested within other loops, to perform a complicated task. The following program, **Asctable.java**, displays the table of ASCII characters in the range 0x20 to 0x7F. The code uses three loops. The first consists of two `for` statements that display the column heads for the table. The second, a `while` loop, takes care of the table's row heads and leading spaces. The third loop, nested in the second, displays a row of 16 ASCII codes. The program's result is a labeled table of the ASCII character codes.

The source file for the program Asctable.java is in the Session 9 directory on the book's CD-ROM.

```java
//    File name: Asctable.java
//    Reference: Session 9
//
//    Java program to demonstrate looping
//    Topics:
//       1. Using several loop constructs simultaneously
//       2. Nested loops
//
public class Asctable
{
  public static void main(String[] args)
  {
    // Local variables
    char hexLetter;            // For table header
    char ascCode = 0x20;        // First ASCII code
    // Counters for rows and columns
    int row = 2;
    int column;

    System.out.print("\n\n");
    System.out.print("                           ");
    System.out.println("ASCII CHARACTER TABLE");
    System.out.print("                           ");
    System.out.println("characters 0x20 to 0xff");
    System.out.print("\n     ");
```

```
// FIRST LOOP
// Display column heads for numbers 0 to F hexadecimal
// Notice that this actually requires two for loops: one
// for displaying the hex number 0 to 9, and another one
// for the hex letters A to F.
for(hexLetter = '0'; hexLetter <= '9'; hexLetter ++)
    System.out.print("    " + hexLetter);
for(hexLetter = 'A'; hexLetter <= 'F'; hexLetter ++)
    System.out.print("    " + hexLetter);

// Blank line to separate table head from data
System.out.println("\n");

// SECOND LOOP
// While ASCII codes smaller than 0x80 display row head
// and leading spaces
// THIRD LOOP (nested in the second loop)
// Display row of ASCII codes for columns 0 to 0x0F.
// Add a new line at end of each row
while (ascCode < 0x80)
{
    System.out.print("    " + row);
        for (column = 0; column < 16; column ++)
        {
            System.out.print("    " + ascCode);
            ascCode ++;
        }
        System.out.print("\n\n");
    row ++;
}
}
}
```

Figure 9-2 is a screen snapshot of the compilation and execution screen for the **Asctable.java** program.

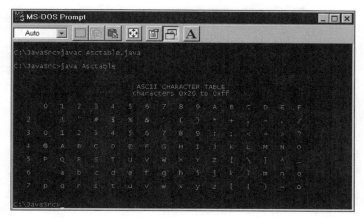

Figure 9-2
Screen snapshot of the asctable.java program

Direct Flow Control

The previous loop statements in this chapter, as well as the decision constructs of Session 8, provide ways of directing program execution. In these cases, execution is directed according to the result of a statement or expression that evaluates to true or false. We can say that these constructs change the flow of a program indirectly because their action depends on the result of a logical expression.

In addition to the indirect flow control statements, Java contains instructions that change execution directly and abruptly. These instructions are *break, continue*, and *return* statements. We discuss the return statement in Session 10.

C and C++ contain an additional statement, goto, **that allows us to direct execution unconditionally to a specific destination. Although** goto **is a Java reserved word, the** goto **statement has not been implemented.**

The break Statement

The Java break statement provides a way to exit a switch construct. In addition, a break statement can be in a for, while, or do-while loop. In this case, execution proceeds at the next line after the currently executing level of the loop.

Notice that we cannot use the break statement outside a switch or loop structure. When we use break in a nested loop, execution exits the innermost loop level.
The following **Break.java** program shows this.

**The source file for the program Break.java is in the Session 9
directory on the book's CD-ROM.**

```java
//    File name: Break.java
//    Reference: Session 9
//
//    Java program to demonstrate direct flow control
//    Topics:
//        1. Action of the break statement
//

public class Break
{

  public static void main(String[] args)
   {
   int number = 1;
   char letter;

   while(number < 10 )
      {
      System.out.println("number is: " + number);
      number ++;
         for (letter = 'A'; letter < 'G'; letter ++)
         {
         System.out.println(" letter is: " + letter);
            if (letter == 'C')
               break;
         }
      }
   }
}
```

The program **Break.java** contains two loops. The first one, a `while` loop, displays a count of the numbers from 1 to 9. The second one, an inner loop, displays the capital letters A to F. However, an `if` statement, and an associated `break` statement, interrupt execution of the nested loop as soon as the letter C is reached. Because the `break` statement acts on the current loop level only, the outer loop resumes counting numbers until the value 10 is reached.

The continue Statement

Although we can use the `break` statement with either a switch or a loop construct, the `continue` statement operates only in loops. We can use it only within a `for`, `while`, or `do-while` construct. The purpose of `continue` is to bypass all statements not yet executed in the loop and to return to the beginning of the loop immediately.

The following program, **Continue.java**, contains a `for` loop designed to display the letters A to D. A `continue` statement in this loop serves to bypass the letter C, which is not displayed.

The source file for the program Continue.java is in the Session 9 directory on the book's CD-ROM.

```
//    File name: Continue.java
//    Reference: Session 9
//
//    Java program to demonstrate direct flow control
//    Topics:
//       1. Action of the continue statement
//
public class Continue
{

   public static void main(String[] args)
      {
      char letter;
      for (letter = 'A'; letter < 'E'; letter ++)
         {
```

```
        if (letter == 'C')
            continue;
        System.out.println("  letter is " + letter);
    }
  }
}
```

The Labeled break Statement

We can use the break statement to exit a loop construct; however, execution continues at the innermost loop level. Occasionally, an application requires the immediate exit of all levels in a loop. One typical case that requires a fast exit occurs when an error condition is detected. One possible solution is to include an if statement in the loop and to add a terminating condition to the loop header. However, when we deal with several nesting levels, extra conditions can be inconvenient.

For these cases, C and C++ contain the goto statement mentioned at the start of this section. The equivalent Java instruction, which provides an immediate and unconditional exit, is the *labeled break*. In the case of the Java break, the identifier of a program label follows the break statement. The label itself is a placemarker that ends with a colon. The general form of the labeled break is as follows:

```
char n;
. . .
FAST_EXIT:
while(. . .)
{
  for(. . .)
    {
        if(n == 'x')
            break FAST_EXIT;
            . . .
    }
}
```

Notice that the label must precede the outermost loop out of which you want to break. Also notice that the use of a labeled break usually implies that code must test for the circumstances that determine the end of the loop.

The following program, called **FastBreak.java**, shows the use of a labeled break to implement an error handler.

The source file for the program FastBreak.java is in the Session 9 directory on the book's CD-ROM.

```java
//    File name: FastBreak.java
//    Reference: Session 9
//
//    Java program to demonstrate direct flow control
//    Topics:
//        1. Action of the labled break statement
//        2. Use of a labeled break in an error handler
//
//    Requires:
//        1. Keyin class in the current directory

public class FastBreak
{

  public static void main(String[] args)
    {
    int number = 1;
    char letter;

    letter = Keyin.inChar("Enter any character, except C: " );

    FAST_EXIT:
    while(number < 10 )
       {
       System.out.println("number is: " + number);
       number ++;
          for (char ch = 'A'; ch < 'D'; ch++)
             {
                System.out.println("  char is: " + ch);
                 if (letter == 'C' || letter == 'c')
                    break FAST_EXIT;
             }
```

Done!

```
      }
   if(letter == 'C' || letter == 'c')
      System.out.println("ERROR, invalid input");
   }
}
```

REVIEW

In Java language, we use loops to implement repetitive tasks. Java contains three fundamental types of loops: the for loop, the while loop, and the do-while loop. Each loop type has its own mode of operation, and is used to solve typical programming problems. Instructions that produce abrupt changes in program execution are the break and continue statements.

QUIZ YOURSELF

1. Write a Java program with a for loop that displays all odd numbers in the range between 0 to 50. (See "The for Loop.")

2. Write a Java program with a loop that displays a single digit the user inserts. The digit 0 terminates the loop. (See "The while Loop.")

3. Explain the difference between the while and the do-while loops. (See "The do-while Loop.")

4. Write a Java program that displays all capital letters in the English alphabet. Use the continue statement to skip the letters "J" and "W." (See "The continue Statement.")

Creating Methods

Session Checklist

✔ Java methods

✔ Modular program construction

✔ The structure of a method

✔ The method declaration

✔ Access specifier, modifier, return type, name, and parameter list

✔ The method call

✔ Returning from a method

✔ Matching arguments and parameters

✔ Scope of method arguments

✔ Global variables

✔ Passing by value and by reference

**30 Min.
To Go**

Very early in the history of software development, programmers discovered that code often contained sections that performed identical operations. For instance, in a geometrical calculations program, the code lines that obtained the area of a circle were repeated. Re-coding the same routine over and over wasted programming effort, made the program larger, and increased the possibility of error. The solution to this problem was the creation of subprograms within the program. The routine in the subprogram could be reused as often as necessary without having to recode it. In addition, subprograms reduced code size and simplified testing and error correction. For example, a subprogram to calculate the area of a circle would receive the radius parameter from the caller. It would then perform the required operations and return the area as a result. This session is about using subprograms in Java programming.

Java Methods

We call Java subprograms *methods,* and they are the building blocks of a Java application. All execution takes place within a Java method. Furthermore, methods are the processing component in Java classes. In this session, we are concerned with methods as subprograms; that is, we are looking at Java methods as an element of the language. Later, we re-examine methods as a class element.

Modular Program Construction

One of the fundamental notions of modern-day programming is modular program construction. The idea is to break a processing task into smaller units that are easier to analyze, code, and maintain. A properly designed method performs a specific and well-defined set of processing operations. Each method has a single entry and a single exit point, and the processing operations are a manageable size. In practice, a well-conceived method rarely exceeds a few pages of code. In general, it is better practice to divide processing into several simpler functions than it is to create a single complex function.

The Structure of a Method

We can describe a Java method as a collection of declarations and statements grouped under a method name and designed to perform a specific task. Every method contains two identifiable elements: the *method declaration* and the *method body*. The method declaration creates and defines the method. The method body contains data and processing operations associated with the method. The following program, **arrayAverage.java**, adds all elements in an array of int type and returns the average value.

The arrayAverage.java program can be found in the Session10 directory on the book's CD-ROM.

```
public static int arrayAverage(int[] intArray)
{
   int sum = 0;           // Local variable

   // Calculate sum of all array elements
   for(int x = 0; x < intArray.length; x++)
       sum = sum + intArray[x];

   // Calculate and return average
   return sum / intArray.length;
}
```

The Method Declaration

The method declaration, sometimes called the header, is a single expression that defines the method name, what the method name returns, and the parameters that the method name sends to the caller. The declaration can contain information such as access specifiers and modifiers that determine the method's visibility and interaction. In addition, the method declaration can contain exception-handling information. We discuss this topic in the context of Java exceptions in Session 19. The following diagram shows the elements of a method declaration:

```
public static int arrayAverage(int[] intArray)
```

Where:

public	=	access specifier
static	=	modifier
int	=	return type
arrayAverage	=	method name
int[] intArray	=	parameter list

Notice that the method declaration does not end with a semicolon.

Access Specifier

The first element of a method declaration is the optional access specifier. As the name implies, the access specifier controls access to the method. Whatever the access specifier, other methods in the same class have access to all methods. The access specifiers are *public*, *protected*, and *private*. Of these, public is the least restrictive. We discuss access specifiers for methods in the context of object-oriented programming starting in Session 11.

Modifier

Modifiers set the properties for the method. The method modifiers are *static*, *abstract*, *final*, *native*, and *synchronized*. Because method modifiers are related to their visibility and attributes within the class structure, we discuss them in this context. We must declare methods unrelated to objects with the static modifier, as is the case with the arrayAverage() method listed previously in this section.

Return Type

The method declaration requires the return type, except in constructor methods, which we discuss in Session 12. Java methods can return any of the eight simple data types such as int, long, boolean, float, and double, or complex types such as objects. This explains why a Java method can return a string even though a string is not a primitive data type. In addition, a method's return type can be void. In this case, the method returns nothing. Unless we use the keyword void as a return type, a method must return the type specified in the declaration.

The following method returns a type boolean.

```
public static boolean isEven(int aValue)
{
  if(aValue % 2 == 0)
    return true;
  else
    return false;
}
```

Method Name

The method's name is a required element in the declaration. The name can be any legal Java identifier. It is popular in Java programming to start method names with a lowercase letter and to start other words on the method name with uppercase, as in the methods arrayAverage() and isEven() listed previously.

Parameter List

The parameter list contains the information the caller passes to the method. There is no limit to the number of parameters the caller can pass. They are formatted as follows:

```
DataType VariableName, DataType VariableName, . . .
```

If a method receives no parameters from the caller, it is declared with an empty parameter list, as follows:

```
public static void eraseBuffer()
```

20 Min. To Go

The Method Call

A method receives control when its name is referenced in a program statement. This reference, or method call, can appear anywhere in the code in which the method called is visible. Furthermore, Java allows a method to call itself. This type of operation, called recursion, is the topic of Session 15.

The following code fragment contains a call to the arrayAverage() method discussed previously.

```
public static void main(String[] args)
{
  // Local variables
    int[] values = {1, 2, 3, 4, 5, 6, 7, 12};
    int average;

    // Call the method named arrayAverage()
    average = arrayAverage(values);

    // Display results
    System.out.println("Average is: " + average);
  . . .
```

In this case, the call is in the following statement:

```
average = arrayAverage(values);
```

Notice that we call the method `arrayAverage()` by referencing its name. The call contains the name of the array values as an argument. This argument becomes the only parameter in `arrayAverage()`.

Returning from a Method

The `return` keyword ends the execution of a method and returns control to the line following the call. A return statement can contain an expression, sometimes in parentheses, that represents the value returned to the caller. The method `arrayAverage()`, listed previously, contains the following statement:

```
return sum / intArray.length;
```

In every case, the value a method returns must match the return type in its declaration. We can use optional parentheses to clarify the above statement, as follows:

```
return (sum / intArray.length);
```

If no value is associated with a return statement, the returned value is undefined. For example, a method defined with the return type void can have the statement:

```
return;
```

If no return statement appears in a method, the method concludes when it encounters the closing roster (}). In this case, we sometimes say the method "fell off the edge." A method can also return a constant to the caller, as in the following example:

```
public static double getPi()
  {
    return 3.141592653589793;
  }
```

The `getPi()` method returns the constant PI to the calling routine.

A return statement can appear anywhere in the method body. A method can contain more than one return statement, and each statement can return a different value to the caller. For example:

```
if ( program_error > 0 )
  return (1);
```

```
else
   return (0);
```

In conclusion, a Java method can contain no return statement, in which case execution concludes at the closing brace (method falls off the edge), and the returned value is undefined. On the other hand, a method can contain one or more return statements. A return statement can return no value to the caller, as follows:

```
return;
```

A return statement can return a constant, optionally in parentheses:

```
return 0;
return (1);
```

Also, a return statement can return a value:

```
return (error_code);
return((r + r) * PI);
return 2 * radius;
```

If a method returns no value, we should declare its return type void. In this case, the return statement, if present, does not contain an expression.

Matching Arguments and Parameters

**10 Min.
To Go**

The declaration statement for a Java method contains (in parentheses) a list of the variables. The caller passes the value of these variables. This element of the declaration is the method's parameter list. The call to the method contains, also in parentheses, the value it receives as arguments. For example, we have a method named `triArea()` that calculates the area of a triangle from its height and base dimensions. In this case, we expect `triArea()` to receive these values as parameters, as follows:

```
double area;
double height = 12.7;
double base = 7.9;
. . .
// Calling the method
area = triArea(base, height);
. . .
// Method
public static double triArea(double b, double h)
```

```
{
    double result = (b * h) / 2;
    return result;
}
```

In this case, the methods parameter list includes two variables of type double: b and h. The method call references the arguments base and height in parentheses; it passes this value to triArea(). Note that the term "argument" refers to elements referenced in the method's call and that the term "parameter" refers to the elements listed in the method's declaration. In other words, a value passed to a method is an argument from the viewpoint of the caller and a parameter from the viewpoint of the method itself.

Note that a method receives data in the order in which the arguments are referenced in the call and that this order must match the one in the method's parameter list. In the case of the method triArea(), listed previously, the first argument in the method's call, the variable base, becomes the parameter b declared in the method's header. The second argument referenced in the call, the variable height, becomes the variable h in the method.

Scope of Method Arguments

The value a method returns is associated with the method's name, not with the variable or variables that appear in the return statement. For this reason, the variable referenced in a method's return statement can be of local scope. Also, observe that a method returns a single value to the caller. This can be inconvenient in cases in which a method must provide several results. In the following sections, we discuss several ways of getting around this limitation.

Methods and Global Variables

In Session 5, we see that the scope of a Java variable is the block in which we declare it. Because we define a method's body within a block, a variable declared inside this block has method (local) scope. For example:

```
public static double triArea(double b, double h)
{
    double result = (b * h) / 2;
    return result;
}
```

In this case, the scope of the variable result is the `triArea()` method. By the same token, data elements declared outside the methods of a class have class (global) scope. Methods can access global data. This provides a simple mechanism whereby a method can return more than one result. The following program, **Circle.java**, contains two global variables and a constant.

The method `circleData()` receives the radius of a circle as a parameter and calculates its area and circumference. The calculated values are stored in global variables; here, the calculated values can be accessed by the caller.

The source file for the program Circle.java is in the Session10 directory on the book's CD-ROM.

```java
//    File name: Circle.java
//    Reference: Session 10
//
//    Java program to demonstrate global variables
//    and their use by methods
//    Topics:
//        1. Global variables
//        2. Variable visibility to methods
//        3. Method that returns several results in
//           global variables
//        4. Data is passed by reference to a method
//
//    Requires:
//        1. Keyin class in the current directory

public class Circle
{
    // Data elements defined at the class level
    static final double PI = 3.141592653589793;
    static double area;
    static double perimeter;

    //*******************************
    //         main() method
    //*******************************
    public static void main(String[] args)
```

```
        {
            // Local variables
            double radius;

            // Input radius from keyboard
            System.out.println("Caculating circle dimensions");
            radius = Keyin.inDouble("Enter radius: ");

            // Call method
            circleData(radius);

            // Display data stored globally
            System.out.println("Radius: " + radius);
            System.out.println("Area: " + area);
            System.out.println("Perimeter: " + perimeter);
        }


    //*****************************
    //      circleData() method
    //*****************************
    public static void circleData(double radius)
    {
        area = PI * (radius * radius);
        perimeter = PI * (2 * radius);
        radius = 0;                         // Fruitless effort!
        return;
    }
}
```

Notice that we define the `circleData()` **method of the preceding program with return-type void. Because we return the values in global variables, the code uses a plain return to end the method's execution.**

Passing by Value and by Reference

Programming languages can pass data to methods in two ways: by *value* and by *reference*. We pass data by value when the method receives a copy of the data contained in the caller's arguments. In this case, the method does not have access to the values stored in the variables. On the other hand, when we pass data by reference, the method receives the addresses of the passed variables as arguments. Any changes the method performs affect the values stored in the variables.

When we pass a primitive data type to a Java method, we pass it is always by value. In the **Circle.java** program, we see that the method `circleData()` receives the radius of the circle as a parameter from the caller. The method attempts to change the value of this variable in the following statement:

```
radius = 0;              // Fruitless effort!
```

Note

In this case, assigning a value to the variable radius is a fruitless effort because the first `println` statement in the caller's code shows that the value of the variable remains unchanged.

Done!

REVIEW

Methods are subprograms in Java. Using methods fosters modular program construction. A method starts with its declaration. The declaration contains the method's name, the access specifier, a possible modifier, the method's return type, and a list of the parameters the caller passes to the method. When processing concludes, the method returns execution to the caller with a possible value associated with the method's name. Variables declared within a method have local scope. Methods can access global variables. This provides a simple mechanism whereby a method can return more than one value to the caller.

QUIZ YOURSELF

1. Write the declaration of a Java method that calculates the average of four variables of type `double` and returns this value in a `float` data type. (See "The Method Declaration.")

2. Describe the purpose of the modifier in a method declaration. (See "Modifier.")

3. Can a Java method return a String object? (See "Return Type.")

4. What happens when a method contains no return statement? (See "Returning from a Method.")

5. How can a method return more than one result? (See "Method and Global Variables.")

6. When a Java primitive data type passes to a method, does it pass by value or by reference? (See "Passing by Value and by Reference.")

PART II

Saturday Morning
Part Review

1. List Java's primitive data types.
2. Describe Java's rules for identifiers.
3. How are Java's primitive data types classified?
4. Write Java code to cast a floating-point variable type into an integer type.
5. Write a Java program to create three arrays: one of type int, one of type double, and an array of String. Display the first element in each array.
6. Use the length operator to obtain the number of characters in each array in the previous exercise.
7. Create a multidimensional array that consists of four columns and three rows. Make sure the program compiles correctly.
8. What is the action of the assignment operator?
9. In a Java expression, what can be to the left of the equal sign?
10. List the arithmetic operations, and describe the action of the remainder (%) operator.
11. Which operator performs string concatenation?
12. Write the simplest Java expression that adds one to the value of a variable.
13. What is the fundamental difference between a computer and a calculating machine?
14. Write an if construct that tests whether a person is a teenager.

15. How can you associate two if statements so that execution takes place only if both statements are true?

16. Describe the purpose of the else clause.

17. Explain the difference between the while and the do-while loops.

18. Write the declaration of a Java method that calculates the average of four variables of type double and returns this value in a float data type.

19. Describe the purpose of the modifier in a method declaration.

20. Can a Java method return a String object?

PART

Saturday Afternoon

Object-Oriented Java

Session Checklist

✔ Object-oriented programming in Java

✔ Rationale of object orientation

✔ Classes and objects

✔ Fundamental principles: Encapsulation and inheritance

✔ Object-oriented modeling

✔ Polymorphism and abstract classes

**30 Min.
To Go**

ava is an object-oriented language. Every statement and every construct of a Java program exists inside a class of objects. The Java libraries are defined as classes. This means that to understand and use Java you must first grasp the fundamental notions of object-oriented programming. This session is about object orientation and its basic elements: classes and objects.

The section that follows presents a short history of object-oriented programming and of the evolution of object-oriented languages. It can be skipped without loss of continuity.

A Brief History

The object-oriented approach appeared in the computing mainstream during the early 1980s, although its origin dates back to the 1960s. Java implements object-orientation by means of two programming constructs: classes and objects. In general, three conceptual elements are associated with object-oriented systems: *data abstraction*, *inheritance*, and *dynamic binding*.

The first notions of data abstraction resulted from the work of Kristen Nygaard and Ole-Johan Dahl at the Norwegian Computing Center, during the early 1970s. Nyaard and Dahl developed a computer language named SIMULA I, which was intended for use in simulations and operations research. A few years later SIMULA I was followed by SIMULA 67. Although this language had little impact on programming, its historical importance was the introduction of the class construct.

 The abbreviation OO is often used in reference to object orientation. Thus, we sometimes speak of OO languages and OO programming.

The basic idea of a class is a template that packages data and processing routines. Note that this definition of class as a template implies that a class is a formal construct, rather than a concrete entity. The programmer creates instances of a class as needed. In Java, the instances of a class are called objects.

Historically, it was Alan Kay who first described a fully operational object-oriented language. Kay's vision was that desktop computers would become very powerful machines, with megabytes of memory executing millions of instructions per second. Kay reasoned that because mostly nonprogrammers would use these machines, a powerful graphical interface would have to be developed to replace the awkward teletype terminals and batch processing methods of the time. Kay's solution to a friendly and easy-to-use interface was an information processing system named Dynabook.

Dynabook consisted of the visualization of a desk in which some documents were visible and others were partially covered. A user selected documents by using the keyboard. A touch-sensitive screen enabled users to move the documents on the desk. The result was very similar to some of our present-day windowing environments. Processing was performed by the Flex programming language that Kay had helped design. Flex was based on SIMULA 67. Kay eventually went to work at the Xerox Palo Alto Research Center (PARC) where these ideas evolved into a mouse-controlled, windowing interface, and eventually into Smalltalk, the first fully operational object-oriented programming language. Led by Adele Goldberg, the work of the Smalltalk design team at Xerox PARC enabled the language to become the de facto description of object-oriented programming. Since then, several object-oriented languages have been developed, the most notable being Eiffel, CLOS, ADA 95, C++, and Java.

Object-Oriented Fundamentals

Different object-oriented languages implement the paradigm differently and to varying degrees of conceptual purity. In recent years, the development and marketing of object-oriented products has become a major commercial venture. Thus, to the natural uncertainties of an elaborate and sophisticated concept, we must add the hype of commercial entrepreneurs and promoters.

The result of the commercialization of object-oriented products is a mixture of valid claims and unjustified praise, some of it originating in the real virtues of a new and useful paradigm, some of it in pure mercantilism.

Problem Set and Solution Set

A computer program, whether it is a major operating system or a small application, is a machine-code solution to a real-world problem. At the beginning of any programming project is a problem set that defines it and, at its conclusion, there is a solution set in the form of a group of instructions that can be executed by a computing machine. The art and science of programming is facilitating the transit from the real-world problem set to the machine-coded solution set. In this conceptualization, programming includes the phases of analysis, design, coding, and testing of a software product.

Many methodologies have been developed to facilitate the transition from a real-world problem to a solution consisting of machine instructions. Assemblers, high-level programming languages, CASE tools, analysis and design methodologies, formal specifications, and scientific methods of program testing are all efforts in this direction. The most significant simplifications are those based on generalized abstractions. Structured programming was one of the first efforts in making programs easier to develop and more dependable. In this sense, structured programming is often considered an abstraction that focuses on the solution-set, whereas the object-oriented approach focuses on the problem set. A project engineered in terms of structured programming is based on a model of the solution set, while a project analyzed and designed using object-oriented methods focuses on the problem set.

Rationale of Object Orientation

The supporters of the object-oriented approach make the following claims:

- Object-oriented-analysis and design methods facilitate communications with clients and users because the model does not require technical knowledge of programming.
- Many real-world problems are easier to model in object-oriented terms than by using structured analysis and design techniques.
- Object-oriented programming languages promote and facilitate code reuse, which eventually increases programmer productivity.
- Object-oriented programs have internal mechanisms that make them resilient to change; therefore, they are better able to accommodate the natural volatility of the problem domain.

Although questions have been raised whether these advantages are worth the complications, the fact is that the programming community is leaning toward the object-oriented approach.

Classes and Objects

An object is an abstraction, not a thing in the real world. It is a conceptual entity related to the problem domain. A conventional fallacy is to claim that an object, in the context of object-oriented programming, is equivalent to an object in the real world. This misconception can become a major obstacle to understanding object orientation. In reality, an object in object-oriented programming is a hybrid that shares some characteristics of common objects with features of a computer construct. Instead of giving a formal definition for an object, we start with a rather simplified listing of its properties:

- Every object belongs to an object class. An object cannot exist without a class that defines it. In this sense we say that an object is an instance of a class. We can visualize the class as a cookie cutter and the object as the cookie.
- An object (and the class that contains it) is an encapsulation that includes data and its related processing operations.

- The object's attributes serve to store and preserve the object's state. They determine what is remembered about an object. An object's methods are the only way of accessing its data or modifying its state. This is accomplished by sending a message to the object.

20 Min. To Go

Fundamental Principles of Object-Orientation

The basic concepts that underlie object-orientated systems are encapsulation and inheritance. Other characteristics that derive from these two are data abstraction, message passing, polymorphism, and dynamic binding. We begin with the elements of encapsulation and inheritance.

Encapsulation

In object-oriented terms encapsulation relates to information hiding. Non-object-oriented systems are based on routines and subprograms that share global data or that receive data passed by the caller. The object-oriented approach, on the other hand, adopts the notion that data and functions should be packaged together in a single capsule. The class construct serves this purpose. A class consists of data elements and processing elements. The data elements of a class are called the attributes and the processing operations are called its methods. Attributes and methods are the class members: the attributes are the data members and the methods are the member functions.

The purpose of encapsulation is to hide the implementation details while stressing the interface. The goal is to create an abstraction that forces the programmer to think conceptually. Typically, the data members of a class are invisible to the user. If a data member must be made accessible to the class' client, then the class provides a method that inspects it and returns its value. When a class exposes its data members it is said to break encapsulation.

Inheritance

In computer science, the notion of inheritance originated in the field of knowledge representation. It refers to the inheritance of properties of a higher-level class to its subclasses, which is a basic mechanism used in scientific classifications. The rule states that knowledge can be organized into hierarchies based on class relationships. Thus, we say that an individual inherits the properties of the class to which it belongs. For example, animals breathe, move, and reproduce. If the subclass bird belongs to the animal superclass, then we can infer that the members of the bird class breathe, move, and reproduce because these properties are inherited from its base class. Figure 11-1 is an inheritance diagram for some classes of animals.

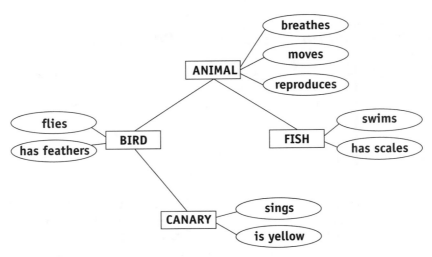

Figure 11-1
An inheritance diagram

Inheritance systems are used in knowledge bases to ensure the highest levels of abstraction. For example, a knowledge base about birds first defines the traits that are common to all birds (fly and have feathers) and then the traits of the particular species (canary sings and is yellow). In this manner, the subclass canary inherits the properties of its parent class, bird, which, in turn, inherits the properties of its parent class, animal. This reduces the size of the knowledge base by requiring that common properties be asserted only once. Inheritance also serves to maintain the consistency of the knowledge base.

In object-oriented systems, inheritance refers to the possibility of a subclass acquiring the public members of its parent class. Class inheritance promotes the highest level of abstraction and simplifies the knowledge base. It enables building a class hierarchy that goes from the most general to the most specific. In the diagram of Figure 11-1 we can say that ANIMAL is a base class, and that BIRD, FISH, and CANARY are derived classes. A derived class incorporates all the features of its parent class, and may add some unique features of its own. Also, a derived class has access to all the public members of its base class. The terms parent, child, and sibling are sometimes used to express degrees of inheritance between classes. As in biological systems, sibling classes do not inherit from each other; therefore, the properties of FISH (in Figure 11-1) are not inherited by its sibling class BIRD.

Object-Oriented Modeling

**10 Min.
To Go**

A model is a simplification of reality that serves to better understand a complex system. An architect creates a scale model of a building that can be shown to clients. An engineer draws a model of a mechanical component that can be used to manufacture the part. An aircraft designer creates a model of an airplane that can be tested in a wind tunnel. The more elaborate or complex a system is, the more useful is a model of the system.

An object-oriented software system is often complex. It may consist of many subsystems of interrelated object classes that connect and interact with each other. The classes and objects within each subsystem inherit properties from their parents and interact with their siblings. In this case, the system designers can work at a higher level of abstraction by using models that show the interaction between the component elements. For a programmer to begin creating a new software system by writing code is as futile as for a mechanical engineer to start building a new automobile by turning parts on a lathe. In either case, engineering is design and design is modeling.

Over the years, the object-oriented community has developed several successful modeling tools. The basic element of these modeling tools is a notation for classes and objects and their relations. A popular model is the result of the work of Coad and Yourdon. Later, Booch, Jacobson, and Rumbaugh created the Unified Modeling Language (UML) that uses a notation similar to the one proposed by Coad and Yourdon. In either case, the notation consists of diagrams that depict relationships between classes. Figure 11-2 shows the diagram of a class.

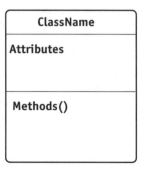

Figure 11-2
Class diagram

Suppose we want to create a class of objects called Dog where each object of the class Dog will be associated with the dog's name, weight, and color. Also, suppose that we want the objects of the class Dog to have the capability to bark and jump. Using the class diagram we can model the class Dog as shown in Figure 11-3.

```
┌─────────────────────────┐
│          Dog            │
├─────────────────────────┤
│  name                   │
│  weight                 │
│  color                  │
│                         │
├─────────────────────────┤
│  Bark()                 │
│  Jump()                 │
│                         │
└─────────────────────────┘
```

Figure 11-3
Modeling the class Dog

The modeling notation must include symbols to represent relationships between classes and objects. There are two basic types of class associations: the subclass is a *kind-of* or a *part-of* the parent class. The kind-of association is also called a generalization-specialization relationship (also called a Gen-Spec association). For example, a classification in which Vehicle is a base class could have the subclasses Automobile and Airplane as specializations. In this case, the Automobile and the Airplane are a kind-of vehicle. On the other hand, a classification could be based on a class being a part-of another class. In this case, the subclass is a component of the parent class and we speak of a Whole-Part association.

A model of the Gen-Spec relationship, in which the subclass is a kind-of the parent class, is depicted using a semicircle to connect the subclasses to the parent class. The Whole-Part association, in which the subclass is a part-of the parent class, is depicted using a triangle to connect the subclasses to their parent. The notation is shown in Figure 11-4.

Figure 11-4 shows a classification in which Vehicle is the base class and Automobile and Airplane are specializations of the base class. In this case, Automobile is a kind-of vehicle and so is Airplane. On the right-hand side the classification is based on the Whole-Part association. In this case, the Chassis and Engine classes are a part-of the Automobile superclass.

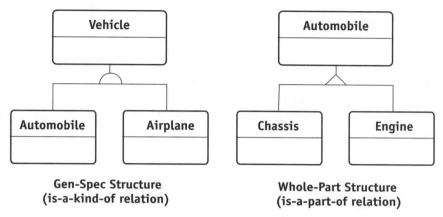

Figure 11-4
Notation for class inheritance

Polymorphism and Abstract Classes

Object-oriented systems support the notion of a class that serves to define the interface but contains no implementation. In Java, this is made possible by using abstract classes and a special type of method called an *abstract method*. An abstract method is a method that defines an interface but contains no implementation. An abstract class is a class that has at least one abstract method. The fundamental purpose of abstract classes is a greater generalization. The abstract class serves as a framework for other classes lower in the hierarchy. The implementation details are left to these lower-level classes. In this manner, the empty method serves as a template for the interface of a family of functions that share the same name.

The concept of abstract classes relates closely to the notion of polymorphism. Polymorphism means many forms. In object-oriented terms, polymorphism relates to several methods that share the same name. The most common implementation of abstract classes is based on several methods with the same name, all located in different classes. The method highest in the class hierarchy is an abstract method. The abstract method defines the interface for all its polymorphic relatives, but provides no implementation. In class diagrams, abstract classes are often modeled by enclosing them in a dashed rectangle.

Example of Classification

Suppose that we have to design and code a graphics system that can display several types of geometrical figures at any screen position. The figures are straight lines, rectangles, circles, ellipses, and parabolas. In analyzing this project we may start by noticing that the circle, ellipse, and parabola belong to a family of curves called the conic sections, which are obtained by sectioning a right-circular cone, as shown in Figure 11-5.

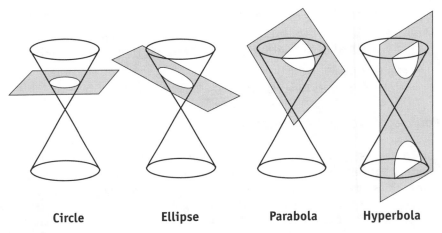

Circle   **Ellipse**   **Parabola**   **Hyperbola**

Figure 11-5
Visualization of the conic sections

We can proceed to model the graphics program by means of a class hierarchy, as shown in Figure 11-6.

In the classification of Figure 11-6, we start by defining the abstract class `GeometricalFigure`. Because a geometrical figure is an abstraction, it can have no attributes. Furthermore, it is impossible to draw a geometrical figure until it has been specified if the figure is a line, a rectangle, a circle, and so on. Line and Rectangle, on the other hand, are concrete classes. Because it is possible to draw a line or a rectangle, these classes can have attributes as well as concrete methods. Circle, Ellipse, and Parabola are also concrete classes of the abstract class `Conic Section`. `ConicSection` is another abstraction and is a subclass of `Geometrical Figure`.

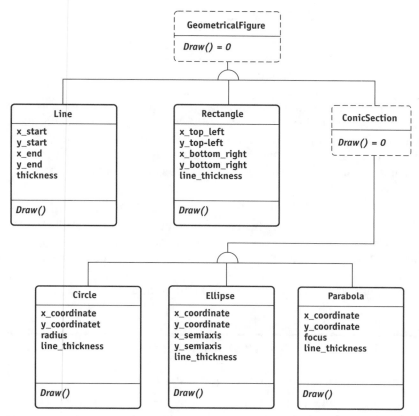

Figure 11-6
Classification for a graphics application

The interface to the drawing application, which is the Draw() method, is defined in the abstract classes GeometricalFigure and ConicSection. However, it is only implemented in the concrete classes. We use the convention of equating the abstract methods to zero.

Virtual functions in abstract and concrete classes are also set in italics typeface.

Done!

Review

Java is a pure object-oriented language. Every statement and construct of a Java program exists inside a class of objects. The history of object-oriented programming started in 1967 at the Norwegian Computing Center with the work of Nygaard and Dahl. Alan Kay described the first object-oriented language in 1970, and Adele Goldberg implemented that language in Smalltalk. The basic goal of object-oriented languages is to provide a smooth transition from the problem set to the solution set of a programming task. Object-oriented languages facilitate modeling, communication with clients, and code reuse. OO programs are also easier to modify.

A class can be described as a classification. The class is often visualized as the cookie cutter, and the object as the cookie. Encapsulation and inheritance are the basic principles of object-orientation. Class diagrams are often used to depict relationships between classes and objects. Abstract classes provide an interface, but no implementation. In OO programming, polymorphism relates to methods with the same name, but which are usually located in different classes.

Quiz Yourself

1. Where did OO originate? (See "A Brief History.")
2. In a programming project, how does an object-oriented language facilitate the transition from the problem set to the solution set? (See "Problem Set and Solution Set.")
3. Why do OO languages facilitate communication with clients and domain experts? (See "Rationale of Object Orientation.")
4. Can an object exist without a class to contain it? (See "Classes and Objects.")
5. What are the data members of a class? (See Encapsulation.")
6. What OO mechanism allows a subclass to access the public members of a superclass? (See "Inheritance.")

Programming with Classes

Session Checklist

✔ Using classes in your Java programs

✔ Classes and objects

✔ Instantiation

✔ Field and method variables

✔ Constructors: the default constructor and overloaded constructors

✔ Modeling with classes

**30 Min.
To Go**

So far, we have programmed in Java by creating small applications that contain a single class and that use static variables and methods. In other words, we have ignored the object-oriented features of the Java language. Now, with the material presented in Session 11 serving as background, we are ready to start creating object-oriented code.

**It takes object-oriented programming to make use of the full
capabilities of the Java language.**

Classes and Objects

Classes are the building blocks of Java programs. A class defines the attributes and behavior of the objects that it creates. It serves as a template for creating objects. In this sense, classes have been said to resemble a cookie cutter, while the object resembles the cookie. Consider the following Java program, **DogAction.java**:

The source file for the program DogAction.java is found in the Session 12 directory on the book's CD-ROM.

```
//*********************************************************
//    File name: DogAction.java
//    Reference: Session 12
//*********************************************************
//
//    Java program to demonstrate a classes and objects
//    Topics:
//        1. Java application with multiple classes
//        2. Object instantiation
//
//    Note:
//        1. Only one class in a file can be public. The public
//           class must have the name of the file.
//        2. The "this" operator refers to the current object.
//        3. Class variables are usually declared with private
//           accessibility in order to preserve encapsulation


//*********************************
//*********************************
//              CLASS Dog
//*********************************
//*********************************
class Dog
{
  // Class variables
  private int dogNum;
  private String dogName;
```

```
//************************
//     setInfo()
//************************
public void setInfo(int aNum, String aName)
{
    this.dogNum = aNum;
    this.dogName = aName;
}


//************************
//     method bark()
//************************
public void bark()
{
    System.out.println("Arf!, Arf!");
}


//************************
//   method sayInfo()
//************************
public void sayInfo()
{
    System.out.println("My name is " + this.dogName);
    System.out.println("I am dog number " + this.dogNum);
}
}


//*********************************
//*********************************
//       CLASS DogAction
//*********************************
//*********************************
public class DogAction
{
    public static void main(String[] args)
    {
        // Declare objects of class Dog
        Dog myDog = new Dog();     // First object is named myDog
        Dog MSUDog = new Dog();    // Second object is MSUDog
```

```
// Assign names to Dog objects using setName() method
myDog.setInfo(1, "Fido");        // myDog's name
MSUDog.setInfo(2, "Maverik");    // MSUDog's name

// Call methods of the class Dog using objects
myDog.bark();              // myDog barks
myDog.sayInfo();               // myDog says its name
MSUDog.sayInfo();              // ... and so on
MSUDog.bark();
  }
}
```

Object Instantiation

The preceding program **DogAction.java** contains two classes in a single Java file. The class DogAction is called the driving class. Every Java program must contain a driving class, and the driving class must contain the main() method. The class Dog is a helper class. In DogAction.java, the class Dog contains a single attribute (the String dogName). It also contains the methods setName(), bark(), and sayName().

To use a class you must first instantiate an object of the class. In DogAction. java, the objects are instantiated as follows:

```
// Declare objects of class Dog
    Dog myDog = new Dog();     // First object is named myDog
    Dog MSUDog = new Dog();    // Second object is MSUDog
```

Sending a message to the object accesses the methods of a class. Each object stores information about its state. To change the state of an object you send messages to its mutator methods.

 An object whose state can be changed externally breaks encapsulation.

Each object has:

- A behavior (defined by its methods)
- A state (determined by its fields)
- An identity that makes it different from all other objects of the same class

In most cases, objects have different states, but two objects of the same class are unique and different, even if they have the same state. For example: a GasGauge object encodes the amount of gasoline in a tank. A truck with two tanks may have two GasGauge objects. These objects would be different, even if by chance both of them represented the same number of gallons of gas.

If two objects have the same state, each one would still have its own identity.

Field and Method Variables

Variables can be of two types in relation to their location within a class. Variables declared outside the methods of a class, usually before any of the methods, are called *field variables*, or just *fields*. Field variables are accessible to all the methods in the class. Variables declared inside methods are called *local* or *method* variables. Local variables have their lifetime limited to the duration of the method. In other words, a local variable exists and is accessible while the method that contains it is executing. For this reason, local variables cannot be accessed by other methods, or by other classes. This also explains why you cannot apply access modifiers to local variables.

In **DogAction.java**, the class Dog contains two data items: one is a variable of type int and the second is a string. Both are declared with the private access modifier in order to preserve encapsulation. The class Dog provides the method setInfo() that assigns a name and a number to each object created from the class. Later, in the section "Constructors," we learn that a special type of method, called a *constructor*, is often used to initialize object data at the time it is created.

Object and Class Variables

Class variables declared without the static keywords are associated with the objects of the class. For example, the variables dogNum and dogName in the class Dog of DogAction.java are object variables. Object variables are associated with the objects of a class.

Another type of class variable is declared with the static attribute. In this case, the variable is related to the class itself, not to the objects. The use of class variables is discussed in the section "Modeling with Classes" later in this session.

**20 Min.
To Go**

Constructors

A constructor is a special method that has the same name as the class where it is defined. If you do not code a constructor, Java supplies one for you, sometimes called the default constructor. The default constructor does nothing, but it enables all variables that are not initialized in their declaration to assume default values, as follows:

- Numeric variables are set to 0
- Strings are set to null
- Boolean variables are set to false

A constructor has no return type. Although a constructor can be public, private, or protected, most constructors are public. A private constructor does not allow other classes to instantiate objects. Therefore, only the static methods of the class are accessible in this case.

 Programmers use private constructors when they want to prevent other classes from instantiating their class, but still want access to their static methods.

Calling the Default Constructor

The constructor method is called when we create an object of the class. For example, in the case of the **DogAction.java** program, the default constructor is called when the objects are created, as in the following statement:

```
// Declare objects of class Dog
    Dog myDog = new Dog();    // First object is named myDog
//                  -----
//                      |_____ call to constructor
```

The default constructor creates the object and sets the field variables that were not initialized in their declaration to the default values mentioned previously. For example, in the case of our sample program **DogAction.java**, the default constructor sets the variable dogNum to zero and the String dogName to null.

Overloaded Constructors

A class can contain more than one constructor, but each different constructor must have a unique signature. Recall that the signature of a method is its unique parameter list. No two constructors can have the same signature. When a class has more than one constructor we say that the constructor is overloaded. This means that there are several methods with the same name but different signatures. Overloaded constructors enable the building of objects in different ways. Java determines which constructor to use by looking at the object's parameters. After you define a constructor, no matter its signature, the default constructor is not used in creating objects. One constructor can call another constructor.

The following program, **Payroll.java**, demonstrates overloaded constructors.

The source file for the Payroll.java program file is found in the Session 12 directory on the book's CD-ROM.

Part III—Saturday Afternoon
Session 12

```
//****************************************************************
//    File name: Payroll.java
//    Reference: Session 12
//****************************************************************
// Topics:
//      1. A class with object and class attributes
//         and object and class methods
//      2. Creating and using constructors
//      3. Polymorphism by overloaded constructors
//***********************************************************

//***************************************
//***************************************
//            Employee class
//***************************************
//***************************************
class Employee
{
  //*****************************
  //      attributes section
  //*****************************
  // field variables
```

```java
private String name = "no name";
private String address;
private String ssn = "xxx";
private int dependants = 1;    // Default for dependants field
private int empNum;

// Class attribute (static qualifier)
private static int consecNum = 0;

//********************************
// methods section - constructors
//********************************
// Fully parameterized constructor for Employee objects
public Employee(String n, String a, String s, int x)
{
    this.name = n;
    this.address = a;
    this.ssn = s;
    this.dependants = x;
    this.empNum = ++consecNum;
}

// Nonparameterized constructor assigns only an employee number
public Employee()
{
    this.empNum = ++consecNum;
}

// Partially parameterized constructor assigns name and
// consecutive employee number
public Employee(String n)
{
    this.name = n;
    this.empNum = ++consecNum;
}

//********************************
// methods section - other methods
//********************************
public void showData()
```

```
   {
      System.out.print("number: " + this.empNum);
      System.out.print("\tname: " + this.name);
      System.out.print("\t\taddress: " + this.address);
      System.out.print("\n\t\tSSN: " + this.ssn);
      System.out.print("\t\tdependants: " + this.dependants +
                       "\n\n");
      System.out.flush();
   }


   // Class method is used to access a class variable without
   // an object reference
   public static void showTotal()
   {
      System.out.println("Total employees: " + consecNum);
      System.out.println();
   }


} // end of class Employee

//*****************************************
//*****************************************
//               Driving class
//*****************************************
//*****************************************
public class Payroll
{
    public static void main(String[] args)
    {
    // First two objects of Employee class are created using the
    // parameterized constructor
    Employee emp1 = new Employee("Jane", "131 Calm Street",
                                 "263", 2);
    Employee emp2 = new Employee("Jim", "42 Curve Road", "261",
                                 6);


        // Third employee object is created with nonparameterized
        // constructor
        Employee emp3 = new Employee();
```

```
// Fourth employee is created with partially parameterized
// constructor
Employee emp4 = new Employee("Mary");

//****************************
//          WARNING
//****************************
// If you coded the following line:
// Employee emp5 = new Employee("Joe", "12 Bridge Drive");
// your program would generate a compiler error stating
// that there is a wrong number of arguments in the
// constructor call

// Display data using an accessor method
emp1.showData();
emp2.showData();
emp3.showData();
emp4.showData();

// Display total number of employees using a class method
Employee.showTotal();
  }
}
```

The class Employee in the **Payroll.java** program contains three constructors, declared as follows:

```
public Employee(String n, String a, String s, int x)
public Employee()
public Employee(String n)
```

The first constructor receives four parameters: three String-type parameters and one int-type parameter. The second constructor is parameterless. This constructor overrides the default constructor, which is not be used. The third constructor receives a single parameter of String type.

 Because their signatures are unique, the three constructors can coexist in the same class.

The data elements for the class Employee in **Payroll.java** are declared as follows:

```
// field variables
private String name = "no name";
private String address;
private String ssn = "xxx";
private int dependants = 1;    // Default for dependants field
private int empNum;

// Class attribute (static qualifier)
private static int consecNum = 0;
```

The class contains five fields and one class variable. The field variables are related to the objects of the class. The class Employee contains the class variable named consecNum. Java creates a single copy of a class variable. The class variable is associated with the class, not with its objects. In this case, the class variable keeps track of the consecutive number of the employee objects.

**10 Min.
To Go**

Modeling with Classes

The following program, **ThrottleDemo.java**, uses a class to make objects that have similar characteristics. In this sense, a class can be considered as an object factory. The Throttle class in **ThrottleDemo.java** builds the throttle object. Each throttle has a maximum position, determined by its range, and a current position that indicates the present setting. Figure 12-1 diagrams the throttle itself and the class that models it.

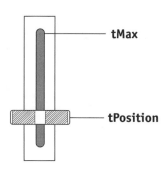

Figure 12-1
Modeling a throttle object

The following is the code listing of the **ThrottleDemo.java** program.

The source file for the ThrottleDemo.java program is found in the Session 12 directory on the book's CD-ROM.

```
//***********************************************************
//    File name: ThrottleDemo.java
//    Reference: Session 12
//***********************************************************
// Topics:
//      1. Modeling a throttle object
//      2. A class as an object factory


//*******************************************
//*******************************************
//              Throttle class
//*******************************************
//*******************************************
class Throttle
{
   //******************************
   //      attributes section
   //******************************
   // Constants
   private static final int MAX_VALUE = 100;   // Maximum
                                               // throttle


   // Instance fields
   private int tMax;        // Maximum throttle position
   private int tPosition;   // Current throttle position

   // Class variable
   private static int tCounter = 0;  // Counts number of objects


   //******************************
   // methods section - constructor
   //******************************
   public Throttle(int x)
```

```
{
    if(x > MAX_VALUE)
        x = MAX_VALUE;

    this.tMax = x;          // Set maximum for this throttle
    this.tPosition = 0;     // Throttle initial position is off
    Throttle.tCounter++;    // Count the throttle object
}


//********************************
// methods section - other methods
//********************************
// Method to move throttle forward or backward
public void moveThrottle(int ammount)
{
    if(ammount > this.tMax - this.tPosition)
        this.tPosition = MAX_VALUE;
    else if (this.tPosition + ammount < 0)
        this.tPosition = 0;
    else
        this.tPosition += ammount;
}


// Method to turn off throttle
public void turnOff()
{
    this.tPosition = 0;
}


// Method to check if throttle is not off
public boolean isOn()
{
     return (this.tPosition > 0);
}


// Method to obtain gas flow at current throttle position
public double getFlow()
{
    return ((double) this.tPosition / (double) this.tMax);
}
```

```
    } // end of class Throttle

    //*******************************************
    //*******************************************
    //              Driving class
    //*******************************************
    //*******************************************
    public class ThrottleDemo
    {
        public static void main(String[] args)
        {
         // Declare throttle objects
         Throttle t1 = new Throttle(50);      // t1 has range 0 to 50;
         Throttle t2 = new Throttle(100);     // t2 has range 0 to 100
         Throttle t3 = new Throttle(10);      // t3 has range 0 to 10

         t1.moveThrottle(10);                 // t1 to 1/5 throttle
         t2.moveThrottle(50);                 // t2 to 1/2 throttle
         t3.moveThrottle(1);                  // t3 to 1/10 throttle

         // Chech that throttle t3 is not OFF
         if(t3.isOn())
           System.out.println("Throttle t3 is ON");

         // Turn t2 OFF
         t2.turnOff();
         // Check that it is off
         if(!t2.isOn())
           System.out.println("Throttle t2 is OFF now");

         // Display gas flow for t1
         double gasFlow;
         gasFlow = t1.getFlow();
         System.out.println("Flow of t1 is " + gasFlow);
        }
    }
```

Done!

REVIEW

The building blocks of OO are classes and objects. Objects are instantiated with the new operator. In addition to its name, each object has a behavior, a state, and an identity. Field variables are related to the objects of a class. They are declared outside methods. Local variables, which have limited scope and visibility, are declared inside methods. Class variables relate to the class itself, not to the objects. Class variables are declared with the static keyword.

Constructors are special methods that have the same name as the class. If you do not code a constructor for a class, Java creates a default constructor for you. Constructors are used in creating objects of a class. The constructor can be overloaded.

QUIZ YOURSELF

1. In which class must the main() method be located? (See "Object Instantiation.")

2. What determines the state of an object? (See "Object Instantiation.")

3. How can you determine if a data element is a field or a method variable? (See "Field and Method Variables.")

4. To what values will the default constructor set uninitialized numeric, string, and Boolean variables? (See "Constructors.")

5. Write Java code that calls a parameterized constructor to create an object. (See "Overloaded Constructors.")

6. Write a Java program that uses classes and object to model a real-world problem. (See "Modeling with Classes.")

Using Class Inheritance

Session Checklist

✔ Inheritance in Java

✔ Extending functionality

✔ Overriding

✔ Abstract classes and methods

✔ Implementing an abstract class

**30 Min.
To Go**

I n Session 11, we looked at inheritance as the mechanism for organizing knowledge into hierarchies. Java inheritance is implemented by means of a class hierarchy in which one class, usually called the *derived class*, inherits the functionality of another class, which is called the *base class*. The terms *super-class* and *subclass* are also used in this context. As in biological inheritance, an object of a class contains the attributes and properties of the class to which it belongs, as well as those of its superclasses. In this session, we learn how to implement inheritance constructs in Java code and how to use inheritance to promote a higher level of abstraction that aids in modeling and simplifies the programming.

Inheritance in Java

The idea behind inheritance is that a class can extend the functionality of another class, thereby fostering reusability and simplifying coding. In Java, inheritance is achieved by declaring that one class extends another class, for example:

```
class Circle extends GeometricalFigure
{
  ...
}
```

In this case the subclass `Circle` inherits all the methods of its superclass `GeometricalFigure`. In addition, the subclass can add methods and attributes of its own.

You can prevent inheritance by making a class final, for example:

```
class final Rectangle
{
  . . .
)
```

In this case, no other class can extend `Rectangle`. Furthermore, if a specific method in a class is declared with the final attribute, that method is not inherited by the subclasses.

Extending Functionality

Inheritance provides a powerful way of modeling classes that are in a kind-of relationship — Generalization-Specialization (Gen-Spec) structure type — and for extending the functionality of subclasses. Inheritance is not suitable for modeling class relationships when the classes are in a part-of relationship (Whole-Part structure type). The keyword super is used in a subclass to refer to a method of the superclass. It is useful in calling superclass constructors and in specifying polymorphic methods.

One advantage of inheritance is that it enables redefining methods for a subclass without changing the operation of the superclass. If a method is not implemented in the subclass, Java searches up the inheritance hierarchy for the first polymorphic method. If none is found, a compiler error is produced.

Overriding

**20 Min.
To Go**

Overloading generates static polymorphism because the method to be used can be determined at compile time. Session 12 showed how constructors with different signatures are overloaded. In inheritance constructs, two or more methods with the same signature coexist in a class hierarchy.

In overriding, the methods have the same signature, whereas overloaded methods have different signatures.

We say that the selection of two or more methods with the same signature is a case of method *overriding*. In this case, which method is linked to the object depends on the position of the method in the hierarchy. Consider a hierarchy consisting of three classes named Class1, Class2, and Class3. Furthermore, assume that two of the three classes have a polymorphic method named MethodA(). Figure 13-1 shows the class diagram.

If an object makes a call to methodA(), which polymorphic implementation is used depends on the object. If the object belongs to Class1, then the implementation of methodA() in Class1 is used. Because Class2 has no methodA() the implementation in Class1 is used if the object of this class calls MethodA(). The general rule is that Java searches the inheritance hierarchy for the closest polymorphic method. If an object of Class3 calls methodA(), then methodA() in Class3 is used.

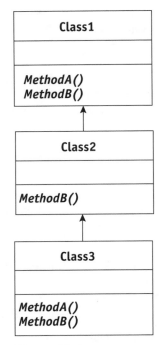

Figure 13-1
Polymorphic methods in an inheritance structure

The program Inheritance.java shows simple inheritance and method selection by overriding. The program is based on the class diagram in Figure 13-2. The source file for Inheritance.java is found in the Session 13 directory on the book's CD-ROM.

**10 Min.
To Go**

Abstract Classes and Methods

An abstract method is one with no body, that is, it performs no processing operations. The abstract method defines a signature that must be used by all polymorphic methods in extended classes. Thus, an abstract method defines an interface in the base class, and leaves the implementation to the derived classes.

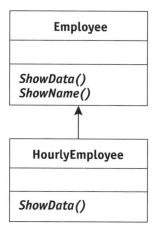

Figure 13-2
Class structure in the program Inheritance.java

Session 12 taught us that an abstract class is a class that contains one or more abstract methods. In Java, an abstract class is declared by including the abstract keyword in the class declaration statement. An abstract class cannot be instantiated; it can, however, be extended. An abstract class can have concrete data and methods that perform normally. An abstract class can also have constructors.

Creating an Abstract Class

Assume that there is a drawing program that manipulates several types of geo-metrical figures, such as ellipses, rectangles, triangles, and so on. Also assume that the common element for all geometrical figures is that they are defined by a bounding rectangle that encloses them. We can model this system by means of an abstract class named GeoFigure with an abstract method named Draw() that takes as parameters the screen location where the figure is to be displayed and the dimensions of the bounding rectangle. The extended classes Ellipse, Triangle, and Rectangle implement the method Draw() for each concrete figure. Clearly the abstract class cannot be instantiated and the abstract method Draw() cannot be referenced because there is no way of creating or drawing a GeoFigure object. However, the abstract method defines the interface for all polymorphic implemen-tations of Draw(), thus making the system more stable. Figure 13-3 shows the class diagram in this case.

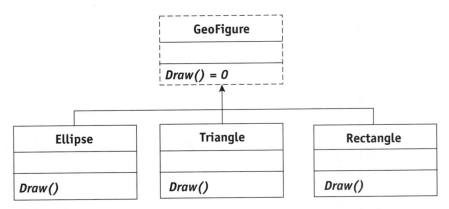

Figure 13-3
System with an abstract class

It is a mistake to think that an abstract class should only have abstract methods. It is always better to have as much functionality as possible in the superclass, whether or not it is an abstract class. Instance fields and nonabstract methods should all be in the superclass. Operations that cannot be implemented in the superclass are the only ones that should appear in the subclasses.

The program, DrawFigure.java, implements the abstract classes in Figure 13-3. Because we have not yet discussed Java graphics, the code merely displays text messages that show that execution is in the corresponding routine. The source file for DrawFigure.java is found in the Session 13 directory on the book's CD-ROM.

Done!

REVIEW

In Java, inheritance is implemented by means of a class hierarchy. In inheritance, one class — called the derived class or the subclass — inherits the functionality of another class — called the base class or superclass. Inheritance promotes a higher level of abstraction and serves to extend the functionality of classes that are in a kind-of relationship. The keyword *extends* is used to implement inheritance in a subclass. When two methods with the same signature exist in a class hierarchy connected by inheritance, the one used is determined by *overriding*, where the method used is the one closest in the inheritance hierarchy to the object making the call. An abstract class is a class that defines an interface but that does not contain implementation. Abstract classes are created with the *abstract* keyword. Abstract classes can have abstract and nonabstract methods.

QUIZ YOURSELF

1. Write Java code that creates a hierarchy in which one class extends another one. (See "Inheritance in Java.")

2. What is the difference between overloading and overriding as a method selection mechanism? (See "Extending Functionality.")

3. In an inheritance hierarchy, when are two methods said to be polymorphic? (See "Overriding.")

4. What Java keyword is used to create an abstract class? (See "Abstract Classes and Methods.")

5. Can an abstract class contain a nonabstract method? (See "Abstract Classes and Methods.")

6. Write a Java program that uses an inheritance hierarchy with a base abstract class and two nonabstract derived classes. (See "Implementing an Abstract Class.")

Using Object Composition

Session Checklist

✔ Object composition

✔ The uses relationship and aggregation

✔ Objects as parameters

✔ Returning an object

✔ Acquaintance relationship

✔ Combining inheritance and object composition

✔ Arrays of objects

✔ Dynamic binding

**30 Min.
To Go**

I n this session, we discuss an alternative to inheritance as a way of reusing class functionality. This method is called *object composition*. In inheritance, reusability is accomplished by extending a superclass. In object composition, a class reuses functionality simply by declaring and holding an object of the class it wants to use. The main advantage of object composition is that reusability is accomplished in a simpler manner and without exposing the class structure.

In general, object composition is a more satisfactory approach to class reuse than inheritance.

Fundamentals of Object Composition

Session 13 shows that a class can extend another class in order to use the methods of that class. The mechanism, called inheritance, is particularly useful when a class is a kind-of another one. However, we often encounter cases in which the class whose functionality we want to reuse is not in a kind-of relationship with the other class. An alternative, and simple approach, is for the class to create an object of the class it wants to reuse, because public methods can always be accessed through objects. In this case we say that reusability is achieved through object composition. Object composition is based on the following facts of the Java language:

- A class can access the public members of another class.
- An object can be a member of a class.
- A class can instantiate an object of another class.

Object composition requires a different way of thinking about the class relationships. In the case of inheritance, we say that a class extends another class in order to use its methods. In object composition a class accomplishes the same purpose by creating or holding an object of the other class.

The uses Relationship

Suppose there is a class Rectangle with a method named Area() that calculates the area of a rectangular figure. Furthermore, assume that there is a class named Window that is rectangular. One way in which the class Window can use the method Area() of the class Rectangle is to make Window extend Rectangle. Because Rectangle is the superclass and Window the subclass, an object of Window can access the Area() method in Rectangle. This inheritance-based reusability assumes that Window is a kind-of Rectangle, which is not an accurate model if Window can also be circular or elliptical in shape.

Alternatively, the class `Window` can use the method `Area()` of `Rectangle` without an inheritance relationship. The alternative is for `Window` to create an object of the `Rectangle` class. In this case, we can say that `Window` "uses" `Rectangle`; this is a more accurate representation of the class relationship. The object `Rectangle` of `Window` is considered a member object.

Aggregation

20 Min. To Go

We speak of a class aggregation relationship when a class contains an object of the class whose methods it wants to reuse. In many of the sample programs listed in previous sessions, the driving class creates objects of other classes in order to access their methods. In fact, aggregation is the simplest and most common way of accessing the public members of another class.

But the fact that an aggregation association is simple and common does not make it any less valuable. In many cases, a simple aggregation association is an alternative to a more elaborate one based on class inheritance. Aggregation is depicted in class diagrams by means of an arrow pointing to the class whose functionality is to be used, as shown in Figure 14-1.

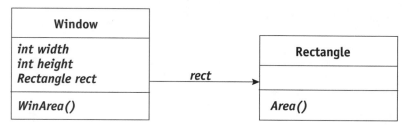

Figure 14-1
Modeling an aggregation association

Sometimes you may want to write the name of the object above the arrow that depicts the class aggregation relationship.

The program Aggregation.java shows the implementation of the class diagram in Figure 14-1 using object composition by aggregation. The source file for Aggregation.java is found in the Session14 directory on the book's CD-ROM.

Objects as Parameters

Any variable — for example, an int, a double, or a string — can be passed as an argument to a method. An object, which is a variable of an abstract data type, can also be passed as an argument. As is the case with primitive types, the method that receives the parameter object can access it using an alias. The difference is that there is only one copy of the object and any change performed by the method also modifies the original. In other words, while primitive data types are always passed by value, objects are passed by reference.

Returning an Object

A method can also return an object. In this case, the method declaration must specify the object's class as the return type. Typically, the returned object is created in the method using the new operator. Methods that receive objects as parameters or that return objects are often of static type. The following program, **PixelOps.java**, demonstrates objects passed as arguments and returned as parameters to a method.

The source file for the program PixelOps.java is found in the Session 14 directory on the book's CD-ROM.

```
//*********************************************************
//*********************************************************
// Program: PixelOps
// Reference: Session 14
// Topics:
//     1. Object passed as an argument to a method
//     2. Method that returns an object
//*********************************************************
//*********************************************************

//****************************************
//          Pixel class
//****************************************
class Pixel
{
    // Attributes
```

```java
   private int x;
   private int y;

   // Constructor
   public Pixel(int pixX, int pixY)
   {
     this.x = pixX;
     this.y = pixY;
   }


   // Method receives Pixel as parameters
   public static Pixel midPix(Pixel p1, Pixel p2)
   {
   int midX = (p1.x/2) + (p2.x/2);
   int midY = (p1.y/2) + (p2.y/2);
   Pixel midOne = new Pixel(midX, midY);
   return midOne;
   }


   // Display the address of a pixel
   public void pixLocation()
   {
     System.out.print("Pixel x : " + this.x + "   ");
     System.out.print("Pixel y : " + this.y + "\n\n");
     System.out.flush();
   }
}


//*****************************************
//*****************************************
//                Driving class
//*****************************************
//*****************************************
public class PixelOps
{

    public static void main(String[] args)
    {
    // Create objects of the class Pixel
    Pixel pix1 = new Pixel(10, 50);
```

```
Pixel pix2 = new Pixel(90, 200);

// Since the method midPix is static, it is called with
// a class reference
Pixel pix3 = Pixel.midPix(pix1, pix2);

// Display location of all three Pixel objects
pix1.pixLocation();
pix2.pixLocation();
pix3.pixLocation();
    }
}
```

**10 Min.
To Go**

Acquaintance

This session began by considering the case of a class that contains an object of another class, or an aggregation relationship. However, in the program PixelOps. java, we see a class that receives as a parameter the object that it uses to access the methods of another one. Because in this case the object is not contained in the class, we speak of object composition by *acquaintance*. In the acquaintance relationship, the binding is looser than in object composition because in the case of acquaintance the object may not be defined until runtime.

It is this looser binding in the acquaintance relationship that makes it possible to use acquaintance to implement dynamic binding.

Suppose there is an application that has access to two methods to calculate areas. Both methods are named Area(). One Area() method, located in a class named Rectangle, calculates the area of a rectangular figure. Another Area() method is located in a class named Circle and calculates the area of a circular figure. Now suppose that we are coding a class named Window, which can be circular or rectangular in shape, and we want to use the area-calculating methods of the classes Rectangle and Circle. One possible approach is to code two methods named WinArea() of the class Window. One method receives a Rectangle object as a parameter and the other method receives a Circle object. Because the WinArea() methods have different signatures they are not polymorphic. Which method is used depends on the object that is received as a parameter. The class diagram in Figure 14-2 shows the class structure in this example.

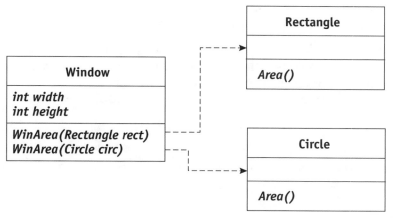

Figure 14-2
Modeling an acquaintance association

Recall that we use a solid line to represent object composition by aggregation. To distinguish object composition by acquaintance, a dashed line is used to represent this relationship, as in Figure 14-2.

The program Acquaintance.java, implements the class diagram in Figure 14-2. The source file for Acquaintance.java is found in the Session 14 directory on the book's CD-ROM.

Combining Inheritance and Object Composition

An object is an instance of a class and a class is a collection of data and methods that work as a unit. The new operator is used in Java to create an object from a class. A class can be defined as an abstract data type. Because it is possible to create an array of any primitive data type, it is also possible to create an array of an ADT (Abstract Data Type).

Arrays of Objects

When we create an array using a class, the result is an array of objects of the class. For example, if there is a class named Employee, we create an array of Employee objects in the same way that we create an array of int:

```
int[] intArray = new int[14];
Employee[] empArray = new Employee[10];
```

After the array of type `Employee` is created, we can store 10 objects of the class `Employee` in it. An interesting variation on arrays of objects is that we can store objects of a subclass in an array of a superclass. In this manner, if the class `HourlyEmployee` extends `Employee`, and emp4 is an object of the subclass, then we can code:

```
empArray[9] = emp4;
```

Notice that the reverse is not true: An array of a subclass cannot store elements of its superclass, except by typecasting.

Dynamic Binding

Arrays can store objects of different types, that is, of the base class and of any of its subclasses. This creates the possibility of defining an array of objects of a superclass and then filling the array at runtime with objects of any class in the inheritance hierarchy. Because the objects are created when the program runs, it is clear that the binding between the object and the method takes place at runtime, which is a case of true polymorphism.

Done!

The program ObjectArray.java uses the classes `Employee` **and** `HourlyEmployee` **to demonstrate dynamic binding with an array of objects. During program execution, the user selects an object of either class, which object is then inserted in the object array. The binding is dynamic because the object is not known until the program runs. The source file for ObjectArray.java is found in the Session14 directory in the book's CD-ROM.**

REVIEW

Object composition provides an alternative way for reusing class functionality. In this case, reuse is based on one class declaring, or receiving as a parameter, an object of another one. An aggregation relationship takes place when the class contains an object of the other one. A method can receive an object as a parameter and return one to the caller. In acquaintance relationships, an object received as a parameter is used to access the functionality of another class. Acquaintance binds looser than aggregation. Objects can be stored in arrays. An array of objects of a superclass can also store objects of a subclass. We can implement dynamic binding by combining inheritance and object composition.

QUIZ YOURSELF

1. List the three facts of the Java language on which object composition is based. (See "Fundamentals of Object Composition.")

2. What type of class association is described as a uses relationship? (See "The uses Relationship.")

3. Code a Java method that receives an object as a parameter. (See "Objects as Parameters.")

4. Can a method return an object to the caller? (See "Returning an Object.")

5. Draw a class diagram that depicts object composition by aggregation and by acquaintance. (See "Acquaintance.")

6. Write a Java program that implements dynamic binding. (See "Combining Inheritance and Object Composition.")

Using Recursion

Session Checklist

✔ Recursion in Java

✔ Understanding recursion

✔ Recursive solutions

*30 Min.
To Go*

Recursion is the process of defining something in terms of itself. Outside the world of mathematics and computing, a recursive definition is often an undesirable one. Imagine a dictionary defining a square as a sort of rectangle and a rectangle as a sort of a square. The circular definition would be useless to the user. In computer programming, a recursive solution to a problem consists of formulating progressively simpler versions of the same problem. Java supports recursion, as is the case with most programming languages developed after Lisp and Algol. This session presents recursion as a problem-solving technique. Recursion is an important programming methodology because some algorithms can be expressed better recursively.

Recursion in Java

The notion of recursion exists both in theoretical mathematics and in programming. In programming, a recursive routine is a routine that calls itself in order to perform a calculation. Although recursion is a natural consequence of subprograms, programming languages must be especially designed to support recursion. Lisp was the first programming language to support automatic recursion. Ada, Algol, Prolog, Pascal, C, Snobol, PL/I, and Java, among many others, also support recursion.

A recursive mathematical definition is one that expresses a calculation in terms of itself; for example, the factorial of a number n (n!) can be expressed as:

```
0! = 1
n! = n * (n - 1)!
```

In Java, the recursive calculation of the factorial can be coded as:

```java
public static int Factorial(int n)
{
    if( n == 0)
        return 1;                    // Stopping case
    else
        return n * Factorial(n - 1);  // Recursive call
}
```

A recursive method contains a call to itself. In the method named Factorial(), listed previously, we see a program line in which the method Factorial() calls the method Factorial(). In addition, in order for a recursive method to execute correctly, it must have a case in which the recursion stops. In the listed factorial recursion, this case is when n == 1. This is called the stopping case, or the base case of the recursion.

Recursion is based on the fact that each time a method executes it is furnished with a unique and fresh copy of the arguments and local variables. This copy of the data is called the *activation record* of the method. A recursive routine can be visualized as a yo-yo, going up and down.

Most recursive routines perform the calculations on the return cycles of the function calls.

Understanding Recursion

We must understand recursion in order to imagine that a particular programming problem could have a recursive solution. We need an even deeper understanding of recursion in order to devise a recursive algorithm to solve a particular problem, and to then implement it in Java code.

**20 Min.
To Go**

Understanding recursion requires grasping the call-return mechanism used by a programming language to access subprograms. In Java, this means visualizing how methods are accessed and how execution returns from the method to the calling code. In the following descriptions, we use the term *client* or *client code* to refer to the routine that makes the call.

The call-return mechanism is easy to follow in the case of client code calling a method in its same class or in another class to which it has access. In this case, the client references the method's parameters in the call and receives an optional return value at the conclusion of the method's execution. Not as evident is the fact that the calling code must also pass to the method the address to which execution is to return. The return operation cannot be performed without this memory address. Figure 15-1 depicts the call-return mechanism.

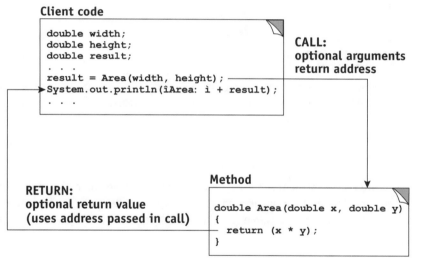

Client code

```
double width;
double height;
double result;
. . .
result = Area(width, height);
System.out.println(îArea: i + result);
. . .
```

CALL:
optional arguments
return address

RETURN:
optional return value
(uses address passed in call)

Method

```
double Area(double x, double y)
{
    return (x * y);
}
```

Figure 15-1
Elements of the call-return mechanism

The parameters and the return address that are passed to a method at call time are known as its *activation record*. Recursion is possible when a programming language maintains a unique activation record for each iteration of a method. One way to visualize this is to imagine that when a method is called the language creates a copy of the code and attaches to it the corresponding arguments and the return address, in other words, its activation record.

For example, suppose that the recursive method to calculate the factorial listed previously is called with an initial value of 3. In this case client code passes its return address and the initial value n = 3 as the activation record for the first iteration of the Factorial() method. The method then decrements the value of n (n = 2) and calls Factorial() recursively. In this case, the activation record for the second iteration of Factorial() is the return address of the line that follows the call and the value n = 2. Processing again decrements the value of n (n = 1) and calls Factorial() for the third time. Again the activation record for the call is the address of the code line following the call and the value n = 1. During the third call to the Factorial() method the value of n is again decremented and the method called for the fourth time. During the fourth iteration of the recursion the value of n is equal to 0. This determines that the terminating condition is encountered and that no further recursive calls are made. The recursion now starts unwinding from its most deeply nested iteration. It is during this unwinding process that the calculations are performed. The process is shown graphically in Figure 15-2.

Recursive Solutions

10 Min. To Go

Many problems in mathematics, as well as in symbolic processing in general, can be expressed recursively. For example, the general expression of the exponential function can be expressed as a recursion:

```
if y = 0 then x^y = 1
x^y = x * x^(y-1)
```

Other more common programming problems can often be solved by means of recursion. Consider the task of displaying the individual digits of an integer number in a vertical stack. For example, displaying the number 13579 as

```
1
3
5
7
9
```

The following program, **StackDigits.java**, displays the digits of an integer number in a vertical stack.

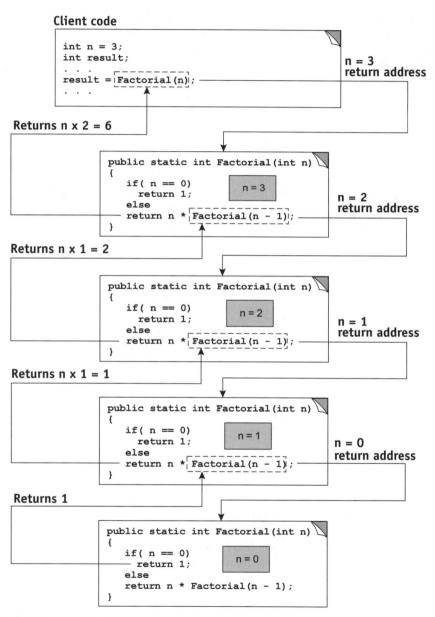

Figure 15-2
Recursive calculation of 3!

The source file for the program StackDigits.java is found in the Session15 directory on the book's CD-ROM.

```
//************************************************************
//************************************************************
// Program: StackDigits
// Topics:
//     1. Program to display digits stacked vertically
//        using recursion
// Requires:
//     1. Keyin class in the current directory
//************************************************************
//************************************************************


//*****************************************
//*****************************************
//              Driving class
//*****************************************
//*****************************************
public class StackDigits
{
    public static void main(String[] args)
    {
    // Input integer from user
    int aNumber;
    aNumber = Keyin.inInt("Enter integer number: ");
    stackDigits(aNumber);
    return;
    }
    //***************************
    //     recursive method
    //***************************
    public static void stackDigits(int x)
    {
       if(x == 0)
         return;
       else
```

```
    {
        stackDigits(x / 10);      // Method calls itself
        System.out.println(x % 10);
    }
  }
}
```

Recursive routines usually do not improve code size or memory use. Recursive versions of most algorithms execute slower than their iterative counterparts. The main advantage of recursion is as a problem-solving tool.

Some sorting algorithms, such as quicksort, are difficult to describe or implement without recursion.

Complex reasoning problems that occur in artificial intelligence lend themselves to recursive solutions. PROLOG is a programming language that uses recursion as its primary control mechanism. Recursion is often used in processing lists. A list is defined as an ordered set of values; for example:

```
    [1, 3, 4, 5, 8, 1, 5]  = listA
```

Where:

1	=	head of the list
3, 4, 5, 8, 1, 5	=	rest of the list

We can use recursion to test whether element x is in list A, as follows: IF_MEMBER function:

- if the list is empty, return NO
- if x is equal to the head of the list, return YES
- call IF_MEMBER with the rest of the list as the argument

The following program, **TwoToTheY.java**, calculates the powers of 2 using recursion.

The code listing for the program TwoToTheY.java is found in the Session15 directory on the book's CD-ROM.

```
//****************************************************************
//****************************************************************
// Program: TwoToTheY
// Topics:
//      1. Program calculate 2 to the y using recursion
// Requires:
//      Keyin class in the current directory
//****************************************************************
//****************************************************************


//*****************************************
//*****************************************
//               Driving class
//*****************************************
//*****************************************
public class TwoToTheY
{

    public static void main(String[] args)
    {
    // Input integer from user
    int power, result;

    System.out.println("Calculates 2-to-the-y power");
    power = Keyin.inInt("Enter an integer power: ");

    result = PowerOf2(power);
    System.out.println(result);
    return;
    }

    //***************************
    //      recursive method
    //***************************
    public static int PowerOf2(int exponent)
    {

        if(exponent == 0)
            return 1;
```

```
        else
          return (2 * PowerOf2(exponent - 1));
    }
}
```

Done!

REVIEW

In programming, a recursive routine is one that performs calculations by calling itself. Many common programming problems can be expressed and solved recursively. Understanding recursion requires visualizing the call-return mechanism used by programming languages. Recursion is made possible when a programming language maintains a record for the data and the address of the calling code passes to each iteration of a called routine. This is called the activation record.

> **Note**
> **Recursive solutions are elegant and powerful, but they often take longer and use up more code than their iterative versions.**

QUIZ YOURSELF

1. List three other programming languages that support recursion. (See "Recursion in Java.")

2. What is the name given to the copy of the local variables passed on to a method at call time? (See "Recursion in Java.")

3. Symbolically describe the process of calculating the exponential function using recursion. (See "Recursive Solutions.")

4. Write a Java program that uses recursion to display the digits of an integer number, stacked vertically, and in reverse order. For example, the number 1357 displays as:

   7.

   5.

   3.

   1.

   (See "Recursive Solutions.")

Abstract Data Types

Session Checklist

✔ Arrays revisited: array alias, cloning an array, arrays as parameters

✔ Abstract Data Types

✔ ADT for a bag of integers

✔ Invariants of an ADT

✔ Removing an element from a bag

✔ Refining the constructor

✔ Manipulating a bag's capacity

30 Min.
To Go

A benefit of object-oriented systems is using the class structure to create our own customized data types. We are already familiar with this concept because we have been using the String class as a data type. This session discusses the mechanisms and language structures that are used to create Abstract Data Types (ADT). We also develop Java code for implementing an ADT called a bag. Other ADTs are discussed in the sessions that follow. Because ADTs are often implemented using arrays, we begin by reviewing Java arrays.

Arrays Revisited

Implementation of Java Abstract Data Types often requires the use of arrays. We begin by reviewing the material on arrays, which were discussed in Session 6, and by introducing several new concepts.

An array is an ordered group of variables of the same type. An array of type `int` is declared as follows:

```
int[] grades;
```

The array is created using the new operator

```
grades = new int[14];
```

You can also create and initialize an array in the same statement:

```
int[] grades = new int[14];
```

The length of an array is the number of elements that it contains. After an array is created or initialized, its length cannot be changed. The `length` operator can be used with an array name to obtain the number of elements in the array. For example:

```
System.out.println("Array grades has" +
                   grades.length + " elements");
```

Array Alias

When an array variable is assigned to an existing array, both variables actually refer to the same array. For example:

```
int[] exams;
exams = grades;
```

Now exams is an alias for the array named grades.

Cloning an Array

To create a new copy of an array you must use the Java built-in `clone()` method of the Object class. The use of `clone()` requires a typecast, as follows:

```
scores = (int[]) exams.clone();
```

Now there are two different arrays: one array named `scores[]` and a second array named `exams[]`. Initially, `scores[]` contains all the values of `exams[]` but if an element is changed in either array the other one is not affected.

Arrays as Parameters

An array can be passed as a parameter to a method. When the method is activated, the array parameter becomes an alias of the array passed as an argument in the call, not a clone. Therefore, the method accesses the same data structure, often using a different name. For example, the following method initializes with zeros all the elements of any array of type `int`:

```
public static void clearAll(int[] anArray)
{
  for(int x = 0; x < anArray.length; x++)
    anArray[x] = 0;
}
```

The method can now be called with an array argument:

```
clearAll(scores);
```

**20 Min.
To Go**

ADT for a Bag of Integers

The programmer creates an ADT by means of a class. The String is a Java ADT. Another simple data type that can be implemented as an ADT is a *bag*. A bag is a collection of elements of the same type that can be taken in any order. A bag can have duplicate elements, for example, the collection:

```
[8, 2, 8, 8, 7, 6, 2]
```

represents a bag of integers. The elements in a bag are in no particular order.

Invariants of an ADT

Java enables implementing a bag of integers ADT using an array of type `int`. In addition, we can use an instance variable for storing the number of elements stored in the bag. The rules that determine how the instance variables of an ADT are managed and used are called the ADT invariants. Determining the invariants is a critical part of the implementation of an ADT. Each method that manipulates the

ADT (except the constructors) assumes that the invariants are valid. Methods are responsible for ensuring that the invariants remain valid when the method finishes.

Invariants are a result of a modern programming tendency called formal and semiformal specifications. This approach fosters a more rigorous definition of program specifications in order to ensure quality and to facilitate development.

The program BagOfInt.java implements a bag of integers ADT. The source file for BagOfInt.java is found in the Session 16 directory on the book's CD-ROM.

10 Min.
To Go

Removing an Element from a Bag

By definition, a bag's elements are in no particular order. To remove an element from a bag, we search for the first occurrence of the element. If the target element is found in the bag, we remove it by taking the last element in the bag and moving it to the position of the found element. The operation reduces the number of elements in the bag by one. Figure 16-1 graphically shows the process of removing element 33 from a bag initially containing seven elements.

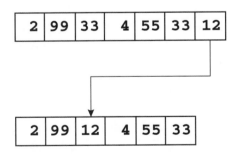

Figure 16-1
Removing an element from a bag

The code for removing an element from a bag is as follows:

```
//*****************************************
//  method to remove an element from a bag
//*****************************************
```

```
// Removes the first occurrence of the target element
// from the current bag.
// Returns true if a target element was found and
// removed. Returns false if the bag is empty or if
// the target element was not found.
public boolean removeElement(int target)
{
  // First check for an empty bag
  if(this.itemsInBag == 0)
    return false;

  // If bag is not empty, attempt to find the target
  // element in the bag
  for(int x = 0; x < this.itemsInBag; x++)
  {
    // Test for target found condition
    if(this.data[x] == target)
      {
        // Copy last element to this element
        this.data[x] = this.data[itemsInBag-1];
        this.itemsInBag--;
        return true;
      }
  }
  // Target not found
  return false;
}
```

The method returns true if the target element was found in the bag; otherwise, the method returns false. Client code can examine the returned value and proceed accordingly.

The previously listed code continues to work if the target element is the only one in the bag. In this case, the number of items in the bag is initially one. The element found is first placed in its same position. Then the number of elements in the bag is reduced by one, creating an empty bag.

Refining the Constructor

The constructor for the IntArrayBag ADT should be refined so that a null bag is never created. This is accomplished by testing the size parameter. If this value is less than 10, then a bag of 10 elements is created by the code. We also provide a parameterless constructor that builds a default bag with 10 elements. The code is as follows:

```
//*****************************
//       new constructors
//*****************************
// Parameterized constructor allows the user to define
// the initial bag size. A minimum of 10 elements is
// used if the user enters a smaller value
public IntArrayBag(int initialSize)
{
  // Create a Bag with at least 10 elements
  if(initialSize < 10)
    data = new int[10];
  else
    data = new int[initialSize]; // Size of bag

  // Initially a bag has no elements
  this.itemsInBag = 0;         // Bag has no elements
}

// A parameterless constructor allows creating a default
// bag of 10 elements
public IntArrayBag()
{
   data = new int[10];
   this.itemsInBag = 0;        // Bag has no elements
}
```

Manipulating a Bag's Capacity

Bag operations should not assume that there is sufficient capacity in the bag to store new elements. Code should first test for space in a bag before inserting a new element. If the bag's capacity is at its limit, then the bag can be expanded before performing the insertion.

The System class in the standard Java package contains a method named `arraycopy()` that copies one array into a second array. The method's signature is as follows:

```
arraycopy( source,           // Source array
           int sourceOffset,  // Offset in source
           destination,       // Destination array
           int destOffset,    // Offset in destination
           int count)         // Number of elements to copy
```

Copying takes place from the array *source*, starting at the location `sourceOffset`, and copies *count* elements into the array *destination*, starting at the location `destOffset`. The action can be seen in Figure 16-2.

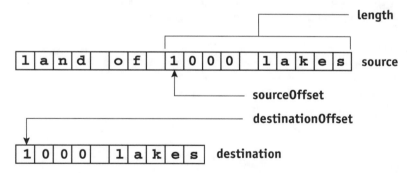

Figure 16-2
Action of the arraycopy() method of the System class

If *source* and *destination* are the same array, then the method creates a temporary storage space to which the items are first copied. This makes it possible to use `arraycopy()` to close gaps by performing an overlapping copy within a single array. The process is shown in Figure 16-3.

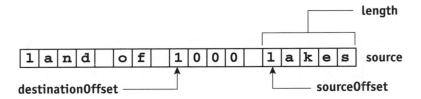

System.arraycopy(source, 13, source, 8, 5);

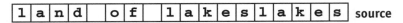

Figure 16-3
Using arraycopy() to close a gap in an array

Notice that when `arraycopy()` is used within the same array, the length of the array is not changed. The following program, **ArrayOps.java**, demonstrates the use of the `arraycopy()` method.

The source file for the program ArrayOps.java is found in the Session 16 directory on the book's CD-ROM.

```
//*********************************************************
//*********************************************************
// Program: ArrayOps
// Reference: Session 16
// Topics:
//      1. Array operations with the arraycopy() method
//          of the System class
//*********************************************************
//*********************************************************


//*****************************************
//               Driving class
//*****************************************
public class ArrayOps
{
```

```java
public static void main(String[] args)
{
// Array declarations
char[] minn = {'l','a','n','d',' ','o','f',
               ' ','1','0','0','0',' ',
               'l','a','k','e','s'};

char[] newMinn = new char[10];

// Display original array
System.out.println(minn);

// Copy to another array
System.arraycopy(minn, 8, newMinn, 0, 10);
System.out.println(newMinn);

System.arraycopy(minn, 13, minn, 8, 5);
System.out.println(minn);

   }
}
```

We can also use `arraycopy()` to expand the capacity of a bag. This can be done by creating a local array that is larger than the original array, copying the elements of the old array into the new array, and then assigning the new array to the object's data variable. The following method, `expandBag()`, adds four elements to an existing array:

```java
public void expandBag()
{
  // Create a new array with 4 more elements than the
  // old one
  int biggerBag[] = new int[this.data.length + 4];

  // Copy the old array into the new one
  System.arraycopy(this.data, 0, biggerBag, 0, this.itemsInBag);

  // Assign new array as object's data
  this.data = biggerBag;
}
```

We can use the `expandBag()` method to modify `addElements()` so that the bag is expanded if necessary.

```java
//******************************
// method to add element to bag
//******************************
// This implementation checks to see if there is room
// in the array to add a new element. If not, then the
// array is expanded by four elements
public void addElement(int element)
{
    // Test for full bag
    if(this.itemsInBag == this.data.length)
      expandBag();

    this.data[itemsInBag] = element;
    this.itemsInBag++;          // Bump bag size
}
```

The program BagADT.java demonstrates the previously described bag operations. The source file for BagADT.java is found in the Session16 directory on the book's CD-ROM.

Done!

REVIEW

An array is an ordered group of variables of the same type. Arrays are created using the new operator. Assigning another name to an existing array creates an array alias. An array clone consists of two different and independent arrays. Java Abstract Data Types are usually created in a class construct. A bag ADT is a collection of elements of the same type, taken in any order. Bag ADTs are often implemented using arrays. The rules that define how the instance variables of an ADT are managed are called the invariants. Minimal implementation of a bag ADT include methods for creating the bag (constructors), as well as to add and remove elements to and from the bag, and to display the bag contents.

QUIZ YOURSELF

1. Can variables of different types be represented in the same array? (See "Arrays Revisited.")

2. Which Java operator would you use to create a clone of an array? (See "Cloning an Array.")

3. What are the invariants of an ADT? (See "Invariants of an ADT.")

4. In what order are the elements placed in a bag? (See "Removing an Element from a Bag.")

5. In expanding a bag's capacity, what method of the System class is used to create a copy of the array? (See "Manipulating a Bag's Capacity.")

PART

III

Saturday Afternoon
Part Review

1. Where did OO originate?
2. Can an object exist without a class to contain it?
3. What are the data members of a class?
4. What OO mechanism allows a subclass to access the public members of a superclass?
5. In which class must the main() method be?
6. How can you determine if a data element is a field or a method variable?
7. To what values does the default constructor set uninitialized numeric, string, and boolean variables?
8. What is the difference between overloading and overriding as a method-selection mechanism?
9. In an inheritance hierarchy, when are two methods polymorphic?
10. What Java keyword do we use to create an abstract class?
11. Can an abstract class contain a nonabstract method?
12. List the three facts of the Java language on which object composition is based.
13. What type of class association do we describe as a uses relationship?
14. Can a method return an object to the caller?
15. List three other programming languages that support recursion.
16. What name do we give to the copy of the local variables that pass to a method at call time?

17. Use recursion to describe symbolically the process of calculating the exponential function .

18. Can we represent variables of different types in the same array?

19. Which Java operator do we use to create a clone of an array?

20. What are the invariants of an ADT?

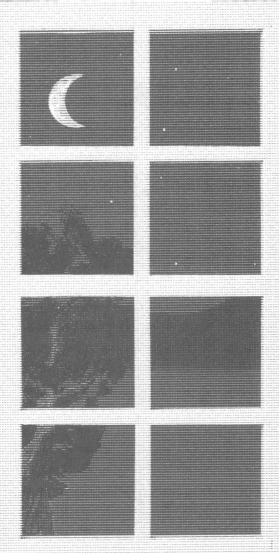

The Linked List ADT

Session Checklist

✔ Linked Lists in Java

✔ Developing the `IntNode` class and `IntNode` methods

✔ Developing the `IntList` class

✔ Manipulating and traversing a linked list

✔ Inserting and deleting elements from a linked list

✔ Implementing the linked list ADT

✔ Multiple links

**30 Min.
To Go**

A linked list is a primitive data structure that provides an alternative mechanism to arrays for implementing abstract data types (ADTs). The linked list is dynamic in the sense that it grows and shrinks as the program executes. In contrast with a bag, the elements in a linked list are arranged in a specific order. Each element is connected to the one that follows by means of a link.

Linked Lists in Java

Linked lists are often implemented by means of individual objects called *nodes*. Each node contains the value of the element as well as a link to the next element in the list. If a node contains a null link then there is no next element in the list. Every list contains a special node called the *head node*, which is always the first element in the list. The last node in the list is called the *tail of the list*. Figure 17-1 shows a possible visualization of a linked list.

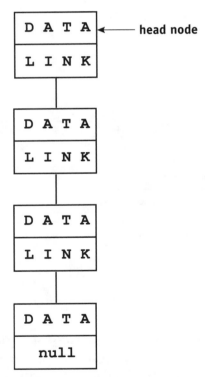

Figure 17-1
Visualization of a linked list

Perhaps linked lists are easier to visualize in programming languages that use explicit pointers, such as C and C++, where the link element of a node is a pointer to the next node in the list. In Java, an object's name is also its address, so the link element is actually the next object in the list. This means that each node, except the last one, contains a reference to another node.

Developing the IntNode Class

We can design a class that creates and manipulates the nodes of a linked list. For instance, a class named IntNode can be used to handle the nodes of a list of integer values. Each node contains a data element and a link. The class can be coded as follows:

```
class IntNode
{
// Invariants:
//   1. The integer variable data holds the node's data element.
//   2. The link component is null for the last node in a list,
//       otherwise the link element references the next node.

   private int data;
   private IntNode link;

//***************************
//        constructor
//***************************
   public IntNode(int initialData, IntNode initialLink)
   {
       this.data = initialData;
       this.link = initialLink;
   }
}
```

IntNode Methods

Notice that the class IntNode has two instance variables. One is of type int (data) and the other one (link) is an object of the class IntNode itself. The notion of a class that contains its own objects may seem strange at first, but in Java, this is the only way in which we can store a reference to another object.

The IntNode class must also provide mutator and accessor methods to manipulate its instance variables. This means that there must be an accessor and a mutator method for each variable. The four methods can be coded as follows:

```
//*************************************
// accessors and mutators methods for
// the IntNote class instance variables
//*************************************
```

```
public int getData()
{
    return this.data;
}

public void setData(int newData)
{
    this.data = newData;
}

public IntNode getLink()
{
    return this.link;
}

public void setLink(IntNode newLink)
{
    this.link = newLink;
}
}
```

Developing the IntList Class

Based on the primitive functionality of the IntNode class we can create an IntList class that implements a linked list of integers. Because IntList contains objects of the class IntNode, we say that IntList is a container-type ADT. An array is the only primitive container type in Java. In a sense, we can say that the IntNode class is also a container type, because it contains its own objects. However, in reality, the objects contained by IntNode are used only as a means for accessing other nodes.

To access a list we must know its head. The IntList class maintains an instance variable called head, of type IntNode, for each list. This variable provides access to the first element of the list. Because each node contains a link to the next one in the list, the entire list can be accessed through the head node. The IntList class can be implemented as follows:

```
//*********************************************
//    class for an int linked list
//*********************************************
class IntList
{
```

```
// IntList is a container class that holds objects of
// the class IntNode
// Invariants:
//    1. IntNode head holds the address of the first node
//       in the list. Mutator methods must always update
//       this object.
//    2. numNodes is a convenience counter so that code
//       need not traverse the list in order to determine
//       the number of elements.

// Instance variables
   int numNodes;        // number of nodes in list
   IntNode head;        // First node in list

// Constructor
   public IntList()
   {
     this.head = null;
     this.numNodes = 0;
   }
}
```

In addition to the constructor, the IntList class can contain methods to manipulate lists, such as methods to insert elements in a list, to delete an element from a list, and to traverse the list. List traversal operations are based on obtaining the node at the head of the list and then following the links until a node is reached in which the link is null. This node is the tail of the list. Coding can be as follows:

```
// Create a variable to walk through the list.
// Variable is an object of IntNode initialized to
// the list's head

   IntNode aNode = this.head;

   while(aNode != null)
   {
     . . . list processing operations here
     // Get next node in list
   aNode = aNode.getLink();
   }
```

The program IntListOps.java demonstrates the use of the
`IntNodes` **and the** `IntList` **classes. With minor modifications,**
the classes can be adapted to operate on linked lists of other
primitive types. The source file for IntListOps.java is found in
the Session 17 directory on the book's CD-ROM.

Manipulating the Linked List

20 Min.
To Go

In addition to the constructors and the classes to hold the data elements, a linked list ADT contains several methods to manipulate the list. A minimal set includes the following functionality:

- A way of traversing the linked list while examining each element
- A way of inserting an element into the list
- A way of deleting an element from the list

Traversing a Linked List

List-processing code must often examine the elements in a list, one by one. This operation is called traversing a linked list. The following method traverses a list by means of a loop. The data variable of each node is displayed as the list is traversed. The routine uses a dummy node variable (called aNode) to walk through the list.

```java
// Method to traverse a linked list displaying all elements
public void showList()
{
   // Display number of nodes in list
   System.out.println("Number of nodes: " + this.numNodes);
   // Create a variable to walk through the list.
   // Variable is an object of IntNode initialized to
   // the list's head
   IntNode aNode = this.head;
     while(aNode != null)
   {
      System.out.print(aNode.getData() + "   ");
      // Get next node in list
      aNode = aNode.getLink();
   }
```

```
    System.out.println();
}
```

Inserting an Element into a Linked List

A new list contains no elements. To insert a new element into a list we create a new node object and reset the links in the other nodes of the list. The simplest insertion takes place at the head of the list. In this case we reset the list's head to the new node, as follows:

```
// Method to insert a new element at the head of
// the list
public void insertAtHead(int item)
{
    // Create a new node
        IntNode aNode = new IntNode(item, this.head);

        this.numNodes++;  // update nodes count
        this.head = aNode;  // set head to new node
}
```

Inserting after a particular element in a list requires traversing the list to locate the target element and then resetting the links. The code is:

```
// Method to insert after a particular element in a
// linked list
public boolean insertAfter(int target, int newValue)
{
    // Check for an empty list
    if(this.numNodes == 0)
        return false;
    // If list is not empty, create a variable to walk
    // through the list.
    Node aNode = this.head;

    while(aNode != null)
    {
        // Check if data element of node is target value
            if(aNode.getData() == target)
            {
                // Target found. Create new node to insert
```

```
            // and set link to next node in list
            IntNode inNode = new IntNode(newValue,
                                         aNode.getLink());
            // Reset link of target node to inserted node
            aNode.setLink(inNode);
            // Bump nodes counter for list
            this.numNodes++;
            return true;
        }
        aNode = aNode.getLink();
    }
    // Target element not found in list
    return false;
}
```

Deleting an Element from a Linked List

Deleting the element at the head of the list consists of resetting the head reference to the next node, as follows:

```
// Method to delete the element at the head of the list
//   Returns true if element was removed and false if not
public boolean removeFromHead()
{
    // Check for an empty list
    if(this.numNodes == 0)
        return false;

    // Remove node by resetting head to next node
    this.head = this.head.getLink();
    this.numNodes--;
    return true;
}
```

Deleting a specific element from a linked list requires traversing the list in search of the target element, and when the element is found, resetting the required links. In this case, the code must keep track of the preceding node so that the target node can be skipped. Coding can be as follows:

```
// Method to delete a particular element in a list
public boolean deleteElement(int target)
```

```
{
    // Check for an empty list
    if(this.numNodes == 0)
        return false;
    // If list is not empty, create two variables to walk
    // through the list. One holds the current element and
    // the other one the previous one
        IntNode nextNode = this.head.getLink();;
        IntNode currNode = this.head;

    // Handle the case of a list with a single node
        if(nextNode == null)
            this.head = null;

    // Traverse list in search of target node
     while(nextNode != null)
     {
        // Check if data element of node is target value
            if(nextNode.getData() == target)
            {
            // Target found. Delete element by skipping over
            // the next node
                currNode.setLink(nextNode.getLink());
            // Decrement nodes counter
                this.numNodes--;
                return true;
            }
        currNode = currNode.getLink();
        nextNode = nextNode.getLink();
     }
    // Target element not found in list
        return false;
}
```

**10 Min.
To Go**

The program LinkedListADT.java demonstrates the operations of inserting and deleting into an integer linked list. The code listing for LinkedListADT.java is found in the Session 17 directory on the book's CD-ROM.

Multiple-Link Lists

Deleting a particular element from a linked list requires that we keep track of the node preceding the one to be deleted, which is sometimes called the predecessor node. This is due to the fact that each node in a linked list contains a reference to its successor node, but not to its predecessor node. Performance can be improved in linked lists by keeping track of both the successor and the predecessor nodes. Furthermore, some linked list implementations also keep track of the tail node in the list and of one or more nodes that relate to current operations. The objection to lists that contain multiple references in each node is the amount of memory taken up by each node. In deciding whether to use linked lists with multiple references you must weigh the additional memory requirement against the gain in performance and the simplification in coding.

A circular list is one in which the last node in the list references the first one. Circular lists are often used in implementing some types of input and output buffers, such as the keyboard buffer used in DOS and Windows.

Done!

REVIEW

The linked list is a dynamic data structure that serves as an alternative to arrays for implementing ADTs. The individual objects of a linked list are called nodes. Each node contains a value and a link to the next element in the list. A node with a null link marks the end of the list. The implementation of a node-based linked list requires accessor and mutator methods for the data and the link elements of each node. The IntList class provides functionality for implementing a linked list containing integer values. The objects of the IntList class contain a count of the number of nodes in the list and a reference to the first node in the list. This first node is usually called the head of the list. Methods to manipulate the linked list include those to insert an element in the list, to delete an element from the list, and to traverse the list visiting each element. Multiple-link lists keep track of other associated nodes, such as the predecessor node. Multiple-link lists provide better performance at the expense of storing more data in each node.

QUIZ YOURSELF

1. Describe the main difference between an ADT implemented as an array and as a linked list. (See "Linked Lists in Java.")

2. List the invariants for an `IntNode` class. (See "Developing the IntNode Class.")

3. Which accessor and mutator methods are required for manipulating the data and the link elements of an `IntNode` class? (See "IntNode Methods.")

4. List the invariants required for implementing an `IntList` class that holds the number of nodes in the list and a reference to the node at the head of the list. (See "Developing the IntList Class.")

5. List the three fundamental methods used in manipulating a linked list. (See "Manipulating the Linked List.")

Stacks, Queues, and Trees

Session Checklist

✔ The Stack: implementing Push() and Pop() and developing a Stack ADT

✔ The Queue: methods to enqueue and dequeue

✔ Trees: binary trees and general trees

✔ Array implementation of binary trees

**30 Min.
To Go**

In addition to bags and linked lists, stacks, queues, and trees are ADTs that applications often require. Some programming languages have built-in support for implementing one or more of these types. We implement stacks, queues, and trees as ADTs. Stack and queues are simple data structures we use often in the temporary storage of program data. A tree is a nonlinear data structure with complex linking among the elements.

The Stack

A stack, sometimes called a *pushdown store*, is a simple data structure in which we order the elements as we enter them. An important characteristic of a stack is that we only have access to the last element we enter. This determines that we must remove items from the stack in the reverse order in which we insert them. The term LIFO (Last-In-First-Out) is sometimes used by programmers to describe the operation of a stack. Coin dispensers sometimes used in buses operate in a stack-like manner.

Traditionally, we associate two methods with stack operations: Push() and Pop(). The Push() method inserts an element at the top of the stack; the Pop() method returns the element to the top of the stack. Figure 18-1 shows the operation of a stack.

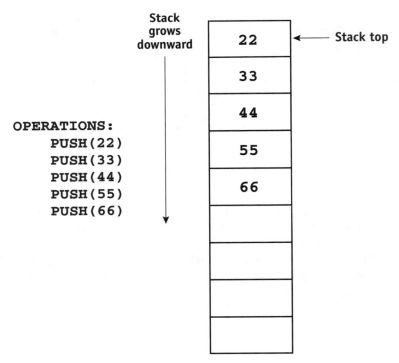

Figure 18-1
Stack operation

Figure 18-1 shows a stack after five elements have been pushed. The last value pushed (22) is now at the top of the stack. If the stack is popped, this element is retrieved.

We can implement a stack by means of a linked list. We can reuse the class IntNode, developed in Session 17, to implement a stack. It may be useful to define an instance variable that keeps track of the number of elements in the stack. This variable prevents us from attempting to pop an empty stack. We can implement the class as follows:

```
class IntStack
{
    // IntStack is a container class that holds objects of
    // the class IntNode
    // Invariants:
    //     1. IntNode top holds the address of the first node
    //        in the stack. Mutator methods must always update
    //        this variable.
    //     2. stackSize records the number of elements in the
    //        stack. Mutator methods must always update this
    //        variable

    // Instance variables
    int stackSize;       // number of elements in stack
    IntNode top;         // Top of the stack

    // Constructor
    public IntStack()
    {
        this.top = null;
        this.stackSize = 0;
    }
}
```

Implementing Push()

The Push() method stores an element at the top of the stack and updates the stack-size variable. We can implement the method as follows:

```
public void Push(int value)
{
```

```
// Create a new node
IntNode aNode = new IntNode(value, this.top);

this.stackSize++;        // update nodes count
this.top = aNode;    // set head to new node
}
```

Implementing Pop()

The Pop() method retrieves the item at the top of the stack if the stack is not empty. It also deletes the stack-top element and adjusts the stack-size variable. We can implement the method as follows:

```
public int Pop()
{
    int element = 0;

    // Check for an empty list
    if(this.stackSize == 0)
      {
        System.out.println("STACK IS EMPTY...");
        return element;
      }

    // If stack is not empty, retrieve element at the
    // top
    element = this.top.getData();
    // Remove node by resetting head to next node
    this.top = this.top.getLink();
    this.stackSize--;
    return element;
}
```

The sample program IntStackADT.java implements an integer-stack- abstract data type. The source file is in the Session 18 directory on the book's CD-ROM.

**20 Min.
To Go**

The Queue

A queue is a simple data structure in which the elements are returned in the same order in which we insert them. Although we define the stack as a Last-In-First-Out (LIFO) structure, the queue is a First-In-First-Out (FIFO) structure. We use queues when code must accommodate devices that operate at different speeds. For example, a computer that sends files to a relatively slow printer uses a queue-based spooler to store the characters until it can process them. Often, we manage input buffers with queue data structures.

Enqueue and Dequeue Methods

Queue operations require one method to insert items in the queue (enqueue) and another method to remove them (dequeue). As with a stack, we can implement a queue with a linked list. In this implementation, we can use two possible approaches:

- Enqueue items at the top of the queue, and remove them from the bottom of the queue.
- Insert items at the bottom of the queue, and remove them from the top.

Implementation of the queue is often easier if we insert items at the bottom and remove them from the top.

You can now implement a queue using the program IntStack ADT.java contained in the book's CD ROM.

Trees

A tree is a nonlinear data structure. The elements in a tree do not form a sequence of first, second, third, and so on. Instead, they have a more complex linking. The fact that trees are nonlinear structures makes them useful when we implement collection classes. Usually, we call the primary element of a tree a *node*.

Binary Trees

A binary tree is a finite set of nodes with the following rules:

- There is a single, special node called the *root*.
- Each node can have no more than two associated nodes: the node's *left child* and *right child*.
- Each node, except the root, has a single parent.
- If you start moving toward a node's parent and then toward the parent of that node, you eventually reach the root.

The following are conventional definitions in regard to trees:

- The parent of a node is the linked node above it in the tree.
- Siblings are nodes that have the same parent.
- A node's parent is its first ancestor, the parent of the parent is the second ancestor, and so on until you reach the root.
- A node's children are also its descendants.
- A node with no descendants is a *leaf*.
- The depth of a node is the number of steps required to get to the root.
- The depth of a tree is the maximum depth of its leaves.

In addition, it is important to understand the concepts of a full and a complete binary tree. In a full binary tree, every leaf has the same depth. A complete binary tree is one in which every level, except the deepest, contains the maximum number of nodes; and the deepest level nodes are as far left as possible. Figure 18-2 shows these concepts graphically.

General Trees

**10 Min.
To Go**

Each node in a binary tree has, at most, two children, although we can extend the notion of a tree so that each node can have any number of children. In this case, we speak of a general tree, which has the following properties:

- There is one special node we call the root.
- We can associate each node with one or more nodes we call its children.
- Each node, except the root node, has one parent.
- If you start moving toward a node's parent and then toward the parent of that node, you eventually reach the root.

Complete and full (depth = 2)

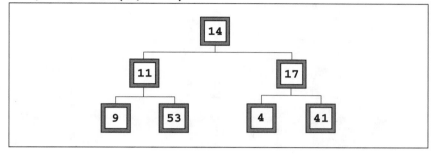

Complete, but not full

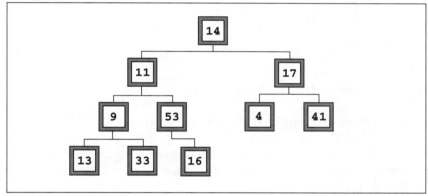

Neither complete, nor full

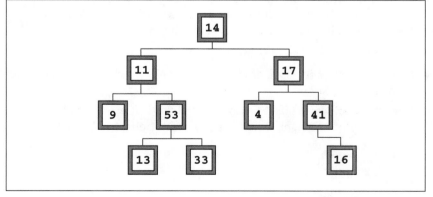

Figure 18-2
Binary trees

Figure 18-3 shows the generalized notion of a tree structure.

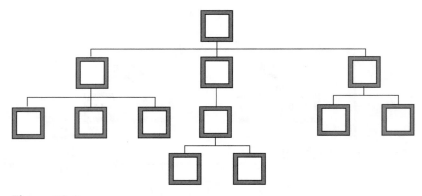

Figure 18-3
A general tree

Array Implementation of Binary Trees

We can implement complete trees by using arrays. Recall that a complete binary tree is one in which all depths are full (except, perhaps, the deepest) and that at the deepest depth the nodes are as far left as possible. Figure 18-4 is a classic representation of a complete binary tree that contains the characters in the word ALGORITHMS.

The lower part of Figure 18-4 shows the 10 characters of the binary tree holding the word ALGORITHMS stored in an array. Starting at the root, we place the characters in the array; then, moving left-to-right, we visit the various depths. Array representations of binary trees obey the following rules:

- We store the root at array index 0.
- If we store a nonroot node at offset [i], we always store the node's parent at offset [(i-1)/2].
- If we store a node at offset [i], the left child (if it exists) is at offset [2i + 1], and the right child (if it exists) is at offset [2i + 2].

Tree representation

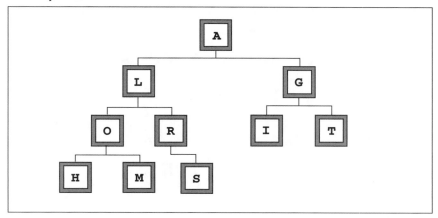

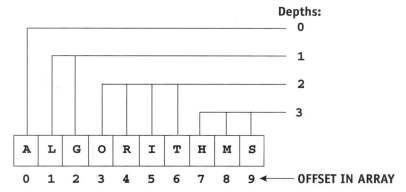

Figure 18-4
Array representation of a binary tree

A Binary Tree Using the Node Class

In a similar manner as we use a linked list, we can use a Node class to represent a binary tree. We store each node as an object of a binary tree Node class. Each node requires four instance variables, as follows:

- Node data
- Node level
- A reference to the node's left child
- A reference to the node's right child

The Node data can be any of the Java data types. The following class provides a Node-based implementation of a binary tree of int type:

```java
//***********************************************
//    class for a binary tree integer node
//***********************************************
class BTNode
{
// Invariants:
//   1. The char variable data holds the node's data element.
//   2. The level variable encodes the node's level, starting
//      with the root at level 0.
//   3. leftChild holds the node's left child
//   4. rightChild holds the node's right child

    private char data;
    private int level;
    private BTNode leftChild;
    private BTNode rightChild;


//****************************
//    constructor
//****************************
    public BTNode(char initialData, int nodeLevel,
            BTNode lChild, BTNode rChild)
    {
        this.data = initialData;
        this.level = nodeLevel;
        this.leftChild = lChild;
        this.rightChild = rChild;
    }


//***********************************
// accessors and mutators methods for
// the instance variables
//***********************************
    public int getData()
    {
```

```java
        return this.data;
    }

    public void setData(char newData)
    {
        this.data = newData;
    }

    public BTNode getLeft()
    {
        return this.leftChild;
    }

    public void setLeft(BTNode child)
        {
        this.leftChild  = child;
    }

    public BTNode getRight()
    {
        return this.rightChild;
    }

    public void setRight(BTNode child)
    {
        this.rightChild  = child;
    }

    public boolean isLeaf()
    {
      if(this.leftChild == null && this.rightChild == null)
        return true;
      return false;
    }
}
```

Done!

REVIEW

A stack is a simple data structure we sometimes call a pushdown store. In a stack, the elements are stored in the order in which we enter them. Because we remove elements from the stack in the reverse order in which we enter them, we call this a Last-In-First-Out (LIFO) structure. The operation to insert an element into a stack is push, and the operation to remove an element is pop. In the queue, we return the elements in the same order in which we enter them. For this reason, the queue is a First-In-First-Out (FIFO) structure. The operations to insert and remove elements from a queue are enqueue and dequeue.

Trees are nonlinear data structures in which the elements have no particular order. The elements of a tree are the nodes. A single node at the base of a tree is the root. A node with no descendents is a leaf. In a binary tree, each node can have no more than two associated nodes, called the node's right child and left child. In a general tree, each node can have more than two associated nodes.

QUIZ YOURSELF

1. What are the names of the two fundamental stack operations? (See "The Stack.")

2. What does the term LIFO stand for? (See "The Stack.")

3. List the invariants for the Stack ADT we develop in the text. (See "A Stack ADT.")

4. In an array implementation of a binary tree, what formulas can we use to find a node's left child and right child? (See "Array Implementation of Binary Trees.")

Errors and Exceptions

Session Checklist

✔ Hardware, software, and algorithmic errors

✔ Exceptions: Java exception handling, exception classes, advertising exceptions

✔ Exceptions programming

✔ Raising, handling, and throwing exceptions

30 Min.
To Go

Errors seem to be in the nature of computer systems. The logical complexity of programs, as well as the mechanical diversity of the hardware, advises that we consider program errors as likely events. Ignoring the possibility of errors leads to a hope-for-the-best attitude in programming that is both immature and dangerous. This session looks at Java's extensive and powerful support for handling program errors.

Error Types

Program errors can originate in hardware, in software, or in algorithmic or logical flaws. The possible solutions and the ideal error-handling techniques differ in each case.

Hardware and Software Errors

A program error can be hardware-related. For example, an application attempts to open a file that does not exist, send characters to a printer that is turned off, or communicate with a serial port that does not respond. Other error conditions are software-related. For example, code attempts to access an element that is beyond the bounds of the array or attempts to store a value that exceeds the capacity of a data format.

Hardware-related errors are usually detected and reported by the system. Software-related errors, on the other hand, must be detected by code. Other errors can be detected either by software, by hardware, or by both. For example, an application may inspect the divisor operand to make sure that a division by zero is not attempted. However, if a division by zero does take place, the hardware in most computer systems produces an error response.

Algorithmic Errors

Another type of error, sometimes called algorithmic errors, relates to flaws or intrinsic limitations of the real-world modeling performed by the computer. One example is the approximation that may take place when converting decimal numbers into binary format. Some decimal fractions have an exact binary representation, as is the case with the values 0.5, 0.25, 0.125, 0.0625, and so on. Other decimal fractions have no exact binary equivalent, in which case, the computer uses the best binary approximation of the decimal fraction according to the machine's word length. This approximation entails a roundoff error that can propagate in the calculations and lead to incorrect results.

Numerical analysis is the discipline that deals with roundoff and truncation errors of various algorithms. The programmer must be aware of the algorithms' error potential and use this knowledge to detect erroneous results or to avoid ill-conditioned data sets. It is algorithmic errors that are most often ignored by programmers.

Exceptions

The term exception is used to denote hardware, software, and algorithmic errors. Thus, an exception can be broadly defined as any unusual event that may require special handling. Exception handling refers to the special processing operations that take place when an exception is detected. Raising an exception refers to the actions that generate the exception itself. The entire process can be described as follows:

- A hardware, software, or algorithmic error takes place.
- The error is detected and an exception is raised.
- An exception handler provides the error response.

The detection of an error condition can originate in hardware or in software. However, the exception itself is a software process. The error handler can consist of many possible options, including:

- The error condition is ignored and the exception is cancelled.
- The exception handler takes no specific action and passes the error condition along to another handler in the hierarchy.
- The exception handler acts and passes the error condition along to another handler in the hierarchy for additional response.
- The exception handler acts and ends the exception response.

Exceptions Handled by the Language

Programming languages differ widely in the level of built-in support for handling exceptions. Some languages provide no exception handling aid, while others contain sophisticated mechanisms to support error response and to ensure that all exceptions are adequately handled.

In the case of languages that contain built-in exception handlers, as does Java, there are various implementation issues and design considerations, including:

- Does the language's runtime environment provide default action for some or all exceptions?
- Can user code raise exceptions?

- Are hardware-detectable errors treated as exceptions?
- Can the language's exception mechanism be temporarily or permanently disabled?
- Where does execution continue after an exception response concludes?

PL/I was the first major language to provide exception handling. The PL/I exception-handling facilities are powerful and flexible; however, most language designers consider them too complex. The most often-mentioned problem is that exceptions are bound dynamically to the handlers. A more reasonable model provides for statically bound exception handlers. The statically bound handlers were adopted in the Ada language, which also includes a mechanism for propagating unhandled exceptions to some other program unit.

Java's Approach

Java's approach to exceptions is based on the model proposed by the 1990 ANSI standardization committee for C++. This model, in turn, is based on the one used in the research language ML (Meta Language) developed at Bell Labs. Most modern versions of the C++ compiler, as well as Java, implement the resulting approach to exception handling.

Java exception handling is based on three basic constructs, named *throw*, *try*, and *catch*. The `throw` keyword is used to raise or re-raise an exception. The `try` and `catch` blocks implement the exception handler. An additional optional block, named *finally*, is used within exception handlers to provide an alternate processing option.

According to their cause, Java exceptions are classifiable into two types: *implicit* and *explicit*. Implicit exceptions occur when the program performs an illegal operation, for example, attempting a division by zero or accessing an element array whose index is out of range. Code cannot recover from this type of exception, although their cause can often be avoided. Explicit exceptions are generated by the application by means of a throw statement in order to handle some special condition. Implicit exceptions are called runtime exceptions in the Java literature, while explicit exceptions are said to be user-defined. Runtime exceptions refer to the fact that the Java runtime library throws implicit exceptions. In reality, all exceptions take place at runtime.

Java's Exception Classes

**20 Min.
To Go**

Java contains several classes that relate to exceptions. The class hierarchy is shown in Figure 19-1.

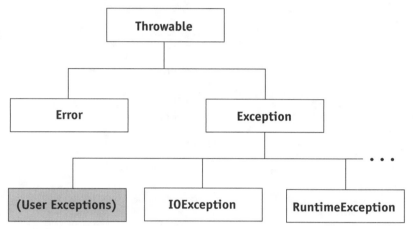

Figure 19-1
Java's exception class hierarchy

The Throwable class is at the top of the exception hierarchy. Throwable is extended by the Error and Exception classes. The members of the Error class are system-level errors thrown by the Java virtual machine. System-level errors are rare, and although it is possible for applications to catch these errors, the recommended approach is to let the system handle them. There is little an application can do if the system runs out of memory or encounters another terminal condition.

The most important part of the Java Throwable hierarchy is the one that goes through the Exception branch. There are currently 29 classes that extend Exception. Figure 19-1 shows the two more notable classes that extend Exception: IOException and RuntimeException. Table 19-1 lists the classes that extend IOException and RuntimeException.

In addition, application code can extend the Java Exception class in order to provide its own exception conditions. The class shows this possibility in a shaded rectangle in Figure 19-1. Providing your own exception handlers is one of the most important topics discussed in the remainder of this session.

Table 19-1
Java Built-in Subclasses of Exception

IOException	RuntimeException
ChangedCharSetException	ArithmeticException
CharConversionException	ArrayStoreException
EOFException	CannotRedoException
FileNotFoundException	CannotUndoException
InterruptedIOException	ClassCastException
MalformedURLException	CMMException
ObjectStreamException	CurrentModificationException
ProtocolException	EmptyStackException
RemoteException	IllegalArgumentException
SocketException	IllegalStateException
SyncFailedException	ImaginingOpException
UnknownHostException	IndexOutOfBoundsException
UnknownServiceException	MissingResourceException
UnsupportedEncodingException	NegativeArraySizeException
UTFDataFormatException	NoSuchElementException
ZipException	NullPointerException
	ProfileDataException
	ProviderException
	RasterFormatException
	SecurityException
	SystemException
	UnsupportedOperationException

Advertising Exceptions

Java specifications state that exceptions that derive from the class Error or from the class RuntimeException are classified as *unchecked* exceptions. All other exceptions are checked. Unchecked exceptions are either beyond program control, as those related to the `Error` class, or relate to conditions that are beyond program action, as is the case with an array index out of bounds. Code must deal with checked exceptions.

A Java method informs the user that it could generate an exception by declaring it in the method header. For example, a method named `WriteToFile()` that can produce an exception named `NameError` is declared as follows:

```
public void WriteTo File()
    throws NameErrorException
```

In this case, the `throws` keyword is used to advertise the exceptions raised by the method. The general rule is that a method must declare all checked exceptions that it throws, but not the unchecked exceptions. This means that all Java exceptions that are part of the `Error` and `RuntimeException` classes need not be advertised.

Exceptions Programming

The rationale behind the exception handling mechanism of Java is based on two assumptions:

**10 Min.
To Go**

1. The compiler should make sure that all error conditions are adequately handled by code.

2. It is preferable to handle errors separately from the program's main task.

James Slack mentions in his book *Programming and Problem Solving with Java* (Brooks/Cole, 2000) that Java's extensive exception-handling support is due to its origin as a programming environment for consumer electronic devices, which are expected to recover from unexpected errors. Therefore, the language makes sure that recovery routines can be easily developed.

The exception-handling strategy of a Java application should consider the following issues:

- Possible additional response to system errors. Code should not intercept the system handler but may provide some additional diagnostics. For example, upon detecting a system-level terminal error caused by a memory shortage, an application may post a message warning the user of possible loss of data.

- Designing or modifying application code in order to avoid exceptions generated in the classes `IOException` and `RuntimeException`. For example, making sure that a division-by-zero error is not produced by previously examining the divisor operand.

- Handling exceptions generated by nonterminal conditions in Java built-in classes. For example, providing code to recover from a file-not-found error.

- Providing application-defined exception handlers for local error conditions. For example, a user-developed method that finds the average value in an integer array generates an exception if the user passes a null array as the argument.

- Deciding what part of the code should handle an exception. This means determining whether a particular exception should be handled within the method that detects it, or if it should be propagated down the program's method hierarchy to be addressed by another handler.

The first these listed issues requires no additional discussion. The remaining four are examined later in this section.

Java Exception Processing

Processing exception conditions in Java code consists of three basic operations:

1. Raising user-defined exceptions by means of a `throw` clause. This usually requires extending the Java Exception class in order to provide the exception response.

2. Handling either system-generated (implicit) or user-defined (explicit) exceptions. Exception handling is based on coding the corresponding `try`, `catch`, and `finally` clauses.

3. Propagating exceptions into the application's method hierarchy by means of a `throws` clause.

Notice that the `throw` keyword is used to raise an exception and the `throws` keyword to propagate it. It is unfortunate that the designers of the Java language were unable to find better mnemonics for two functions that produce such different results. This book tries to reduce the confusion by referring to the action of the `throw` keyword as raising an exception and that of the `throws` keyword as throwing an exception.

Raising Exceptions

Code can use its own exception classes in order to accommodate specific error conditions. This can be accomplished by defining subclasses of `Exception` or, more commonly, by extending Java's Exception class. The Java Exception class contains two constructors, which are defined as:

```
Exception()
Exception(String s)
```

The easiest way to create an exception handler is to extend the Java Exception class and to call its parameterized constructor. For example, the following method provides an exception handler for a division by zero error; the following class extends the Java Exception class and provides a simple handler for a division by zero error:

```
class DivByZeroException extends Exception
{
   // Parameterized constructor
   public DivByZeroException(String message)
   {
     super(message);
   }
}
```

The method that intends to use the handler in the `DivByZeroException` must declare that it throws a `DivByZeroException`. This done, a `throw` clause gains access to the exception handler code, as shown in the following code fragment:

```
public class DivByZeroDemo
{
    public static void main(String[] args)
      throws DivByZeroException     // Declaring exception
    {
      int dividend = 100;
      int divisor, result;

      divisor = Keyin.inInt("Enter divisor: ");
      if(divisor != 0)
        {
          result = dividend / divisor;
          System.out.println("result = " + result);
```

```
        }
    else
        throw new DivByZeroException("Invalid divisor");
    }
}
```

Notice that the throws clause is used in the signature of the main( ) method to declare that the method raises a DivByZeroException. Because DivByZero Exception is a checked exception, not advertising it results in a compiler error.

Handling Exceptions

Code can handle exceptions raised in other methods, whether these are local methods or part of the Java libraries. For example, attempting to open a nonexisting file raises the FileNotFoundException class of IOException (see Table 19-1) exception. Your code can be designed to intercept Java's error-response mechanism for this error and provide alternate processing. A possible advantage of intercepting the error-response chain is the prevention of a terminal error that terminates execution. Exception handlers can also refer to extrinsic extension.

Three Java keywords are used in coding exception handlers: try, catch, and finally. The try block contains the processing operations and its execution continues until an exception is raised. The catch block contains the actions to take place if an exception is raised. The catch block is skipped if no exception is raised in the try block. The finally block, which is optional, executes whether or not an exception is thrown. The finally statement is often used in deallocating local resources. The following code fragment shows an exception handler designed to intercept a system's division by zero error.

The following program, **CatchDBZ.java**, intercepts the Java ArithmeticException error response in the case of a division by zero. Because ArithmeticException is unchecked it does not have to be advertised in the header of the main( ) method.

The source file for the program CatchDBZ.java is found in the Session 19 directory on the book's CD-ROM.

```
//************************************************************
//************************************************************
// Program: CatchDBZ
// Reference: Session 19
```

```
// Topics:
//    1. Catching Java's ArithmeticException error in a
//       division by zero
// Requires:
//    1. Keyin class in the current directory
//***********************************************************
//***********************************************************

public class CatchDBZ
{
    public static void main(String[] args)
    {
        int dividend = 100;
        int divisor, result;

    while(true)
    {
        divisor = Keyin.inInt("Enter divisor (100 to end): ");

        if(divisor == 100)
            break;

        try
        {
            result = dividend / divisor;  // May raise exception
            System.out.println("result = " + result);
        }
        catch(ArithmeticException msgText)
        {
            System.out.println("Error is : " + msgText);
        }
    }
  }
}
```

The **CatchDBZ.java** program enables the user to enter the divisor of an integer division operation. A special value of 100 is used to terminate execution. The main() method's signature contains a throws clause for Java's ArithmeticException class. The try clause performs the division operation. If an ArithmeticException error is produced, execution continues in the catch clause, which displays a message followed by the string returned by the ArithmeticException handler. In this case, the program recovers and prompts the user for another divisor.

Throwing Exceptions

The basic rule of Java's error-handling mechanism is that an exception must either be handled by the method in which it is raised, or passed along the call chain for another method to handle. If it is passed along, we say that the exception has propagated along the call hierarchy. The principle is this: A Java method must either handle or declare all exceptions.

The declaration of an exception refers to the throws clause that is part of the method's signature. What this means is that code can refuse to handle a possible exception raised by the method being called. For example, suppose a call chain consists of methodA(), which calls methodB(), which calls methodC(). Furthermore, suppose that methodC() can raise Exception1. In this case, methodC() can either handle Exception1 or pass it along the call chain so that it is handled by methodB().If methodB() does not handle the exception, Java continues looking up the call chain for a handler, in this case, in methodA(). Finally, if no handler is found within the application's code, Java generates the exception and terminates execution.

The program Handler.java demonstrates exception propagation and handling. The source file for Handler.java is found in the Session 19 directory on the book's CD-ROM.

Handler.java contains two classes. The driving class (Handler) includes the methods main(), PreDivide(), and Divide(). The class DivisionException extends Exception and provides a handler for a division by zero error.

The division by zero error is raised in the method Divide() but it is not handled in that method. Notice that Divide(), which does not contain a try block, throws the DivisionException in the method's signature. Neither does the PreDivide() method handle the exception. Here again, the exception is passed along the call chain by the throws clause in the method's signature. The main() method, on the other hand, handles the exception that was raised in the Divide() method. For this reason, main() contains a try block with the corresponding catch clause. The exception-handling chain, in this case, ends in main().

Done!

REVIEW

Because of the complexity of software and the limitations of computer hardware, our programs must make allowances for errors. Errors can originate in hardware or software. Algorithmic errors are related to limitations in the real-world modeling performed by the computer. The term exception relates to the handling of hardware, software, or algorithmic errors. Java contains exception handlers that provide an automatic response to certain errors. Exception handling is implemented by means of the throw, try, and catch clauses. Java exceptions are classified as implicit or explicit. The Java Throwable class is at the top of the exception hierarchy. The main subclasses are IOException and RuntimeException. Unchecked exceptions are beyond program control. Checked exceptions are advertised by means of the throws keyword. Exceptions programming consists of raising, handling, or propagating exceptions.

QUIZ YOURSELF

1. What are the three fundamental error types? (See "Error Types.")
2. Give an example of an algorithmic error. (See "Algorithmic Errors.")
3. List the three steps associated with raising an exception. (See "Exceptions.")
4. What are the three basic constructs used in Java exception handling? (See "Java's Approach.")
5. What Java keyword is used to advertise an exception? (See "Advertising Exceptions.")

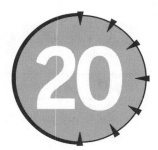

Input and Output

Session Checklist

✔ Java input and output: character data and the java.io package

✔ InputStream and OutputStream classes

✔ Standard streams

✔ Developing the Keyin class

✔ Flushing the input stream

✔ Reading character data and numeric data

30 Min. To Go

Compared to its predecessor languages C and C++, Java contains little support for input and output operations. The reason for this lack of input and output functions is not some deficiency in the language's design or some flaw in its implementation; it is because Java is based on a different model. Perhaps because of their Unix origin, C and C++ assume that the computer system interface consists of a text-based console and keyboard with characters in a western European alphabet. Java, on the other hand, makes no assumption about input characters or devices and barely contains elementary support for a text-based console device and a command-line interface.

Input and Output

The two limitations most often mentioned about Java input and output functions relate to the difficulty in obtaining alphanumeric data from the keyboard and in formatting output to the console device. We have been using an as-yet unexplained Keyin class to obtain keyboard input. This session explores Java input and develops routines for obtaining alphanumeric data from the keyboard. However, keyboard-processing functions that are common in other languages do not exist in Java. Most notably missing are functions to implement a live keyboard because there is no Java primitive to detect a single, raw keystroke.

 Another limitation is that alphanumeric output-formatting operations are also unavailable in Java.

The explanation for this apparent limitation is that in Java, the text-based interface that we are using in our programs is considered obsolete. The language assumes that modern-day applications are developed using a graphical user interface (GUI), which Java extensively supports and which is discussed in Session 24. The minimal support that Java provides for the text-based console is intentionally rudimentary.

Java Character Data

Java input/output (I/O) often relates to text, and text consists of characters. Because data are stored in computer memory as binary values, a conventional numeric encoding represents characters. In ASCII encoding, the letter A is mapped to the number 65, the letter B to the number 66, the blank space to the number 32, and the digit 1 to the number 49.

Code must keep track of whether a stored value represents a binary number, a portion of a binary number, or an alphanumeric character. Some I/O devices are designed to assume that data always represent some specific character encoding. For example, when we send the value 66 to the console device, the device knows to look up a bitmap for the letter B and display it on the screen.

For many years computer technology assumed that character data consisted of the 10 decimal digits, the uppercase and lowercase letters of the English alphabet, and a few dozen additional symbols, such as punctuation marks. Some systems later added a few other characters that were necessary in the western European languages and in mathematical expressions. However, these character sets do not enable representing characters in Arabic, Japanese, Chinese, Russian, Greek, and many other languages.

Java, on the other hand, was conceived as a universal language, and it supports dozens of character sets, including ASCII, ISO Latin-1, and Unicode.

The simplest and most limited Java character set is defined by the American Standard Code for Information Interchange, or ASCII, discussed in Session 4. This set contains 128 characters in the range 0 to 127. Some of these are control codes; for example, the value 10 is interpreted as a linefeed, the value 13 as a carriage return, and the value 8 as a tabulation code. The digits 0 to 9 are represented by the values 48 to 57. The uppercase letters A through Z of the English alphabet are encoded in the values 65 to 90. The lowercase letters are the values 97 to 122. Value 32 represents a space. The remaining values are used for symbols, such as !"#$%&'()*+,-./:;<=>?{|} and ~.

The program AsciiSet.java, in the Session20 directory on the book's CD-ROM, displays the characters in the ASCII set.

A second character set supported by Java is defined by the International Standards Institute Latin-1 standard, commonly referred to as ISO Latin-1. This character set consists of a byte value in the range 0 to 255. The first 128 values are the same as those of the ASCII set. The remaining ones, in the range 128 to 255, are the characters needed to represent non-English languages, including French, Spanish, Italian, and German (in Roman script), typesetting symbols, the Greek letters that are often used in mathematics, mathematical symbols, copyright and trademark glyphs, common fractions, and others.

The program LatinSet.java, in the Session20 directory on the book's CD-ROM, displays the ISO Latin-1 character set.

Because DOS-based consoles do not support the first 32 character in ISO Latin-1, the first one displayed corresponds to the value 160.

The third and most comprehensive character set supported by Java is Unicode. Unicode characters are encoded in 16 bits, which allows values in the range 0 to 65,535. This is the same range as the Java char primitive data type. Unicode enables representation of the characters of most modern languages, including

Cyrillic, Greek, Arabic, Hebrew, Persian, Chinese, and Japanese. The first 256 characters of the Unicode character set coincide with the ISO Latin-1 set.

The fact that Unicode characters are encoded in two bytes may create problems when using stream-based read and write operations. Streams have traditionally assumed that alphanumeric data consists of single bytes. In order to read Unicode characters from the stream, code reads a first byte, shifts all the bits eight positions to the left, reads the second byte, then AND the low 8-bits of the second byte to the shifted bits of the first one. The result is that both bytes are placed side-by-side, with the first byte to the left of the second one. Alternatively, the same results are obtained by multiplying the first byte by 256 and adding the second one. One risk of reading 16-bit data 8 bits at a time is that code may "lose step" and combine the second byte of one character with the first byte of the next one.

Java readers and writers are designed for handling any of the supported character sets. If the host system is set for ASCII or ISO Latin-1, readers and writers operate one byte at a time. If the system is set for Unicode, then data is read from the stream two bytes at a time. Furthermore, because streams are not intended for character-based data, they do not support string operations. In this session, we use readers and writers for performing file-based input and output.

The java.io Package

**20 Min.
To Go**

Input and output operations, I/O for short, are the subject of the java.io library. This library is part of the Java application programming interface (API), which includes java.io, java.lang, java.math, java.net, java.text, and java.util. Although most of the Java I/O support is in java.io, there are a few I/O facilities located in the other packages.

Java I/O is divided into two general types: byte-based I/O and character-based I/O. Java input and output streams handle byte-based I/O and readers and writers handle character-based I/O. In either case, the general approach is to make an abstraction of the data source and of the destination. This makes possible using the same methods to read and write from a file, a text-based console, or a network connection. In other words, Java code need not be concerned with where the data comes from or where it goes. Once the I/O stream is defined, it is possible to automatically receive, send, format, filter, compress, and encrypt the data.

Streams

The fundamental element of Java I/O is the stream. The stream concept is a metaphor for a stream of water. A data stream is defined as an ordered sequence of bytes of undetermined length. An input data stream moves bytes from some external source and an output data stream moves bytes to some external destination.

The java.io package contains two stream-based abstract classes: InputStream and OutputStream. Table 20-1 lists the subclasses.

Table 20-1
Abstract Classes in java.io and Subclasses

InputStream	OutputStream
ByteArrayInputStream	ByteArrayOutputStream
FileInputStream	FileOutputStream
FilterInputStream	FilterOutputStream
InputStream	OutputStream
ObjectInputStream	ObjectOutputStream
PipedInputStream	PipedOutputStream
SequenceInputStream	
StringBufferInputStream	

Other stream-related classes are derived from the ones listed in Table 20-1.

Recall that streams are designed to operate on numeric data and that the stream's data unit is the byte. The byte is one of the Java integral data types and is defined as an 8-bit number, in two's complement format, encoding a value in the range –128 to 127. The maximum positive value for a byte operand is 127. Therefore, the values 128 through 255 are not legal.

Two's complement representations are an encoding scheme for signed binary integers designed to facilitate machine arithmetic. The value of the two's complement is the difference between the number and the next integer power of two that is greater than the number. A simple way of calculating the two's complement of a binary number is negating all the digits and adding one to the result. An additional advantage of two's complement representations is that there is no encoding for a negative zero.

A difficulty of Java stream operations is that the byte data type is not convenient. While many of the methods in the stream classes are documented to accept or return byte arguments, in reality, they operate on `int` data. The main reason is that there are no byte literals in Java, although the compiler sometimes makes automatic assignment conversions, for example:

```
byte val1 = 22;          // Valid assignment
byte val2 = 44;          // Valid assignment
```

however,

```
byte val3 = val1 + val2;  // Illegal. Requires type cast
byte val4 = 1 = 3;        // Illegal. Requires type cast
```

The small range of the byte data type explains why they are often converted to `int` in calculations. Later the calculated values are typecast back into the byte format. This means that although a stream is defined to operate on byte data, internal processing of numeric data by string-based classes is often done on `int` data types.

The InputStream Class

The `InputStream` class, located in the java.io package, is the abstract class on which all input streams are based. The class contains several methods associated with input streams, including reading data from the stream, closing and flushing streams, and checking how many bytes of data are available. Table 20-2 lists the methods of the `InputStream` class.

Table 20-2
Methods of java.io.InputStream Class

Returns	Name	Description
int	available()	Returns the number of bytes that can be read (or skipped over) from the current input stream without blocking.
void	close()	Closes this input stream.
void	mark(intreadlimit)	Marks the current position in the input stream.
boolean	markSupported()	Tests if this input stream supports the mark and reset methods.

Returns	Name	Description
int	read()	Reads the next byte of data from the input stream.
int	read(byte[] b)	Reads a number of bytes from the input stream and stores them into the bigger array b.
int	read(byte[] b, int o, int l)	Reads up to l byte of data from the input stream into an array b at offset o.
void	reset()	Repositions this stream to the position at the time that the mark method was last called.
long	skip(long n)	Skips over and discards *n* bytes of data from this input stream.

The read()method is designed to obtain byte data from the input stream. Table 20-2 shows that the read() method is overloaded in three different implementations: read(), read(byte[] b), and read(byte[] b, int off, int len).

The first implementation of read() has the following signature:

```
public abstract int read()
   throws IOException
```

This version reads the next byte of data from the input stream. The method waits until a byte of data is available or until the end of the stream is reached or an exception is raised. The value is returned as an int in the range 0 to 255. The value –1 is returned if the end of the stream is reached. This is an abstract method that cannot be instantiated.

The second implementation of read() has this signature:

```
public int read(byte[] b)
   throws IOException
```

This version reads a number of bytes from the input stream and stores them in an array of type byte. The value returned is the number of bytes actually read. This method waits until input data is available, the end of file is detected, or an exception is raised. If the array passed to the method is null, a NullPointer Exception is raised. If the length of the array is zero, then no bytes are read and 0 is returned. If no byte is available because the stream is at end of file, the value

−1 is returned. The bytes read are stored in the array and passed as an argument to the method.

The third variation of read() has this signature:

```
public int read(byte[] b, int o, int l)
   throws IOException
```

The method reads up to 1 byte of data from the input stream. The data is stored at offset 0, on the array b passed in the call. The method attempts to read byte lengths, but a smaller number may be read, possibly zero. The return value of type int is the number of bytes actually read. This method waits until input data is available, end of file is detected, or an exception is raised.

The OutputStream Class

The OutputStream class, also located in the java.io package, is the abstract class on which all output streams are based. The class contains several methods associated with output streams, including methods for writing data to the stream and for closing and flushing streams. Table 20-3 lists the methods of the OutputStream class.

Table 20-3
Methods of java.io.OutputStream

Returns	Name	Description
void	close()	Closes the current output stream.
void	flush()	Flushes this output stream. This forces any buffered output bytes to be written.
void	write(int b)	Writes the specified byte to the output stream.
void	write(byte[] b)	Writes b length bytes from the specified byte array to this output stream.
void	write(byte[] b, int o, int l)	Writes 1 byte from the specified byte array starting at offset 0 to this output stream.

OutputStream is an abstract class. Table 20-3 shows that the method named write() is overloaded in three different implementations. Two are concrete and one is abstract. The first implementation of write() has this prototype:

```
public abstract void write(int b)
   throws IOException
```

The method writes the specified byte to the current output stream. The byte to be written is defined as the eight low-order bits of the argument b, which is of type int. The 24 high-order bits of this byte are ignored. Subclasses of OutputStream provide the implementation of this method. An IOException is raised if an I/O error occurs or if the output stream has been closed.

The second implementation of write() has this prototype:

```
public void write(byte[] b)
   throws IOException
```

This method writes b length bytes from the byte array passed as an argument to the current output stream. The method raises an IOException if an I/O error occurs. The third implementation of write() is prototyped as follows:

```
public void write(byte[] b, int o, int l),
   throws IOException
```

This method writes 1 byte from the byte array specified as an argument, starting at offset 0, to the current output stream. This variation of the write() method of OutputStream calls the write() method on each of the bytes to be written. Subclasses override this method and provide a more efficient implementation. If the array passed as an argument is null, a NullPointerException is thrown. If 0 is negative, or 1 is negative, or 0 + 1 is greater than the length of the array b, then an IndexOutOfBoundsException is thrown. An IOException is raised if an I/O error occurs or if the output stream is closed.

Standard Streams

Applications often use the keyboard as the input stream and the display system as an output stream. In this case, it is said that the keyboard is the standard device for console input and that the video display is the standard device for console output. In addition, an error stream is provided for directing error messages during debugging. The System class in the java.lang package contains three fields that relate to the standard streams, as follows:

```
public static final InputStream in;    // Standard input
public static final PrintStream out;   // Standard output
public static final PrintStream err;   // Standard error output
```

PrintStream extends FileOutputStream, which extends OutputStream. PrintStream adds functionality by enabling the display of various data types.

In addition, PrintStream contains the println() method, which we often used in preceding sessions. This method adds a newline character (\n) at the end of the string or array and automatically flushes the stream.

The standard streams are always open and ready for use. This makes them convenient for Java console applications, such as those developed previously in this book.

Coding the Keyin Class

**10 Min.
To Go**

Thus far, we have used a class named Keyin that performs basic console input for character and numeric types.

The Keyin class contains six static methods:

1. inString() allows the promptless input of a string. This method is used internally by the class to obtain the individual characters in an int or double variable.

2. inputFlush() makes sure that there is no data available in the input stream. If data is found, the read() method is called to remove it. InputFlush() is called by the data input methods in the Keyin class.

3. inString(String prompt) is used to input a user string. The string passed as an argument is displayed as a prompt.

4. inInt(String prompt) allows the input of an int type value. The string passed as an argument is displayed as a prompt.

5. inChar(String prompt) allows the user to input a single value of type char. The string passed as an argument is displayed as a prompt.

6. inDouble(String prompt) allows the user to input a floating-point value and returns it as a value of type double. The string passed as an argument is displayed as a user prompt.

All methods of the Keyin class catch some of the exceptions raised by the read() method of the InputStream class. The methods that input character data (inString and inChar) catch IOException. The methods that input numbers in int and float format catch the NumberFormatException.

Flushing the Input Stream

The OutputStream class contains a method to flush the stream but there is no flush() method in InputStream. This means that occasionally code may call the read() method and encounter unexpected characters that have not yet been removed from the stream. This is likely to happen when we attempt to remove a single character from the stream, as is the case when attempting to retrieve a single character. One Keyin class method, called inputFlush(), addresses this potential problem by ensuring that there are no data bytes pending in the input stream.

The inputFlush() method uses the available() method of the InputStream class. This method returns the number of bytes that can be read without being blocked. The method returns zero if there is no data pending to be removed in input stream. This can be interpreted to mean that the stream is clear and that the next call to the read() function will be blocked. The code for the InputFlush() method is as follows:

```
public static void inputFlush()
{
    int dummy;
    int bAvail;

    try
    {
    while((System.in.available()) != 0)
       dummy = System.in.read();
    }
    catch(java.io.IOException e)
    {
      System.out.println("Input error");
    }
}
```

The inputFlush() method contains a while loop that repeats while the input stream is not clear. In each iteration, the byte in the input stream is read into a variable named dummy and discarded. When the method returns, code can assume that the input stream contains no spurious data.

Reading Character Data

Two methods of the Keyin class read character data. One reads and returns a string and the other one a char variable. The method named inChar() is used to input a single character.

```java
public static char inChar(String prompt)
{
    int aChar = 0;

    InputFlush();
    printPrompt(prompt);

    try
        {
          aChar = System.in.read();
        }

    catch(java.io.IOException e)
        {
          System.out.println("Input error");
        }
    inputFlush();
    return (char) aChar;
}
```

Because there is no "raw mode" console input in Java, the method to read a single character waits until the user presses the key that terminates input, usually <Enter> or <Return>. In fact, inChar() returns the first character typed but it cannot prevent the user from typing more than one character. For this reason the method calls inputFlush() before exiting. Also notice that the input, which is of type int, is typecast into a type char in the return statement.

Capturing an input string requires a bit more processing. The method inString, listed here, performs the processing:

```java
public static String inString()
{
    int aChar;
    String s = "";
    boolean finished = false;
```

```
while(!finished)
  {
    try
    {
      aChar = System.in.read();
      if (aChar < 0 || (char)aChar == '\n')
        finished = true;
      else if ((char)aChar != '\r')
        s = s + (char) aChar;   // Append to string
    }

    catch(java.io.IOException e)
    {
      System.out.println("Input error");
      finished = true;
    }
  }
  return s;
}
```

The inString() method contains a while loop that terminates when the user presses the input terminator key or when read() returns –1. If the keystroke is not the <Return> key the input value is cast into a char type and appended to a local string variable. This string is returned to the caller when the method terminates.

An overloaded version of the inString() method flushes the input stream, displays the user prompt, and then calls inString() to obtain input.

Reading Numeric Data

Obtaining numeric data from the keyboard is a two-step process: first, we must retrieve the string of numeric characters typed by the user. Commonly, this string is in ASCII format. Second, we must convert the string of ASCII digits into the desired Java primitive. The first step offers no difficulties. We can use the inString() method, previously developed, to obtain the digit string. Parsing the string of digits into a binary value is another matter.

One approach is to take on the conversion task directly. In the case of a decimal integer string, we can isolate each string digit, proceeding left to right. Convert the ASCII value to binary by subtracting 0×30. Then, multiply each digit by the power of 10 that corresponds to its place value, and accumulate the total. The processing for an integer conversion is relatively straightforward and can be accomplished in a few lines of code. Much more complicated is the conversion of a decimal number in floating-point format. In this case, we must be familiar with the binary encoding defined in the ANSI-IEEE 754 Standard, which is adopted by Java. These formats were designed for computational efficiency; therefore, they are neither simple nor intuitive.

Fortunately, the parsing of the strings into binary formats can be easily accomplished using methods provided in the java.lang library. In this processing, we use the inString() method, developed in the preceding section, to input the string. The expression for obtaining the string and converting into an integer format is:

```
int aValue = Integer.valueOf
             (inString().trim()).intValue();
```

In this case, we use the trim() method to eliminate all spaces at either end of the string obtained by the inString() method. The intValue() method of the Integer class (located in java.lang) returns the integer value of the expression. Then the parsing into an int type is performed by the valueOf() method of the Integer class. A similar processing can be used for converting to other numeric types. For example, to convert into a double format we can use the following statement:

```
double aValue = Double.valueOf
                (inString().trim()).doubleValue();
```

The functions named inInt() and inDouble() in the Keyin class perform input of these two types.

The program Keyin.java, is found in the Session 20 directory on the book's CD-ROM.

Done!

REVIEW

The Java language contains little built-in support for input and output. Input and output programming requires using the classes in the Java support libraries. Java supports several character sets including ASCII, ISO Latin 1, and Unicode. A stream is a sequence of bytes of undetermined length. Java's support for stream operations is mostly located in the classes InputStream and OutputStream, which are part of the java.io package. The Java standard streams are named InputStream, OutputStream, and PrintStream. PrintStream is used for error output.

The Keyin class performs basic input for character and numeric types. It contains six static methods: InputFlush(), inInt(), inChar(), and inDouble(), and two versions of inString().

QUIZ YOURSELF

1. List four languages supported by the ISO Latin 1 character set. (See "Java Character Data.")
2. What is the difference between byte-based and character-based I/O? (See "The java.io Package.")
3. What are basic types of streams? (See "Streams.")
4. What is the purpose of the read() methods of the InputStream class? (See "The InputStream Class.")
5. What is the purpose of the write() methods of the OutputStream class? (See "The OutputStream Class.")
6. List the Java standard streams. (See "Standard Streams.")
7. Why is it necessary to flush the input stream in the Keyin class? (See "Coding the Keyin Class.")

PART

IV

Saturday Evening Part Review

1. Describe the main difference between an ADT implemented as an array and as a linked list.

2. List the invariants for an `IntNode` class.

3. Which accessor and mutator methods are required for manipulating the data and the link elements of an `IntNode` class?

4. List the invariants required for implementing an `IntList` class that holds the number of nodes in the list and a reference to the node at the head of the list.

5. List the three fundamental methods we use to manipulate a linked list.

6. What are the names of the two fundamental stack operations?

7. What does the term LIFO stand for?

8. List the invariants for the Stack ADT we develop in the text.

9. In an array implementation of a binary tree, what formulas can we use to find a node's left child and right child?

10. What are the three fundamental error types?

11. Give an example of an algorithmic error.

12. List the three steps associated with raising an exception.

13. What are the three basic constructs we use in Java's exception handling?

14. What Java keyword do we use to advertise an exception?

15. List four languages the ISO Latin 1 character set supports.

16. What is the difference between byte-based and character-based I/O?

17. What are basic types of streams?
18. What is the purpose of the `read()` methods of the `InputStream` class?
19. What is the purpose of the `write()` methods of the `OutputStream` class?
20. List Java's standard streams.

☑ Friday

☑ Saturday

 ☑ Sunday

PART

V

Sunday Morning

File Operations and I/O

Session Checklist

✔ File Properties

✔ Filename and filename extension

✔ Directories and paths

✔ The File class: fields, constructors, and methods

✔ File I/O classes

✔ Input and output streams

✔ Filtered streams

**30 Min.
To Go**

In addition to console input and output, Java streams are also attached to files and to network connections. As regards files, code can use the classes FileIntputStream and FileOutputStream found in the java.io package. Both are concrete subclasses of java.io.InputStream and java.io.OutputStream; they were discussed in the previous session. This session examines operations performed at the file level. These file-level operations are preparatory and usually precede or follow the actual reading and writing of file data. For example, we need to create or open a file, find out whether a file is readable or writeable, or close a file after access operations have concluded. The functionality for performing common housekeeping operations on files, as well as for manipulating file meta-information, is mostly located in the `java.io.File` class.

File Properties

Files are machine dependent. The structure of filenames, attributes, relative and absolute paths, and file properties change considerably from one environment to another environment. Thus, files on a Unix system, which is typically a multiuser platform, require controls that are unnecessary on a Macintosh, which is designed as a single-user machine. Therefore, we begin with a platform-independent overview of file properties and structures.

The Filename

A file is identified by a filename whose format is determined by the operating system. In most operating systems, the filename specification has evolved over the various versions. For example, a DOS filename consists of up to eight ASCII characters optionally followed by an extension of up to three characters.

If an extension is present, a period is used to separate it from the name. Control characters or punctuation symbols (+=/[]";:,?*\<>|) cannot be used in filenames. Since Windows 95, filenames can contain up to 255 characters. Several characters that are illegal in DOS are valid in Windows 95 and later versions. In particular, the characters +,;=[].

Macintosh filenames can contain up to 31 characters. The filename can include / and \ symbols, but not the :. In the U.S., Macintosh uses the 8-bit MacRoman character set. Macintosh software usually interprets a filename beginning with a period as a device driver. In contrast, many standard Unix files begin with a period. To accommodate these differences it is a good idea to use the following rules in creating cross-platform filenames:

1. Use only ASCII characters. The period and the underscore characters are allowed, but should not be the first character in the name.

2. Special characters should be limited to @ and _. Punctuation characters should be avoided whenever possible, except the period as a separator.

3. Always begin a filename with an alphanumeric character.

4. Mixed case is allowed in filenames but do not assume that case alone will serve to distinguish names that are otherwise identical. For example: MyList.DAT and mylist.dat could represent the same file in some systems.

5. Keep filenames to less than 32 characters.

The Filename Extension

A filename extension provides a short code for identifying the type of file. For example, the extension .txt represents an ASCII text file, .java a Java source file, and .class a Java bytecode file. Although the idea of encoding the file type in a filename extension is basically sound, it does have limitations. The first problem is that there is no formal standard for filename extensions.

Note Although a Multipurpose Internet Mail Extension (MIME) standard does exist, it has not been adopted outside the Web.

A second problem relates to the fact that users can easily change filenames and extensions by means of operating system functions. Thus, there is no assurance that the original extension with which a file was created will be preserved over time. In other words, there is no guarantee that a file with the extension .java is actually a Java source. Table 21-1 lists some of the more common filename extensions used in the PC environment.

Table 21-1
PC Filename Extensions

Extension	File type	Extension	File type
.txt	Text	**filegif**	GIF image
.jpg	JPEG image	**.asm**	Assembler source
.html	HTML text	**.doc**	Microsoft Word document
.class	Java class	**.java**	Java source
.c	C source	**.cpp**	C++ source
.zip	ZIP archive	**.bak**	Backup file
.exe	Executable	**.dll**	Dynamic link library

How the operating system handles the various file types is also environment dependent. For example, double-clicking on an executable file in Windows runs the program, while double-clicking an image file displays it in the program currently registered as a viewer for the file type. On the Macintosh, double-clicking an image file opens the file using the application that created it, if it is available.

Directories and Paths

Operating systems organize files into a hierarchical structure of drives, directories, and subdirectories. Directories and subdirectories have names and attributes, but not necessarily following the same format rules as for the filename. Furthermore, drives, directories, and subdirectories are separated using special characters that vary among operating systems. For example, in DOS and Windows the colon separates the drive from the rest of the path name, and the backslash symbol separates directories and subdirectories. On the Macintosh, the colon separates directories and subdirectories, while Unix uses the forward slash to separate directories and subdirectories. For example:

```
Windows           C:\myDir\myFile.txt
MacOS             Macintosh HD:mydir:myfile.txt
Unix              mydir/myfile.txt
```

In Java, filenames can be relative or absolute. An absolute filename contains the entire path from the disk or root directory to the file. A relative filename refers only to the file and assumes the current directory.

One difficulty with absolute paths relates to variations in the root directories and drive specifications. In DOS and Windows, drives are assigned letters. Letters A and B are reserved for floppy disk drives. The letter C designates the primary hard disk drive. Other letters are assigned to additional drives or to drive partitions. CD-ROM, Zip, and other drives are also assigned drive letters. In Unix, all mounted drives are combined into a virtual file system, the root directory is designated with the / symbol, and two periods (..) refer to the parent of the current directory. On the Macintosh, each disk or partition is designated with a symbolic name, instead of a letter code. The primary hard drive is usually labeled Macintosh HD, but the user can change this. In the following sections, we learn that Java provides some support for system-independent disk access.

These variations make it difficult to implement cross-platform code that reads and writes to the disk. It is probably this difficulty that determines that Java applets can not write to the disk.

The File Class

An object of the class java.io.File represents a single disk file or a directory pathname. The purpose of the abstract File class is to simplify file operations by encapsulating machine-specific information. An object of the class File can be a future file; therefore, it can be instantiated before the file actually exists. In this sense, an object of the class can be a placeholder for a particular file. The same File object can be instantiated to several different files during program execution.

The File classes use an abstract, system-independent concept, for a pathname. The abstraction consists of two components:

1. An optional system-dependent prefix string, such as a disk-drive specifier (/) for the UNIX root directory, and

2. A sequence of zero or more filename strings.

Except for the last name in a pathname, each name represents a directory. The last name may be either a directory or a file.

File Class Fields

The File class contains fields that can be accessed by application code. The fields are defined in Table 21-2.

Table 21-2
File Class Fields

Field	Function
public static final String pathSeparator	This is the system-dependent path-separator character, represented as a string.
public static final char pathSeparatorChar	This is the system-dependent path-separator character.
public static final String separator	This is the system-dependent name-separator character, represented as a string.
public static final char separatorChar	This is the system-dependent default name-separator character.

By declaring public fields, Java software breaks a principle of encapsulation. Furthermore, it is conventional style to type constants in all caps, which Java does not follow in this case.

The file-separator character is the one used to separate two files. This is the backslash (\) in DOS and Windows, the forward slash (/) in Unix, and the colon (:) on the Macintosh. The path separator character is used to separate two paths. This is the semicolon (;) in DOS and Windows, and the colon (:) in Unix.

File Class Constructors

When using these constructors of the File class it is important to remember that File objects are actually filenames. The File class does not actually create files; therefore, we cannot assume that a File object represents an actual file on the disk.

The File class contains three constructors, shown in Table 21-3:

Table 21-3
File Class Constructor

Constructor	Function
File(String pathname)	Creates a new instance of File by converting the pathname string passed as an argument into an abstract pathname.
File(String parent, String child)	Creates a new instance of File from a parent pathname string and a child pathname string.
File(File parent, String child)	Creates a new instance of File from a parent abstract pathname and a child pathname string.

The first constructor, which is also the simplest one, has a single argument. This argument can be an absolute or a relative path. Java implementations allow using file specifications valid in the host operating system. Thus, on a Unix machine we can create a an object of the File class as follows:

```
File file1 = new File("/mach1/html/lesson7.doc");
```

In DOS and Windows, the equivalent File object is created with the statement:

```
File file1 = new File("C:\\mach1\\html\\lesson7.doc");
```

Notice that the double backslash symbols are required because the \ is the escape character in a literal string.

File Class Methods

The current implementations of the Java `File` class contain 39 methods that provide information about files and manipulate `File` objects. Table 21-4 lists a few of the most used methods. Pleas note that the method labled JDK 1.2 are available only in this and later versions of the JDK.

Table 21-4
Often-Used Methods in java.io.File

Returns	Name	Description
boolean	canRead()	Tests whether the application can read the specified `File` object.
boolean	canWrite()	Tests whether the application can write to the specified `File` object.
boolean	createNewFile()	Creates a new, empty file if and only if a file with this name does not exist. JDK 1.2.
boolean	delete()	Deletes the file or directory object contained in the argument.
void	deleteOnExit()	Requests that the file or directory object be deleted when the virtual machine terminates. JDK 1.2.
boolean	exists()	Tests whether the file object exists.
File	getAbsoluteFile()	Returns the absolute form of this abstract pathname. JDK 1.2.
String	getAbsolutePath()	Returns the absolute pathname string of this abstract pathname.
String	getName()	Returns the name of the file or directory.

Continued

Table 21-4 *Continued*

Returns	Name	Description
String	getPath()	Converts this abstract pathname into a pathname string.
boolean	isAbsolute()	Tests whether this abstract pathname is absolute.
boolean	isDirectory()	Tests whether the file denoted by this abstract pathname is a directory.
boolean	isFile()	Tests whether the file denoted by this abstract pathname is a normal file.
boolean	isHidden()	Tests whether the file is a hidden file.
long	length()	Returns the length of the file.
String[]	list()	Returns an array of strings naming the files and directories in the directory denoted by this pathname.
boolean	mkdir()	Creates the specified directory.
boolean	mkdirs()	Creates the specified directory, including any necessary but non-existent parent directories.
boolean	renameTo(File dest)	Renames the file.
boolean	setReadOnly()	Marks the file or directory so that only read operations are allowed.

CD-ROM

The program FileOps.java demonstrates some of the methods of the File class. The source file for the program FileOps.java is found in the Session21 directory on the book's CD-ROM.

File I/O Classes

10 Min. To Go

Java provides a rich set of classes for performing file input and output. When you start programming Java file I/O, this abundance of classes and methods can be intimidating, especially when the methods are overloaded several times. There are several reasons for this profusion, including the fact that Java supports many data encodings, and character sets and the design of the language, in order to ensure platform independence, are among them. Perhaps the most important reason is that Java file processing includes operations that are usually not part of a programming language. These include data encryption, compression and decompression, and interthread communications. Our discussion is limited to essential file manipulations.

Much of what has been said about input and output also applies to files. The notion of a stream accepts a file as a source or a destination. As regards file operations, the InputStream and OutputStream classes are extended by classes that allow defining a file as a stream source or destination. These, in turn, are extended by other classes that improve file access by providing buffered input and output of data. Other subclasses of InputStream and OutputStream enable reading and writing typed data in a machine-independent way. Yet other classes in the hierarchy provide additional functionality to file operations. Figure 21-1 shows a portion of the Java class hierarchy that relates to file I/O.

File Input and Output Streams

The classes FileInputStream and FileOutputStream allow attaching a file to the input and output streams. Like their parent classes, InputStream and OutputStream, they provide support for reading and writing at the byte level. Figure 21-1 shows that other classes do not extend FileInputStream and FileOutputStream, thereby limiting their functionality to methods that overload those of InputStream and OutputStream, as listed in Tables 20-2 and 20-3. This means that the methods of FileInputStream and FileOutputStream cannot be used to write typed data to disk, except bytes and byte arrays. The program **InFile.java** creates a FileInputStream using the name of its own source file and displays the contents on the console.

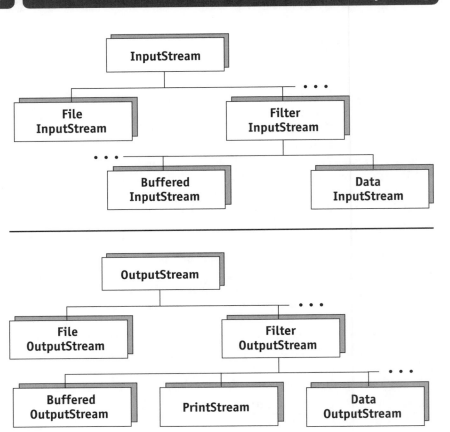

Figure 21-1
Part of Java's file stream I/O class hierarchy

The source file for the program InFile.java is found in the Session21 directory on the book's CD-ROM.

```
//*********************************************************
//*********************************************************
// Program: InFile
// Reference: Session 21
// Topics:
//   1. Reading data from a disk file using the
```

```
//       FileInputStream class
//**********************************************************
//**********************************************************
import java.io.*;

public class InFile

{
   public static void main(String[] args)
   throws java.io.IOException
     {
     int fileData;
     // Open a stream using the program's own source file
     FileInputStream aFile =
          new FileInputStream("InFile.java");

     while((fileData = aFile.read()) > 0)
        System.out.print((char)fileData);

     aFile.close();
     }
}
```

Filtered Streams

The notion of an input or output filter relates to a mechanism for transforming data along its way to the destination or providing some additional functionality. The classes FilterInputStream and FilterOutputStream override the methods in their parent classes, InputStream and OutputStream, and provide some new ones. The only constructors of these classes are defined as follows:

```
FilterInputStream(InputStream in)
FilterOutputStream(OutoutStream out)
```

Done!

The filter themselves are furnished in classes that extend FilterInputStream and FilterOutputStream. For example, the buffered stream classes provide buffered input and output functions to the stream and the data stream classes provide input and output of typed data.

REVIEW

Java streams can also be attached to files. The classes `File`, `FileInputStream`, and `FileOutputStream`, in the java.io package, provide much of the functionality for file manipulation and I/O. File properties are machine-dependent. These properties include the filename, the filename extension, directories, and paths. An object of the Java `File` class represents a single disk file. The `File` class allows treating files in a machine-independent fashion. The methods of the `File` class enable obtaining information about a file and its attributes and the setting some of the file properties. The File I/O classes are used to implement file input and output operations. The `FileInputStream` and `FileOutputStream` classes enable attaching files to input and output streams. Additional manipulations are possible with filtered streams.

QUIZ YOURSELF

1. In addition to the console, to what other objects can Java streams be attached? (See "File Operations and I/O.")
2. List three rules that foster the creation of cross-platform filenames. (See "The Filename.")
3. List four common filename extensions that are used on DOS systems. (See "The Filename Extension.")
4. Describe the difference between a directory name and a path name. (See "Directories and Paths.")
5. What machine-dependent information is encoded in the `pathSeparator` and `pathSeparatorChar` fields of the `File` class? (See "The File Class.")

Reading and Writing Text

Session Checklist

✔ Readers and writers

✔ Writing text: the `FileWriter`, `OutputStreamWriter`, `PrintWriter`, and `BufferedWriter` classes

✔ Compounding stream classes

✔ Programming text write operations

✔ Reading text: `FileReader`, `InputStreamReader`, and `BufferedReader` classes

✔ Programming text-read operations

**30 Min.
To Go**

Readers and writers are the names we give to java classes intended for text operations. Readers and writers are to text what streams are to bytes. The principal feature of readers and writers is their capability to parse any character encoding the Java language supports, such as ASCII, ISO Latin-1, and Unicode.

Readers and Writers

When you are familiar with streams, readers and writers are easy to use. The names and signatures of the methods of the reader classes are similar to those of the stream classes for input, and the methods of the writer classes are similar to those of the stream classes for output. The main difference is that stream classes are byte-based, and readers and writers are character-based. The base classes are the abstract classes java.io.Reader and java.io.Writer. Figure 22-1 shows a portion of the Java Reader/Writer class hierarchy.

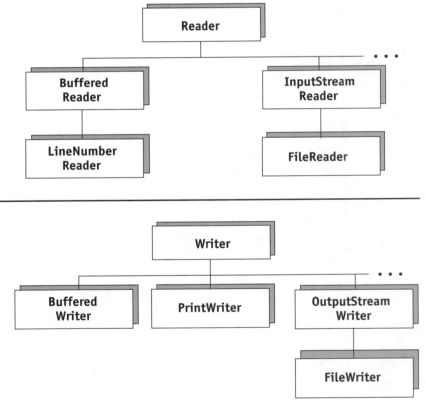

Figure 22-1
Part of Java's Reader/Writer class hierarchy

Reader is the abstract base class for reading character streams, and Writer is the abstract base class for writing them. The methods of the Reader class are in Table 22-1.

Table 22-1
Methods in java.io.Reader Class

Returns	Name	Description
void	close()	Closes the stream.
void	mark(int readAheadLimit)	Marks the present position in the stream.
boolean	markSupported()	Determines whether the stream supports the mark() operation.
int	read()	Reads a single character.
int	read(char[] b)	Reads characters into an array.
abstract	int read(char[] b, int o, int l)	Reads one character into offset 0 of array b
boolean	ready()	Determines whether the stream can be read.
void	reset()	Resets the stream.
long	skip(long n)	Skips characters.

The overloaded read() methods of the Reader class have the same signature as the overloaded read() methods of the InputStream class. Table 22-2 shows the methods of the Writer class.

Table 22-2
Methods in java.io.Writer Class

Returns	Name	Description
void	close()	Closes the stream.

Continued

Table 22-2 *Continued*

Returns	Name	Description
void	flush()	Writes out any buffered characters.
void	write(char[] b)	Writes an array of characters.
void	write(char[] b, int o, int l)	Writes l characters into array b starting at offset o.
void	write(int c)	Writes a single character.
void	write(String str)	Writes a string.
void	write(String s, int o, int l)	Writes l characters in string s starting at offset o.

Writing Text

We can write text to a disk file by combining the functionalities of several Java Writer classes. In Table 22-2, we isolate some of the most common classes.

FileWriter Class

The class FileWriter, which extends OutputStreamWriter, is a convenient class for writing character data to a file. The FileWriter object represents a character output stream, and it is the text-based equivalent of FileOutputStream class. The constructors of the FileWriter class are as follows:

```
FileWriter(File file)
FileWriter(FileDescriptor fd)
FileWriter(String fileName)
FileWriter(String fileName, boolean append)
```

The first constructor uses a File object as its argument. The other constructors allow you to create a FileWriter object using a file descriptor or a filename defined in a string. The append option of the last constructor allows you to add information at the end of a file.

FileWriter **does not declare any methods of its own but inherits methods from the** OutputStreamWriter **class.**

OutputStreamWriter Class

The OutputStreamWriter class extends java.io.Writer. OutputStreamWriter writes characters to the output stream and translates the character source into byte-sized units according to the encoding. Therefore, the class serves as a filter for converting character streams into byte streams. The constructors of the OutputStreamWriter class are as follows:

```
OutputStreamWriter(OutputStream out)
OutputStreamWriter(OutputStream out, String enc)
```

The first constructor takes an output stream as an argument. In this case, the character-to-byte conversion assumes the default character encoding. The second constructor uses the encoding in the named character string. The OutputStream Writer class implements the methods in Table 22-3.

Table 22-3
Methods in java.io.OutputStreamWriter Class

Returns	Name	Description
void	close()	Closes the stream.
void	flush()	Flushes the stream.
String	getEncoding()	Returns the name of the character encoding the stream uses. This is the default encoding the one-parameter constructor uses.
void	write(char[] b, int o, int l)	Writes l characters into array b starting at offset o.
void	write(int c)	Writes a single character.
void	write(String s, int o, int l)	Writes l characters into string s starting at offset o.

PrintWriter Class

The `PrintWriter` class extends Writer and provides a character-level implementation of the methods in the `PrintStream` class for byte output. The class declares the following constructors:

```
PrintWriter(OutputStream out)
PrintWriter(OutputStream out, boolean autoFlush)
PrintWriter(Writer out)
PrintWriter(Writer out, boolean autoFlush)
```

The first constructor constructs a `PrintWriter` object using an output stream. The second constructor provides automatic flushing of the output buffer whenever the `println()` method is called. The last two constructors are similar to the first two but use a Writer object as their first argument. Table 22-4 lists the methods in the `PrintWriter` class.

Table 22-4
Methods in java.io.PrintWriter Class

Returns	Name	Description
boolean	checkError()	Flushes the stream and check its error state.
void	close()	Closes the stream.
void	flush()	Flushes the stream.
void	print(boolean b)	Prints a boolean value.
void	print(char c)	Prints a character.
void	print(char[] s)	Prints an array of characters.
void	print(double d)	Prints a double-precision number.
void	print(float f)	Prints a floating-point number.
void	print(int i)	Prints an integer.
void	print(long l)	Prints a long integer.
void	print(Object o)	Prints an object.
void	print(String s)	Prints a string.

Returns	Name	Description
void	println()	Terminates the current line by writing the line separator character.
void	println(boolean x)	Prints a boolean value and an end line.
void	println(char x)	Prints a character and an end line.
void	println(char[] x)	Prints an array of characters and an end line.
void	println(double x)	Prints a double-precision number and an end line.
void	println(float x)	Prints a floating-point number and an end line.
void	println(int x)	Prints an integer and an end line.
void	println(long x)	Prints a long integer and an end line.
void	println(Object x)	Prints an Object and an end line.
void	println(String x)	Prints a String and an end line.
protected	void setError()	Indicates that an error.
void	write(char[] b)	Writes an array of characters.
void	write(char[] b, int o, int l)	Writes l characters to array b starting at offset o.
void	write(int c)	Writes a single character.
void	write(String s)	Writes a string.
void	write(String s, int o, int l)	Writes l character to string s starting at offset o.

The richness of methods in the PrintWriter class makes it one of the most useful classes for performing character output operations.

BufferedWriter Class

The BufferedWriter class improves the performance of write operations we perform at the character level. When we use a buffered writer, we optimize write operations independently of the number of write() calls in the code. The class declares the following constructors:

```
BufferedWriter(Writer out)
BufferedWriter(Writer out, int s)
```

The first constructor creates a buffered character output stream using the default buffer size, currently 8K. The second constructor allows us to specify the buffer size. Larger buffers allow us to store more characters internally before the actual disk-write operations take place.

The only new method BufferedWriter implements is newLine(). This is the recommended way of writing the system-independent line separator character.

Embedding platform-dependent line separator characters into strings or into the character stream is an incorrect programming practice.

Compounding Stream Classes

The BufferedWriter class adds a specific functionality to writer objects. Also, the class' constructors take an object of the Writer class as their first argument. Because Writer is an abstract class, the object passed as an argument must be overridden. We discuss the possibility of passing an object as a parameter to a method (in this case, the constructor) in Chapter 12, in relation to object composition by acquaintance. Putting all this together, we see that we can create an object of the class FileWriter (which extends Writer) and can use it to create a BufferedWriter object, for example:

```
File outFile = new File("demo.dat");
 . . .
FileWriter fw = new FileWriter(outFile);
BufferedWriter bw = new BufferedWriter(fw);
```

Because the PrintWriter object takes a Writer object as an argument, we can continue coding:

```
PrintWriter pw = new PrintWriter(bw);
```

We can make the process more compact by using cascaded constructors, as follows:

```
PrintWriter pw =
                new PrintWriter
                    (new BufferedWriter
                        (new FileWriter(outFile)));
```

This cascaded constructor is a viable option if we do not need to access the intermediate objects (in this case, FileWriter and BufferedWriter) independently. However, if we need to use some of the methods of the intermediate objects, we must declare them independently. For example, we use the BufferedWriter method newLine() to add a platform-independent line terminator character. To use this method, we need to declare an object of the BufferedWriter class.

Programming Text Write Operations

The PrintWriter class contains methods similar to those we use to display typed data on the console using System.out. However, the PrintWriter class constructor requires either an OutputStream or a Writer object. Because we want to output to a disk file, we must first create a File object. We use this object as an argument to create a FileWriter object, which we use in turn to create a BufferedWriter and a PrintWriter, as in the preceding section. We can use the result to write typed data to disk because the methods of the PrintWriter class (see Table 22-4) are available.

In the program FileWrite.java **we define data items of type** String, int, **and** double **and write this data to disk using the** println() **of the** PrintWriter **class. The source file for the program FileWrite.java is in the Session22 directory on the book's CD-ROM.**

**20 Min.
To Go**

Reading Text

The process we use to read text from a disk file is similar to the process we use to write it. The classes we use most often to read file text are in the upper section of Figure 22-1.

FileReader Class

The FileReader class is the reader equivalent of the FileWriter class we use in character write operations. FileReader defines the following constructors:

```
FileReader(File file)
FileReader(FileDescriptor fd)
FileReader(String fileName)
```

The first constructor receives a File object as a parameter; the second constructor receives a file descriptor, and the third constructor receives a filename encoded in a string. FileReader does not declare any methods of its own but inherits those of the InputStreamReader class.

InputStreamReader Class

The InputStreamReader class, which extends the abstract class Reader, reads bytes from the stream and converts them into a character stream. The method has two constructors, declared as follows:

```
InputStreamReader(InputStream in)
InputStreamReader(InputStream in, String enc)
```

Both methods take an InputStream object as the first argument. The first method uses the default character encoding, and the second method allows defining a particular encoding in a string. Table 22-5 lists the methods of the InputStreamReader class.

Table 22-5
Methods in java.io.InputStreamReader Class

Returns	Name	Description
void	close()	Closes the stream.
String	getEncoding()	Returns the name of the character encoding the stream uses.
int	read()	Reads a single character.
int	read(char[] b, int o, int l)	Reads characters l, into array b, starting at offset o.
boolean	ready()	Reports whether the stream is readable.

BufferedReader Class

The BufferedReader class allows us to read text from a character-based input, and to buffercharacters to improve performance. The class defines two constructors, as follows:

```
BufferedReader(Reader in)
BufferedReader(Reader in, int s)
```

The first constructor creates a buffered reader using the default-size buffer, currently 8K. The second constructor allows us to specify cache size.

Table 22-6 lists the method of the BufferedReader class.

Table 22-6
Methods in java.io.BufferedReader

Returns	Name	Description
void	close()	Closes the stream.
void	mark(int readAheadLimit)	Marks the present position in the stream.
boolean	markSupported()	Tests whether the stream supports the mark() operation.
int	read()	Reads a single character.
int	read(char[] b, int o, int l)	Reads l characters into array b, starting at offset o.
String	readLine()	Reads a line of text. Line terminators are lf, cr, and lf + cr.
boolean	ready()	Tests whether the stream is readable.
void	reset()	Resets the stream to the most recent mark.
long	skip(long n)	Skips n number of characters.

The class `LineNumberReader` extends `BufferReader`. This class allows us to keep track of the number of lines read from the input stream.

Programming Text Read Operations

The `BufferedReader` class contains a good selection of methods for reading character data, as in Table 22-6. The `BufferedReader` constructors require a `Reader` object. Because `FileReader` extends `InputStreamReader`, which extends `Reader`, we can use a `FileReader` object as an argument to the `BufferedReader` constructor.

We can read from a file by means of a `FileReader` object, wrapped in a `BufferedReader` class. We call the `FileReader` constructor with the target file as a parameter and then use the `BufferedReader` methods to access the file, as in the following code:

```
File thisFile = new File("FileRead.java");
  . . .
FileReader fr = new FileReader(thisFile);
BufferedReader br = new BufferedReader(fr);
```

As an alternative, we can use a cascaded constructor, as in the following statement:

```
BufferedReader br
                = new BufferedReader
                        (new FileReader(thisFile));
```

ReadFile.java uses a `BufferedReader` to read data from a disk file. The program reads its own source file and displays it on the console CD-ROM. The source file for the program FileRead.java is in the Session22 directory on the book's CD-ROM.

Applications often need to manipulate and process data read from a disk file. In this case, code often reads the file, or a portion of the file, into an array of type `char`. The `BufferedReader` class does not contain a method for reading file data into an array, but the `Reader` class does. Because a `FileReader` object inherits the public members of `Reader`, an object of the `FileReader` class can use the overloaded `read(char[] b)`.

Done!

ArrayRead.java reads an entire file into an array of type char. The processing is similar to the processing in the FileRead.java program previously listed. The source file for the program ArrayRead.java is in the Session22 directory on the book's CD-ROM.

REVIEW

The Java classes intended for text operations are readers and writers. The File Writer, OutputStreamWriter, PrintWriter, and BufferedWriter classes contain much of the necessary functionality for performing typical text write operations. Programming usually consists of creating a FileWriter object, wrapped in a BufferedWriter object, in turn wrapped in a PrintWriter object. We use methods of the BufferedWriter class to write data to disk. Often, we perform reading text by using the Java FileReader, InputStreamReader, and BufferedReader classes. Programming often consists of wrapping a FileReader object in a BufferedReader object and using the methods of the BufferedReader class to read file data.

QUIZ YOURSELF

1. What is the principal feature of readers and writers? (See "Readers and Writers.")
2. List three Java classes used often in text-write operations. (See "Writing Text.")
3. What is the advantage of using buffered readers and writers? (See "Buffered Writer Class.")
4. What are the advantages and disadvantages of using cascaded constructors? (See "Compounding Stream Classes.")
5. List three Java classes used often in text-read operations. (See "Reading Text.")

Operations on Blocked Data

Session Checklist

✔ Writing and reading blocked data

✔ Delimiting text fields

✔ Parsing operations

✔ Converting numeric data

✔ Writing and reading numeric types

**30 Min.
To Go**

Usually, applications that write disk files must operate with several data types. For example, a typical payroll program defines several fields to represent information for each employee. Typically, these fields include the employee's name, address, and social security number as strings; the number of dependents as an int; the base salary as a double; the additional income tax deduction as a double; and other data the employee's corresponding data types. In this session, we look at how we can block data, how we can write it to a disk, and how we can read it from a disk.

Writing and Reading Blocked Data

We call the organization of data into data fields *file* or *data blocking*. Once we define blocking, code can store and retrieve information according to the sequential types in the data structure. For example:

```
class Employee
{
  private String firstName;
  private String lastName
  private String aAddress;
  private String SSN;
  private int    dependents;
  private double baseSalary;
. . .
```

Delimiting Text Fields

Storing blocked data in text format requires reserving some characters as separators. If we use no separators, some of the data fields can become mangled. For example, for an employee with 12 dependents and a base salary of 14.95/hour, the data appear in the disk file as follows:

```
1214.95
```

When we read this data from the file, we cannot tell whether the employee has one dependent and a base salary of 214.95, 12 dependents and a base salary of 14.95, or 121 dependents and a base salary of 4.95. To delimit the output fields, we select a character not used in the file text. Usually, we call this character the *token*. If we use the vertical bar (|) as a separator, we store the data for the previously mentioned employee as follows:

```
12|14.95
```

The processing software can detect the end of the field that encodes the number of dependents from the field that encodes the employee's base salary. The following program, **BlockedFile.java**, shows how blocked data is written to disk:

The source file for the program BlockedFile.java is in the Session 23 directory on the book's CD-ROM.

```
//**********************************************************
//**********************************************************
// Program: BlockedFile
// Reference: Session 23
// Topics:
//    1. Writing blocked data to disk
//**********************************************************
//**********************************************************/

import java.io.*;

public class BlockedFile

{   public static void main(String[] args)
      throws java.io.IOException

    {
      // Field data
      char delim = '|';
      String firstName = "Joe";
      String lastName = "Smith";
      String address = "121 Calm Ct. SW Mapleton, MN";
      String ssn = "263-87-9870";
      int dependents = 2;
      double baseSalary = 16.22;

    // Initialize the output file
      File outFile = new File("employee.dat");
      if(!outFile.exists() || outFile.canWrite())
    {
    // Create a buffered output stream wrapped by a PrintWriter
    // object
      PrintWriter fos =
                      new PrintWriter
                      (new BufferedWriter
                      (new FileWriter(outFile)));

    // Write data to disk file
    fos.print(firstName);
    fos.print(delim);
```

```
fos.print(lastName);
fos.print(delim);
fos.print(address);
fos.print(delim);
fos.print(ssn);
fos.print(delim);
fos.print(dependents);
fos.print(delim);
fos.print(baseSalary);
fos.flush();
fos.close();
}
 else
{
   System.out.println("Cannot create output file");
   return;
}
 System.out.println("\nBlocked Data was writen to disk");
 System.out.println("Use DOS type command to view" +
                    " employee.dat\n");
 return;
}
}
```

**20 Min.
To Go**

Parsing Operations

Grammatically speaking, to parse a sentence is to separate its parts, explaining the grammatical form, function, and interrelation of these parts. In computer science, parsing has a similar connotation. For example, a text-processing operation may consist of parsing the individual fields by detecting the tokens.

We parse by reading the file into a buffer and then by scanning the text to search for the tokens that serve as field delimiters. Once we find a token, we process the text field according to the file blocking. For example, we can store data for a employee as follows:

```
Joe|Smith|121 Calm Ct. SW Mapleton, MN|263-87-9870|2|16.22\n
```

Because the text line terminates in a newline character (\n), we can use the readLine() method of the BufferedReader class (see Table 22-6) to move each line into a local array. Now the logic can parse the data into previously blocked fields, as follows:

```
Joe
Smith
121 Calm Ct. SW Mapleton, MN
263-87-9870
2
16.22
```

As an alternative, we can parse by using one of the Java token-manipulating classes, such as `StreamTokenizer` or `StringTokenizer`. Later in this section, we discuss the `StringTokenizer` class.

Numeric Conversions

We can represent numeric data in memory and can store it on disk in either text or binary form. The Java libraries offer an abundant selection of methods for performing conversions between numeric binary encodings and text strings. In this section, we develop a program named **TokenRead.java**, which takes as input the file named **employee.dat**, created by the **BlockedFile.java** program listed earlier in this session. To convert the text representations of numeric data back to Java binary primitives, the **TokenRead.java** program uses several classes in the Java libaries: `NumberFormat`, `StringTokenizer`, `Integer`, and `Double`. These classes are diverse and rich in functionality, but this discussion only covers the functions in the **TokenRead.java** program.

NumberFormat Class

The class `java.text.NumberFormat` extends `Format`. It is an abstract class that provides the interface for methods we use to format and to parse numbers, as well as to obtain information about numeric fields.

Java uses the term locale in reference to the number formatting style of a local culture, language, script, and group. For example, in the United States, the number format locale uses a period to separate the decimal fraction of a floating point number, commas to partition large numbers into 3-digit groups, and the $ to represent currency. Some European countries reverse the function of the period and the comma and use other currency symbols.

In the program **TokenRead.java**, listed later in this section, we use two methods of the `NumberFormat` class: `GetInstance()` and `parse()`.

The `GetInstance()` method of the `java.text.NumberFormat` class overloads twice. The first version takes no parameters and returns the default number format for the current locale. The second version takes a locale parameter and returns the number format.

The `parse()` method of the `NumberFormat` class also overloads twice. Both versions take a string as an argument. The method parses the string into a numeric variable. The parameterless version assumes that parsing starts at the beginning of the string. The second version of `parse()` allows us to specify a position within the string where the parse begins. In either case, `parse()` returns a type `long` if the string has no fractional part; otherwise, it returns a `double`.

StringTokenizer Class

This class, part of `java.util` package, allows application code to break a string into its blocked fields using one or more separator tokens. Java literature refers to each substring the method returns as a token. The class declares three constructors, as follows:

```
StringTokenizer(String str)
StringTokenizer(String str, String delim)
StringTokenizer(String str, String delim, boolean returnTokens)
```

All three overloads use the tokenized string as the first parameter. The first constructor assumes the default delimiter string, defined as " \t\n\r\f". This means that any `space`, `tab`, `newline`, `return`, or `formfeed` character serves as a terminator. The second constructor allows us to define a string that contains one or more delimiters. The third constructor also contains a flag that determines whether the delimiter characters return as tokens. The delimiters serve as separators only if this flag is false.

Table 23-1 lists the methods in the `StringTokenizer` class.

Table 23-1
Methods in java.util.StringTokenizer

Returns	Name	Description
int	countTokens()	Calculates the number of times we can call the nextToken() method before it generates an exception.

Returns	Name	Description
boolean	hasMoreElements()	Returns the same value as the hasMoreTokens() method.
boolean	hasMoreTokens()	Returns true if there are more tokens available from the target string.
Object	nextElement()	Returns the same value as the nextToken() method, but its declared return value is Object rather than String.
String	nextToken()	Returns the next token in the target string.
String	nextToken(String delim)	Returns the next token

Double and Integer Classes

These classes of java.lang provide methods for converting a primitive data type, int or double, into a string and a string into an int or double primitive type. These classes also contain many other useful methods for manipulating data in the corresponding primitive types. The following code fragment shows the use of the NumberFormatr, StringTokenizer, Double, and Integer classes in parsing and converting numeric data stored on disk:

```
// Create string tokenizer defining a storage buffer and
// a token
String aLine;
StringTokenizer tk =
                new StringTokenizer(aLine, "|");
// Create a NumberFormatter object
NumberFormat nf
            = NumberFormat.getInstance();
. . .
// Read numeric data from text stored in string aLine and
// store results in local variables of int and double
// type
int dependents = nf.parse(tk.nextToken()).intValue();
double baseSalary = nf.parse(tk.nextToken()).doubleValue();
```

The program **TokenRead.java** reads the data file the **BlockedFile.java** program creates. The source file for the program **TokenRead.java** is in the Session 23 directory on the book's CD-ROM.

10 Min. To Go

Writing and Reading Numeric Types

In this section, we explore ways to store numeric data on disk in binary format and ways to retrieve this data in variables of the corresponding types. Previously in this session, we develop the **BlockedFile.java** program, in which we use the print() methods of the PrintWriter class to convert numeric data to string and to store these strings on disk. However, storing numeric data as strings has limitations. One possible limitation is the loss of precision when we convert binary variables to strings. Another limitation is that string representations of numbers require more storage space than their binary forms. Finally, the conversion of binary encodings to strings, which are often read back to other binary encodings, is a wasted effort.

Most applications that manipulate numeric data store values in binary form. Java supports the ANSI-IEEE 754 Standard for Binary Floating-Point Arithmetic. We encode the Java floating-point primitives float and double in ANSI-IEEE 754 formats.

The stream classes DataInputStream and DataOutputStream allow reading and writing of typed data. For example, the DataOutputStream class contains the method writeDouble(), which converts a variable in double format into eight digits that represent this value in ANSI-IEEE 754 format for binary numbers. The following program, **WriteDouble.java**, uses the sqrt() methods of the java.lang. Math class to calculate the square root of the integers in the range 0 to 19. We store the resulting values in a file named **doubles.dat** using the writeDouble() method of the DataOutputStream class.

The source file for the program **WriteDouble.java** is in the Session 23 directory on the book's CD-ROM.

```
//**********************************************************
//**********************************************************
// Program: WriteDouble
// Reference: Session 23
// Topics:
//    1. Writing floating point numbers to a disk file in
//       ANSI-IEEE double precision format.
```

```
//***********************************************************
//***********************************************************/

import java.io.*;

public class WriteDouble

{  public static void main(String[] args)
      throws java.io.IOException

      {

      FileOutputStream fos = new FileOutputStream("doubles.dat");
      DataOutputStream dostr = new DataOutputStream(fos);

      // Loop calculating 20 square roots
      for(int i = 0; i < 20; i++)
         dostr.writeDouble(Math.sqrt(i));
      dostr.flush();
      dostr.close();

      System.out.println("\nDone!");
      System.out.println("Use DOS type command to inspect");
      System.out.println("the file \"Doubles.dat\"");
      return;
      }

}
```

If you execute the preceding program and then use the DOS type command
to inspect the file **doubles.dat,** you see that the screen does not show the stored
numbers. You see a series of meaningless characters. This occurs because the calculated square roots are encoded in binary format; each floating point number is
represented in eight bytes according to the ANSI-IEEE 754 encoding for doubles.
Code can read these binary values to variables of type double using the
ReadDouble() method of the DataInputStream class.

The following program, **ReadDoubles.java**, reads the 20 binary encodings in the
doubles.dat file and displays the results on the console:

**The source file for the program ReadDouble.java is in the
Session 23 directory on the book's CD-ROM.**

```
//**********************************************************
//**********************************************************
// Program: ReadDouble
// Reference: Session 23
// Topics:
//    1. Reading a file containing floating point numbers
//       in ANSI-IEEE double precision format.
// Requires:
//    1. The file "doubles.dat" created by the program
//       WriteDouble.java must be in the current directory
//**********************************************************
//**********************************************************/

import java.io.*;

public class ReadDouble

{   public static void main(String[] args)
       throws java.io.IOException

    {

      double aNum;

      FileInputStream fis = new FileInputStream("doubles.dat");
      DataInputStream dis = new DataInputStream(fis);

      for(int x = 0; x < 20; x++)
      {
         aNum = dis.readDouble();
         System.out.println(aNum);
      }
      dis.close();
      return;
    }
}
```

Done!

REVIEW

Applications often associate several data types with the same item. We call delimiting the individual elements for organizational or storage purposes data blocking. Often, we delimit blocked fields by means of a separator character. Processing software uses the separator to detect blocking. In this sense, we "parse" blocked data into its original fields by detecting the field delimiters.

We can store numeric data in text form or in binary encoding. In Java, the term *locale* refers to the number-formatting style of a local culture, language, or group. The StringTokenizer class in the java.util package allows code to use separators (tokens) to break a string into its blocked fields. The classes Double and Integer, of the java.lang package, contain methods for converting the corresponding primitive data types into strings. The classes DataInputStream and DataOutputStream allow us to read and to write typed data.

QUIZ YOURSELF

1. Define data fields, and create blocking for identifying an individual book in a library database. (See "Writing and Reading Blocked Data.")

2. Write the logic used for parsing the data blocks in the previous Quiz questions in this section.. (See "Parsing Operations.")

3. What is the meaning of the Java term "locale"? (See "Number Format Class.")

4. What is the use of the StringTokenizer class? (See "StringTokenizer Class.")

Computer Graphics in Java

Session Checklist

✔ Introducing computer graphics

✔ The GUI, text-based, and graphical programs

✔ Programming models: event-driven programming

✔ Elements of a graphics application: the main window and program controls

✔ Java graphics: applets and applications

✔ The Java foundation classes

**30 Min.
To Go**

S o far, we have been developing programs that execute on the system console. Because of its simplicity, console-level programming is useful as you learn the fundamentals of the Java language. However, most current commercial applications are graphical. Text-based programming is almost an anachronism.

In this session, we introduce graphics programming in Java. We begin with an introduction to computer graphics and to the programming models in this field. Graphics programs are based upon a different paradigm from the one used in text-based applications. Graphics programmers must adopt this new model and change their mind-sets accordingly. We then discuss the basic components of a graphics application. The session concludes with an overview of the Java resources we use to develop graphics applications.

Computer Graphics

The operating systems used in the first generation of digital computers required the user to toggle a series of binary switches (typically, each switch had an attached light) to enter data into the machine. In the first generation of computing machines, programming consisted mostly of switch-toggling and button-pressing.

To become a proficient programmer at that time, you had to belong to a select class of binary-speaking, hexadecimal-minded experts who devoted most of their lives to deciphering the arcane mysteries of hardware and software.

During the late 50s and early 60s, several inventions simplified computer use and programming. The IBM Corporation, who had developed punched cards for their business machines, adapted this technology to its first line of computers. At that time, teletype machines (called TTYs) were widely used in the communications industry. A TTY had a typewriter-like keyboard and produced a paper printout. In addition, the TTY usually produced a strip of paper or mylar tape in which the characters were encoded in rows of punched holes. The punched tapes provided a convenient way to transfer data and programs from the TTY into the computer. When programmers adapted teletype machines for use as computer input devices, they ended the age of input through mechanical switches. Not long after, programmers developed the Cathode Ray Tube (CRT), already in use in commercial television, to display computer text. An added bonus was that the CRT could also display pictures.

Some of the devices invented during these years later became standard elements of computer technology, yet other devices disappeared. The most common devices include the CRT, the lightpen, the touch screen, the graphic tablet, the joystick, and the mouse. The common element in all of these devices is that they allow the user to interact visually with the machine. The idea for an interactive input device came from the work of Allan Kay at the Xerox Palo Alto Research Center in the early 1970s. Dr. Kay was attempting to design a computer that preschool children could use, children who were too young to read or to type commands in text form. A possible approach was to use small screen objects, called icons, that represented some object familiar to the child. A mechanical device (now called the mouse) allowed the user to move these graphics objects on the screen. Interactive graphics and the graphical user interface are the result.

Steve Wozniak, one of the founders of Apple Computers, relates that he visited Xerox PARC and saw the mouse and the graphical user interface in action. He immediately concluded that interactive computer interfaces were the way of the future. Back at Apple, Wozniak started to develop an operating system that supported graphical, mouse-controlled, icon-based user interaction. After one or two unsuccessful tries, the Macintosh computer was released. Not long after, Microsoft started to develop a graphical operating system for the PC; we call this system Windows.

The GUI

Many researchers realized the advantages of an easier interaction with a computing machine. Douglas Engelbart devised a viable mouse interface in 1968, although it was another 15 years before the mouse became a common computer component. To implement a graphical user interface, or GUI (pronounced Gu-ee), it was necessary to have not only a pointing device that worked but also a graphics-capable video terminal. Furthermore, operating system software would have to provide graphics services in a device-independent manner.

In the PC world, the evolution of hardware and software components into a graphical operating system took almost one decade. The first versions of Windows were rather crude and achieved little acceptance. It was not until Windows 95 that Microsoft Windows became the standard.

Text-based and Graphical Programs

Roughly, we can classify operating systems into two types: single-user, single-task, command-driven systems, like DOS; and multiple-task, GUI-based systems, such as Windows, X Windows, and the Mac operating system. Single-user, single-task systems allow unrestricted access to the machine's resources. When the application code gains control, it can do whatever it pleases. Its only limitations are hardware capabilities and the programmer's skills. Although the designers of DOS-like operating systems often list rules that well-behaved programs should follow, there is no way of enforcing these rules. Intentionally or not, these programs can raise havoc with the system by deleting or modifying files, interfering with other applications, or even damaging the hardware. A DOS-like application has control over all system resources. It can allocate all memory to itself, set whatever video mode is convenient, control the printer and the communications lines, and manage the mouse and the keyboard. Resources need not be shared because the operating system is dormant while an application is in control. In this environment, a single application executes at a time.

Multitasking systems, on the other hand, share resources among themselves and with the operating system. Multitasking systems share memory, CPU, display hardware, communications lines and devices, mouse, keyboard, and disk storage. Each program operates in its private address space and has limited access to other memory areas. Code cannot access the hardware devices directly but must to do so through operating system services, usually called the Application Program Interface, or API.

In the multitasking model, the operating system controls access to all devices and resources, including memory, the video system, communications devices, and input and output. Figure 24-1 shows how single-tasking and multitasking programs access system resources.

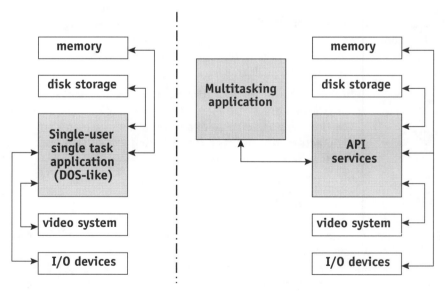

Figure 24-1
Application access to system resources

A multitasking operating system can have a text-based interface or a graphical interface. If the system has a text-based interface, it is command-driven, and we access the operating system services and functions using commands we enter from the console. If the system has a graphical interface, we access services and commands by means of a graphical user interface (GUI).

Programming Models

The nature of the operating system environment determines programming models. In command-driven, single-user, single-task operating systems (such as DOS), a program is "the god of the machine." The running code has unrestricted access and control. It executes on its own, implements its functionality, and calls the operating system only to request a specific service. It shares the machine with no other program. Therefore, the programming model for a single-task, single user program is a set of sequential instructions and program constructs. Control does not return to the operating system until the application terminates. This form of interaction between the application and the operating system gives rise to the sequential programming model.

The conceptual model for a graphical-based, multitasking program is quite different from the command-driven, single-user model. The code has no direct access to devices and resources and must share the machine with other applications and with the operating system itself. In pre-emptive multitasking, the operating system can switch the foreground (CPU access) from one application to another. If an application misbehaves, the operating system can simply turn it off. In this model, the operating system that is "the god of the machine," not the running program.

Event-Driven Programming

We need a different programming model from the one used in command-driven, single-user systems, to accommodate this mode of interaction between an application and the system. Sometimes, we call this model *event-driven* programming. In event-driven programming, synchronization between the operating system and the application is in the form of program events. For example, when we change the size of an application's window (a user event), the operating system takes the appropriate action and then notifies the application code (a system event). The application, in turn, may decide to take its own action to update its display area, or it may decide not to take any action. In either case, control returns to the operating system.

The event-driven model is simple and effective. We implement it by messages passed between the user and the system. Events in the environment generate these messages. For example, we click and drag the window border to resize it. This generates a hardware event and informs the operating system of the mouse action. The operating system responds to this event by resizing the application window. It then informs the application that the size of the window has changed so that application code can update the display as necessary. This interaction among the hardware, the user, and the system, based on events and their associated messages, the core of the multitasking, GUI-driven architecture. Figure 24-2 shows the action of the event-driven programming model.

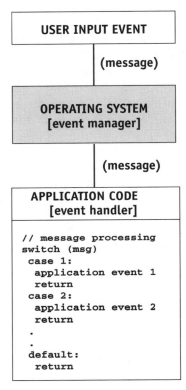

Figure 24-2
Event-driven programming model

**10 Min.
To Go**

Elements of a Graphics Application

A graphics application has a characteristic appearance that makes it different from a text-based program. The characteristic elements of a graphical program relate either to the application's main window or to the input/output controls we use to implement the graphical user interface, such as buttons, scrollbars, checkboxes, and list selectors.

The Program's Main Window

The main window is an application's principal means of input and output and is an application's only access to the video display. In Java, *frame* is the program's main window.

The following are the building blocks of a program window:

- The main window has a title bar. The title bar can display a caption or can be blank.

- On the right-hand side of the title bar, buttons minimize, maximize, and close the program window. The application can select the control buttons to display.

- The optional menu bar is below the title bar. A typical menu bar contains one or more drop-down menus. Each drop-down menu consists of commands you can activate with a mouse click or with the Alt key and the underlined letter code. Trailing ellipses indicate menu commands that expand into submenus.

- The program main window, as well as many input/output controls, can have vertical or horizontal scroll bars. The operating system notifies the application of your action on the scroll bars, but the application must provide the required processing.

- The screen zone assigned to each program window is called the client area. The dimensions and graphics attributes of the client area can be obtained from the operating system.

Figure 24-3 shows the basic components of a program window.

Controls

The program window in Figure 24-3 contains several controls: the buttons on the title bar, the menu items and menu commands, and the scroll bars. Buttons, scroll bars, and menu commands are just a few of many control components available in a graphics application.

Generically, we call the components we use to implement input/output and program manipulation operations *controls*.

Some controls have been around since the original GUI operating systems.

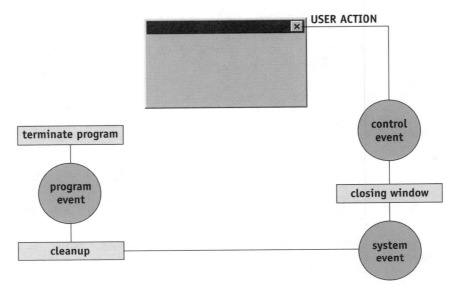

Figure 24-3
Components of a Program Window

Java Graphics

Perhaps the greatest challenge the creators of the Java language faced was the implementation of a cross-platform Graphical User Interface. The specific windowing environments, such as MAC OS, X-Windows, and the various versions of Microsoft Windows, implement features not available in the other windowing environments. Java designers had to find common elements in the supported platforms and ignore those that were exclusive to a particular operating system or version. Their first task was finding the common graphics functionality, and their second task was making sure the Java virtual machines would accommodate the unavoidable differences.

The task was enormous, and the solutions, so far, are not free from problems.

The event model Java adopted originally was based on inheritance. The short-comings of using inheritance to implement event handling led Java to adopt a delegation-based model. This second model solved some of the problems but at the expense of greater complexity. Furthermore, in order to maintain compatibility, the current Java versions continue to support the inheritance-based model. Java 1.2 has two different, sometimes conflicting implementations of event-driven programming.

The first implementation of the GUI was the Java Abstract Windowing Toolkit or AWT. Java literature states that the original AWT was developed in six weeks. It is not surprising that it had major shortcomings and several nasty bugs. The new versions solve many of these limitations.

Applets and Applications

In Session 1, we mention that the World Wide Web is at the heart of the Java language and continues to be one of its principal fields of application. Java became famous for its use in the World Wide Web, and this continues to be one of its most important applications.

Small Java programs, called applets, execute within a Web browsers such as Netscape Navigator and Internet Explorer. These Java programs expand the functionality of the browser by providing the logic and data processing capabilities of Java. Although applets require a Java-enabled browser, we should mention that, currently, you have a difficult time finding a web browser that is not Java-enabled.

Most of the support Java graphics require at the applet level is within the browser. This means that the browser must solve all of the platform-dependency issues. Java applications, on the other hand, are full-fledged Java programs that the Java interpreter executes. So far, the programs we have developed in this book are applications.

The Java Foundation Classes

We perform graphics programming in Java by means of a set of packages we call the Java Foundations Classes. In Java 1.2, the foundations classes include the following APIs:

- Abstract Windows Toolkit or AWT
- Swing components
- Java 2D
- Java Accessibility

AWT

The Java AWT is the core package graphics. The AWT contains classes for creating and operating a Graphical User Interface and for performing drawing and painting operations. In addition, the current versions of the AWT provide support for clipboard-based transfers, image manipulations, fonts, printing, 2D geometrical operations, and input; also, the current versions provide an event handling mechanism.

One of the most useful classes of the AWT is `java.awt.Component`. In Java, a component is a button, a menu, a scrollbar, or any graphical element displayed on the screen that can interact with the user. In Windows terminology, we call components controls. Currently, 66 classes extend the `Component` class. In the sessions that follow, we examine some of these classes.

Swing

The original designers of the AWT decided to use the functionality of the underlying operating systems instead of coding the user interface toolkit from scratch. The AWT is actually a thin software layer that provides access to the system's application programming interface. *Peer classes* are the underlying classes that provide the specific windowing functions. For example, if a Java application uses the AWT to create a button control, the resulting component is a standard Windows button, a Macintosh button, or a Motif button, according to the operating system on which the application executes.

 Java documentation refers to elements that use the underlying APIs as heavyweight components and to elements that we implement in Java code as lightweight components. In this sense, the AWT consists of all heavyweight components. The Swing components, on the other hand, are mostly lightweight.

Peer classes facilitated the development of the original Java toolkits and gave applications the look and feel of their host operating system. However, using peers brings about a performance penalty for Java applications and has been the source of bugs and system dependencies. Java 1.2 addresses these problems by means of Swing, a new set of APIs.

In contrast with API components, Swing components are designed to work the same on all platforms. Swing architecture addresses the following areas of application.

- New components that add functionality to those in the AWT. The classes that implement these components start with the letter "J."

- The possibility of selecting the application's "look and feel." For example, an application using Swing components can look like a Win32, a Motif, or a Mac program.

- The implementation of a Model-View-Controller (MVC) architecture. Each component has an associated `Model` class and an interface it uses.

- The possibility of handling keyboard events in nested components.

- Swing is designed to manage nested containers. Virtually, we can nest any component within another. For example, we can nest a graphic component in a list and a combo box in a toolbar.

- The support of a multiple document interface based on virtual desktops.

- We can specify the space between the edges of the component and the area it is drawn in (the inset) with a blank border. In addition, it makes available many border styles that can be combined to create compound borders.

- Support for message dialogs and user-choice dialogs in a variety of formats. The message displayed in the dialog can be a string, a string-generating object, or an arbitrary component.

- Support for standard dialog classes.

- Support for structured tables and trees.

- Expanded text manipulations. Swing provides support for a field for hidden input and a class for displaying multi-font text. In addition, it provides editing capabilities for multi-font text.

- The undo package provides generic undo capabilities we can use in a variety of situations.

- Built-in support for products that increase accessibility to handicapped persons.

Java 2D

The Java 2D API is a designation for an extension of the AWT that includes enhanced graphics, text operations, image handling, color definition and composition, hit detection, and device-independent printing. The Graphics2D class, which extends the AWT Graphics class, is the fundamental class of Java 2D.

Done!

The Graphic2D class was designed to ensure backward compatibility with java.awt.Graphics. Applications that use Java 2D functionality start by creating an object of the Graphics class and then casting it into one of the Graphics2D classes. The result is that the methods of both Graphics and Graphics2D become accessible to code. In the chapters that follow, we see how we can use the Graphics and Graphics2D.

REVIEW

The first generation of computers required pressing buttons and toggling switches to enter data and programs in binary or hex code. In the 1940s and 50s, IBM introduced punched cards to store data and programs. Later came teletype machines (TTYs), which had a typewriter-like keyboard and produced punched tape as output. The Cathode Ray Tube (CRT), already in use in televisions, and the keyboard both appeared in the late 60s. At that time, Doug Englebart demonstrated a mouse-driven interface, but it took many years for the industry to adopt it.

The graphical user interface, GUI, made a new, event-driven, programming model necessary. Event-driven programming is suitable for multiple-user, multitasking systems. The model is based on message passing between the event-manager (operating system) and the event handler (application code).

Java graphics have been difficult to implement because of cross-platform requirements. A Java applet is a small application that executes within a Java-enabled Web browser. We develop full-featured graphics applications in Java using the libraries in the Java foundation classes. These include the Abstract Windows Toolkit (AWT), Swing, and Java 2D.

QUIZ YOURSELF

1. What does the acronym GUI stand for? (See "The GUI.")
2. How do applications access system resources in a mutitasking environment? (See "Text-based and Graphical Programs.")
3. List four different controls. (See "Controls.")
4. What is the difference between a Java applet and a Java application? (See "Applets and Applications.")

Programming the AWT Classes

Session Checklist

✔ The AWT classes

✔ Frame class

✔ Window class

✔ Container class

✔ Component class

**30 Min.
To Go**

J ava proposes to be a portable language, but the graphics platforms present the biggest challenge to its portability. The hardware variations and the uniqueness of the various operating systems result in GUIs with substantial differences. Windows, Macintosh, X Windows, and Motif, among others, present individualities that are often difficult for Java to accommodate. The Java AWT provides facilities for manipulating images and generating graphics across all supported platforms. The results are not always perfect, but they are often good enough for the task at hand. In any case, regarding portable graphics, Java is still the only game in town.

AWT Classes

In Java graphics terminology, a frame is a top-level window. The Java frame concept includes the client area, the window's title bar, and border. The Frame object can resize itself when you drag the edge or the corner of the window to change its size. You can also reposition a frame by dragging it to another position on the visual desktop. A frame can contain other graphics objects, such as text fields, buttons, and controls.

The AWT provides a Frame class that includes much of the functionality we need to implement a typical application window. The default frame has a title bar and a border. However, applications are expected to provide processing for handling tasks such as resizing or closing the frame. This means that if we do not provide code for handling the frame closing operation, we can close the program window only by system-level commands. In Windows, this requires using the <Ctrl-Alt-Del> keystrokes, which are not only inconvenient but can lead also to an unexpected system reboot and to possible loss of data. In Session 26, we address the problem of creating a frame you can close.

The Java Frame class is in a class hierarchy in which the Component class is the highest level. Although all the classes in this hierarchy are important in graphics programming, in this session we concentrate on the core classes: Frame, Window, Container, and Component. Figure 25-1 shows the classes in this hierarchy.

Graphics programming is a complicated art. This session contains tables of functions for the following AWT classes: Frame, Windows, Container, **and** Component. **Although these tables are a selection of the most popular methods, some of them are rather extensive. We intend them as an overview of AWT functionality and as a programming reference. A light reading of these tables provides the required familiarity for understanding the sessions that follow.**

Frame Class

We use the Frame class to create a window with a title bar, a border, and an optional menu bar. A frame can also contain gadgets such as buttons to resize, minimize, or maximize the window. The Frame class, which extends Window, provides methods for configuring and manipulating frames. Table 25-1 lists some of the most popular methods in the Frame class.

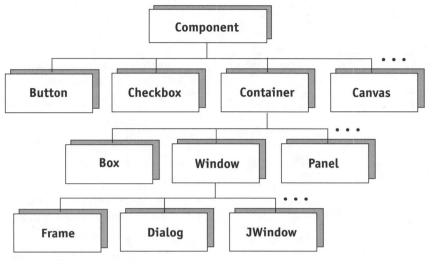

Figure 25-1
Selected classes in the component hierarchy

Table 25-1
Selected Methods of java.awt.Frame

Returns	Name	Description
void	addNotify()	Makes the frame displayable by connecting it to a native screen resource.
static Frame[]	getFrames()	Returns an array containing all Frames the application creates.
Image	getIconImage()	Displays the image in the minimized icon.
MenuBar	getMenuBar()	Retrieves the frame's menu bar.
int	getState()	Retrieves the frame's state.
String	getTitle()	Retrieves the frame's title.

Continued

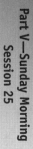

Table 25-1 *Continued*

Returns	Name	Description
boolean	isResizable()	Indicates whether you can resize the frame.
String	paramString()	Returns the frame's parameter String.
void	remove (MenuComponent m)	Removes the frame's specified menu bar.
void	removeNotify()	Makes the frame undisplayable by removing its connection to its native screen resource.
void	setIconImage (Image image)	Sets the image you want to display in the minimized icon for the frame.
void	setMenuBar (MenuBar mb)	Sets the menu bar for the frame to the specified menu bar.
void	setResizable(boolean resizable)	Sets whether you can resize the frame.
void	setState(int state)	Sets the frame's state.
void	setTitle(String title)	Set's the frame's title.

20 Min. To Go

Window Class

Usually, a graphics application needs to access the functionality of the Window class. A window object represents a top-level window with no border or menu. When we construct a window object, it must have a frame, a dialog, or another window object as its owner. Window objects generate events to signal that the window is open or closed. Table 25-2 lists some common methods in the Window class.

Table 25-2
Selected Methods of java.awt.Window

Returns	Name	Description
void	addNotify()	Makes the window displayable by creating the connection to its native screen resource.
void	addWindowListener (WindowListener l)	Adds a window listener to receive events from the window.
void	dispose()	Releases all of the native screen resources used by the Window.
Locale	getLocale()	Gets the Locale object associated with the window if one is defined.
indow[]	getOwnedWindows()	Returns an array containing all the windows the window owns.
Window	getOwner()	Returns the owner of the window.
void	hide()	Hides this Window.
boolean	isShowing()	Checks if the Window is displayed.
void	pack()	Fits the window to the preferred size and to the layouts of its subcomponents.
void	processEvent (AWTEvent e)	Processes events on the window.
void	processWindowEvent (WindowEvent e)	Processes events on the window by dispatching them to any registered WindowListener objects.
void	removeWindowListener (WindowListener l)	Removes the specified window listener.
void	setCursor(Cursor cursor)	Set the cursor image to a specified cursor.
void	show()	Makes the Window visible.
void	toBack()	Moves the window to the back.
void	toFront()	Moves the window to the front.

Container Class

The `java.awt.Container` class defines a generic container object that can contain other containers or components. In Java, a container object is a conceptual element with a rectangular area in which you can place other program elements. The `Container` class is a subclass of `Component`. This means you can nest container objects. Figure 25-2 shows a frame with two containers.

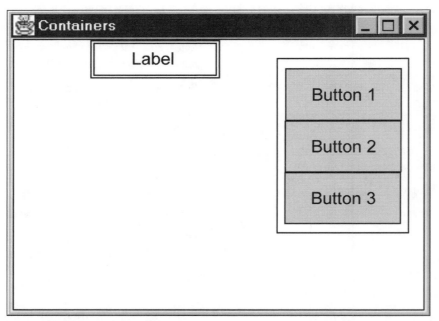

Figure 25-2
Java container objects

The object named "Label" in Figure 25-2 holds a labeling string, a text area, and another container. The nested container holds three buttons. Table 25-3 lists some of the most frequently used methods in the `Container` class.

Table 25-3
Selected Methods of java.awt.Container

Returns	Name	Description
Component	add(Component comp)	Adds the specified component to the container.
Component	add(Component comp, int index)	Adds the specified component to the container at the given position.
void	add(Component comp, Object constraints)	Adds the specified component to the end of the container with the given constraints.
void	add(Component comp, Object constraints, int index)	Adds the specified component to the container with the specified constraints at the specified location.
Component	add(String name, Component comp)	Adds the component specified by its name to the container.
void	addContainerListener (ContainerListener l)	Adds the specified container listener to receive container events from the container.
void	addNotify()	Makes the container displayable by connecting it to a native screen resource.
Component	findComponentAt (int x, int y)	Locates the child component that contains the specified position.
Component	findComponentAt(Point p)	Locates the child component that contains the specified point.

Continued

Table 25-3   *Continued*

Returns	Name	Description
float	getAlignmentX()	Returns the x axis alignment.
float	getAlignmentY()	Returns the y axis alignment.
Component	getComponent(int n)	Returns the component in the container.
Component	getComponentAt(int x, int y)	Locates the component that contains the specified x,y position.
Component	getComponentAt(Point p)	Gets the component that contains the specified point.
int	getComponentCount()	Gets the number of components in the panel.
Component[]	getComponents()	Gets all the components in this container.
Insets	getInsets()	Determines the size of the container's border.
LayoutManager	getLayout()	Gets the layout manager for this container.
Dimension	getMaximumSize()	Returns the container's maximum size.
Dimension	getMinimumSize()	Returns the container's minimum size.
Dimension	getPreferredSize()	Returns the preferred size of the container.
void	invalidate()	Invalidates the container.
boolean	isAncestorOf (Component c)	Checks if the component is in the component hierarchy of the container.

Returns	Name	Description
void	list (PrintStream out, int indent)	Prints a listing of the container to the specified output stream.
void	list (PrintWriter out, int indent)	Prints a list, starting at the specified indentation, to the specified print writer.
void	paint (Graphics g)	Paints the container.
void	paintComponents (Graphics g)	Paints each component in the container.
protected	String paramString()	Returns the parameter string representing the state of the container.
void	print(Graphics g)	Prints the container.
void and protected	printComponents (Graphics g)	Prints each component in the container.
void and protected	processContainerEvent (ContainerEvent e)	Processes container events occurring in the container by dispatching them to any registered Container Listener objects.
void	processEvent(AWTEvent e)	Processes events in the container.
void	remove(Component comp)	Removes the specified component from the container.
void	remove(int index)	Removes the component specified by index.
void	removeAll()	Removes all the components from the container.

Continued

Table 25-3 *Continued*

Returns	Name	Description
void	removeContainerListener (ContainerListener l)	Removes the specified container listener.
void	removeNotify()	Makes the container unable to display by removing its connection to its native screen resource.
void	setCursor(Cursor cursor)	Sets the cursor image to the specified cursor.
void	setFont(Font f)	Sets the font of the container.
void	setLayout (LayoutManager mgr)	Sets the layout manager for the container.
void	update(Graphics g)	Updates the container.
protected	validate()	Validates the container.

10 Min. To Go

Component Class

The highest level class in the hierarchy is Component. The Java Component class defines objects we can display on the screen and with which we can interact. The notion of a component is similar to that of a Windows control, described in Session 24. Examples of components are buttons, checkboxes, scrollbars, and menus. We implement the graphical user interface by means of components. The Component class is one of the richest in the AWT. Information regarding the Component class is found in the JDK.

Done!

REVIEW

The Java AWT provides facilities for manipulating images and generating graphics across all supported platforms. Providing portable graphics is one of the greatest challenges of Java. A frame is a top-level window. The Java frame concept includes the window's title bar and border. The Component class hierarchy contains the graphics functionality of the AWT. The Component class is at the top of the hierarchy. Other classes are Container, Window and Frame.

We use the Frame class to create a window with a title bar, a border, and an optional menu bar. The Frame class, which extends Window, provides methods for configuring and manipulating frames.

We use the Window class to produce objects that represent a top-level window with no border or menu. A Window object must have a frame, a dialog, or another window object as its owner. Window objects generate events to signal that the window is open or closed.

A Container object is a conceptual element with a rectangular area in which we can place other program elements. The Container class is a subclass of Component. We can nest Container objects.

We can display a Component object on screen and can interact with it. It is similar to the notion of a Windows control. Buttons, checkboxes, scrollbars, and menus are Components. We implement the GUI by means of components. The Component class is one of the richest in the AWT.

QUIZ YOURSELF

1. What is the biggest challenge to Java's portability? (See "Session Checklist.")
2. What elements does a Java Frame object include? (See "AWT Classes.")
3. What are the characteristics of an object of the Window class? (See "Window Class.")
4. List three elements that can be inside a Container object. (See "Container Class.")
5. List three Component objects that can interact with the user. (See "Component Class.")

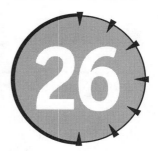

Creating the Graphics Application

Session Checklist

✔ The "closeable" frame problem

✔ Using the `ActiveFrame` class

✔ The Windows display context and Java's Graphics class

✔ Java `update()` and `paint()` methods

✔ Manipulating fonts and displaying text.

**30 Min.
To Go**

Graphics is one of the most demanding and difficult specialties in the programming field. By the same token, graphics programmers traditionally receive some of the highest salaries in the industry. In Sessions 26 and 27, we present an overview of graphics programming in Java. Be warned that we treat many important topics lightly and even skip some topics. Our purpose is merely to give you a taste of what Java graphics programming is about.

The "Closeable" Frame Issue

In Session 25, we mention that we expect Java graphics applications to provide processing for handling events such as resizing or closing the frame. If the program does not provide this logic, we can use only system-level commands to close the window. In Windows, the system-level command is the Ctrl+Alt+Del keystrokes. Using a system-level command to close a program window is not only inconvenient but can lead to an unexpected reboot.

Creating a frame we can close by means of the control button on the title bar (or any other application-level function) requires implementing event-handlers and using event-handling code. With the previous version of the AWT, this task posed no great problems because the event-handling model was simple and intuitive. However, the original event-handling model, based on inheritance, had serious limitations, which led Java to adopt a complex, delegation-based model. Although code that uses the old model still works in Java 1.2, Java declares this support will end in the near future.

To make the frames "closeable," we use an ActiveFrame class. Later in this session, we develop the ActiveFrame class. Because ActiveFrame extends Frame, the methods of the Frame class remain available to our code.

The following are default properties of an ActiveFrame object:

- The frame's default size is 300 by 200 pixels.
- The default location is the top-left screen corner.
- The title bar displays the name of the class.

Using the ActiveFrame Class

To avoid the frame-closing problem, we develop a class that contains code to receive window events. This requires us to implement a WindowListener object by means of the WindowAdapter class, part of the java.lang package. The windowClosing() method of the WindowAdapter class takes a WindowEvent object as a parameter. We invoke this method when we close the application window, thus providing implementation of a "user-closeable" window. The ActiveFrame class that follows extends the Java Frame class and provides the necessary code for conventional closing of the program window. We define ActiveFrame as follows:

```
import java.awt.*;
import java.awt.event.*;
```

```java
public class ActiveFrame extends Frame
{
 //*************************
 //      Constructors
 //*************************
  public ActiveFrame()
   { addWindowListener
    (new WindowAdapter()
      { public void windowClosing(WindowEvent e)
        { System.exit(0);}
     }
    );
    setSize(300, 200);
    setTitle(getClass().getName());
   }
}
```

In addition to creating a closeable window, the ActiveFrame class sets the window size to 300 by 200 pixels and displays the name of the driving class as the program title. Code can modify these default values if you desire.

 The program GFrame.java uses the ActiveFrame **class to create a program window. The source code for GFrame.java is found in the Session 26 folder on the book's CD ROM.**

The resulting window overrides the default size (300 by 200 pixels) defined in the ActiveFrame class. Also, the program's title, as displayed in the title bar, changes. Because we extend ActiveFrame, we can use conventional controls to close the program window. In Windows, we activate the closing action by clicking the title bar button labeled X or by selecting the Close command in the system menu. Figure 26-1 is a screen snapshot of the resulting program window.

The **GFrame.java** program, listed previously, provides a simple shell in which to use the ActiveFrame class to create a graphics window. In your own programs, you probably need to configure the window to suit your purposes. For example, your program may need to execute in a window of a different size from the one in the sample code, which you can initially locate at a different position in the desktop area; the window probably has a title of its own. You can change all of these program parameters by calling the corresponding methods of the superclasses discussed in Session 25: Component, Container, Window, and Frame. For example, we can resize the program window by calling the setSize() method of the Component class, as in the **Gframe.java** program.

Figure 26-1
Screen snapshot of the GFrame program

**20 Min.
To Go**

Display Context and Java's Graphics Class

In Windows, we call a data structure that stores information about a device, such as the video display or a printer, a *device context*. The Java counterpart for a device context is an object of the Graphics class. The Graphics object contains information necessary for drawing operations, such as the following:

- The object to receive the drawing. This is normally a Component, but it can also be an off-screen image.
- A coordinate translation mode that controls the object's position on the screen.
- A clipping rectangle that limits output to the current frame.
- A color used for drawing.
- A font used for text output.

Every Java program that renders text or graphics in a frame must reference a Graphics object. The Graphics class, part of the AWT, contains over 35 methods that draw lines, arcs, rectangles, characters, bytes, bitmaps (called images in Java), ellipses, and polylines, among many others. The Graphics class is an abstract class, so you cannot instantiate objects of this class directly.

Java update() and paint() methods

A graphical Java program that uses the AWT is event-driven. The programmer codes the operations that draw the program's client area but does not perform the drawing directly. Instead, the code waits for a system-generated or user-generated event to draw to the window. For example, the event can be the program window you display for the first time or the program window you uncover, resize, minimize, maximize, or otherwise modify. When the Java event handler needs to redraw a window, it triggers a call to a method called update(), located in the Component class. The update() method erases the window background and then calls the paint() method in the Java Canvas class. An application typically redefines the paint() method so that the new implementation receives control whenever the program's client requires updating. The paint() method receives a Graphics object as its only parameter. For example:

```
public void paint(Graphics g)
{
    g.drawString("Hello World!!!", 50, 100);
}
```

In this case, the code redefines paint() with its own version so that it receives control whenever a screen update is required. The only output operation is using the drawString() method of the Graphics class to display a message on the screen. The second and third parameters to drawString() are the x and y pixel coordinates in the client area.

Manipulating Fonts

A font is a set of characters of the same typeface, style, and size. In the AWT, the typefaces available are SansSerif, Serif, Monospaced, Dialog, and Windows Dialog. The styles are bold, italic, bold-italic, and plain. We express the size in units called points, each point being 1/72th of an inch.

In Java, an attribute of the Graphics object contains the default font that we use to draw text to the screen. Applications can select other fonts and point sizes by instantiating an object of the Font class. The Font constructor is as follows:

```
public Font(String name, int style, int size)
```

Where:

String name can be SansSerif, Serif, Monospaced, Dialog, or DialogInput.

int style can be BOLD, ITALIC, BOLD/ITALIC, OR PLAIN.

int size is point size

An application can create a font object as follows:

```
Font f = new Font("SansSerif", Font.BOLD, 14);
```

Using the setFont() method of the Component class, an application installs the font in the device context, as follows:

```
g.setFont(f);
```

 The program WindowText.java demonstrates the fundamental manipulations required for a Java graphics application that displays text on the screen: The source code for the program WindowText.java is found in the Session26 directory on the book's CD-ROM.

Figure 26-2 is a screen snapshot of the **WindowText.java** program.

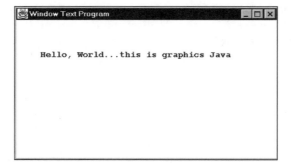

Figure 26-2
Screen snapshot of the WindowText program

Done!

REVIEW

Graphics Java applications must provide logic to support a program window that you can close with an application-level command. A way of doing this in the

AWT is to call the `windowClosing()` method of the `WindowAdapter` class. The `ActiveFrame` class, developed in the text, provides this support.

The classes described in Session 25 (`Component`, `Container`, `Window`, and `Frame`) provide much of the functionality needed in a Java graphics application. The `setSize()` method allows you to change the default size of the program window. We use the `setLocation()` method to position the program window in the desktop area. We use the `setTitle()` method to display a program name in the title bar.

The display context is a Windows structure that contains information about a graphics device, such as the video display. In Java, this information is in an object of the `Graphics` class. AWT programs are event-driven. The `update()` method of the `Component` class erases the window background and calls the `paint()` method of the `Canvas` class. In PC programming, the `paint()` method is an intercept for the WM_PAINT message we describe in Session 25. Applications usually redefine the `paint()` method to receive control when Windows sends WM_PAINT to the application.

A font is a Java object that the application can manipulate. When we construct the font object, we set its type, style, and point size. We can then select the font object into the device context by means of the `setFont()` method of the `Component` class.

QUIZ YOURSELF

1. Does the AWT provide support for closing a program window by means of user-level commands? (See "The 'Closeable' Frame Issue.")

2. Which Java classes provide support for implementing a "closeable" frame? (See "Using the ActiveFrame Class.")

3. What is the Java equivalent of the Windows device context? (See "Display Context and Java's Graphics Class.")

4. Does the Java device context include a default font? (See "Display Context and Java's Graphics Class.")

5. How does a Java application intercept the Windows WM_PAINT message? (See "Java update() and paint() Methods.")

6. Write Java code to set a font that is monospace, bold, and 12-point size. (See "Manipulating Fonts.")

PART

V

Sunday Morning Part Review

1. In addition to the console, to what other objects can we attach Java streams ?

2. List three rules that foster the creation of cross-platform filenames.

3. List four common filename extensions we use on DOS systems.

4. What is the principal feature of readers and writers?

5. List three Java classes we use often in text-write operations.

6. What is the advantage of using buffered readers and writers?

7. What are the advantages and disadvantages of using cascaded constructors?

8. What is the meaning of the Java term "locale"?

9. What is the use of the StringTokenizer class?

10. What does the acronym GUI stand for?

11. How do applications access system resources in a mutitasking environment?

12. List four different controls.

13. What is the difference between a Java applet and a Java application?

14. What is the biggest challenge to Java's portability?

15. What elements does a Java Frame object include?

16. Does the AWT provide support for closing a program window by means of user-level commands?

17. Which Java classes provide support for implementing a "closeable" frame?

18. What is the Java equivalent of the Windows device context?

19. Does the Java device context include a default font?

20. How does a Java application intercept the Windows WM_PAINT message?

PART

VI

Sunday Afternoon

Vector and Raster Graphics

Session Checklist

✔ Translating the frame origin

✔ Color in Java graphics: RGB format

✔ Using the Java Graphics class: vector-drawing methods and geometrical transformations

✔ Raster graphics in Java: creating the Image object and displaying the bitmap

**30 Min.
To Go**

We use two technologies to generate and display images on the graphics screen: *vector* and *raster* graphics. Vector graphics describe images mathematically. For example, the screen location of its start and end points, and a circle or an ellipse by the coordinates of the rectangle that tightly contains it, describe a straight line. A complex graphical object consists of the descriptions of all components that form the object. We can manipulate Vector-based objects by transforming the values that represent the object's coordinate points. Thus, we can move, scale, and rotate images on the screen. Raster graphics, on the other hand, are defined in terms of the individual screen dots that form them. The dots are in rows and columns, and each dot is associated with a color attribute. AWT and other Java graphics packages support both vector and raster graphics.

Translating the Frame Origin

We must address a geometrical issue before we attempt to draw graphic objects on the video display. Figure 26-2, in the previous session, shows a typical Java frame. Notice that the frame includes the title bar and the window border. Because applications cannot draw on the title bar or the border, it is useful to change the frame origin to the top-left corner of the client area, which is the screen area that applications can access. Figure 27-1 shows the frame origin and the client area origin.

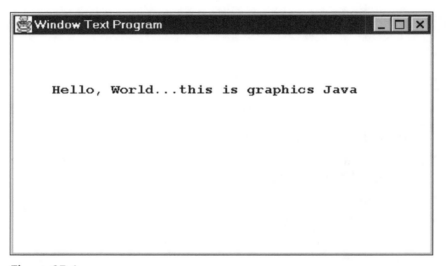

Figure 27-1
The frame origin and the client area origin

To translate the drawing origin from the frame area to the client area, we can use the `translate()` method of the graphics class. The method receives two parameters that represent the x and the y values where we wish to move the origin. We can obtain the size of the title bar and the frame border when we use the `getInsets()` method of the `Container` class, as follows:

```
getInsets().left --> returns the width of the border
getInsets().top  --> returns the width of the titlebar
```

The call to `translate()` is made as follows:

```
g.translate(getInsets().left, getInsets().top);
```

After the `translate()` method executes, the origin of the drawing is at the top-left corner of the application's client area. In most cases, this simplifies programming.

Color in Java Graphics

Today, most video systems display color graphics. In these systems, color is an attribute of the Graphics object (Windows device context). Once we set a color, we use it for all drawing operations that follow. To draw in multiple colors, you must select them in succession.

The `Color` class of Java's AWT encapsulates colors. Several methods you can use to define colors are available. The simplest method consists of using one of the pre-defined color names. The Java standard colors are the following:

black	*green*	*red*	*pink*
blue	*light-gray*	*white*	
cyan	*magenta*	*yellow*	
dark-gray	*orange*	*-gray*	

RGB Color Format

As an alternative, we can define a color by its red, green, and blue components. We call this the RGB format. Constructors of the `Color` class allow us to create a custom color by specifying its red, green, and blue components. One constructor specifies RGB values as floating-point numbers in the range 0.0 to 1.0. Another constructor allows us to use integers in the range 0 to 255 to specify RGB values. The latter constructor reflects the architecture of the most common video cards that use a byte value to encode each RGB component.

We can create objects of the `Color` class, as follows:

```
Color myRed = new Color(200, 0, 0);
Color skyBlue = new Color(0, 0, 180);
Color pinkish = new Color(200, 50, 50);
Color darkest = new Color(0, 0, 0);
Color brightest = new Color(255, 255, 255);
```

Once we define a color, we can install it as an attribute of the Java Graphics object when we use the setColor() method of the Graphics class. The method setColor() takes a Color object as a parameter, which we can create using one of the pre-defined Java standard colors or ; a customized color object. For example:

```
g.setColor(myRed);
g.setColor(Color.orange);
```

We can create a customized color and can install it as an attribute of the Graphics object in the same statement:

```
g.setColor(new Color(0, 128, 128));
```

**20 Min.
To Go**

Using the Java Graphics Class

The Java Graphics class is the abstract base class that allows an application to draw onto the various devices, as well as onto off-screen images. A Graphics object contains information that defines the basic rendering operations Java performs. This state information, the equivalent of the Windows device context, includes the following properties:

- The Component object on which drawing takes place.
- A translation origin for rendering and for clipping coordinates.
- The current clipping rectangle.
- The current color.
- The current font.
- The current logical pixel operation function.
- The current XOR alternation color.

We have discussed some of these attributes, such as the Component, the translation origin, the color, and the font. In Java, rendering operations modify only pixels that lie within the area the current clipping rectangle bounds, which is one of the attributes of the Graphics object. Table 27-1 lists some of the methods in the Java Graphics class.

Table 27-1

Often-used Methods in java.awt.Graphics

Returns	Method	Function
abstract void	clearRect(int x, int y, int width, int height)	Clears the specified rectangle by filling it with the current background color.
abstract void	clipRect(int x, int y, int width, int height)	Intersects the current clip with the specified rectangle.
abstract void	copyArea(int x, int y, int width, int height, int dx, int dy)	Copies an area of the component by a distance that dx and dy specify.
abstract Graphics	create()	Creates a new Graphics object that is a copy of the current one.
Graphics	create(int x, int y, int width, int height)	Creates a new Graphics object based on the current object but with a new translation and clip area.
abstract void	dispose()	Disposes this graphics context and releases any system resources that uses.
abstract void	drawArc(int x, int y, int width, int height, int startAngle, int arcAngle)	Draws the outline of a circular or elliptical arc the specified rectangle defines.
void	drawBytes(byte[] data, int offset, int length, int x, int y)	Uses the current color and font to draw the text the specified byte array provides.

Continued

Table 27-1 *Continued*

Returns	Method	Function
void	drawChars(char[] data, int offset, int length, int x, int y)	Uses the current font and color to draws the text in the specified character array.
abstract void	drawLine(int x1, int y1, int x2, int y2)	Uses the current color to draw a line between point (x1, y1) and point (x2, y2).
abstract void	drawOval(int x, int y, int width, int height)	Draws the outline of an oval its bounding rectangle defines.
abstract void	drawPolygon(int[] xPoints, int[] yPoints, int nPoints)	Draws a closed polygon arrays of x and y coordinates define.
void	drawPolygon (Polygon p)	Draws the outline of a polygon the specified polygon object defines.
abstract void	drawPolyline(int[] xPoints, int[] yPoints, int nPoints)	Draws a sequence of connected lines that the corresponding arrays of x and y coordinates define.
void	drawRect(int x, int y, int width, int height)	Draws the outline of the specified rectangle.
abstract void	drawRoundRect (int x, int y, int width, int height, int arcWidth, int arcHeight)	Uses the graphics context's current color to draw an outlined round-cornered rectangle.

Returns	Method	Function
abstract void	drawString(String str, int x, int y)	Uses the graphics context's current font and color to draw the text the specified string provides.
void	fill3DRect(int x, int y, int width, int height, boolean raised)	Paints a 3-D highlighted rectangle filled with the current color.
abstract void	fillArc(int x, int y, int width, int height, int startAngle, int arcAngle)	Fills a circular or elliptical arc defined by the specified bounding rectangle.
abstract void	fillOval(int x, int y, int width, int height)	Fills an oval defined by the specified bounding rectangle, using the current color.
abstract void	fillPolygon(int[] xPoints, int[] yPoints, int nPoints)	Fills a closed polygon defined by arrays of x and y coordinates.
void	fillPolygon (Polygon p)	Fills the polygon defined by the specified Polygon object , using the graphics context's current color.
abstract void	fillRect(int x, int y, int width, int height)	Fills the specified rectangle.
abstract void	fillRoundRect(int x, int y, int width, int height, int arcWidth, int arcHeight)	Fills the specified rounded corner rectangle using the current color.

Continued

Table 27-1 *Continued*

Returns	Method	Function
void	finalize()	Disposes of this graphics context once it is no longer eferenced.
abstract Shape	getClip()	Gets the current clipping area.
abstract Rectangle	getClipBounds()	Returns the bounding rectangle of the current clipping area.
abstract Color	getColor()	Gets this graphics context's current color.
abstract Font	getFont()	Gets the current font.
boolean	hitClip(int x, int y, int width, int height)	Returns true if the specified rectangular area intersects the bounding rectangle of the current clipping area.
abstract void	setClip(int x, int y, int width, int height)	Sets the current clip to the rectangle specified by the given coordinates.
abstract void	setClip (Shape clip)	Sets the current clipping area to an arbitrary clip shape.
abstract void current color.	setColor(Color c)	Sets the graphics context's
abstract void	setFont(Font font)	Sets the graphics context's font.
abstract void	setPaintMode()	Sets the paint mode of the graphics context to overwrite the destination with the graphics context's current color.

Returns	Method	Function
abstract void	setXORMode (Color c1)	Sets the paint mode of the graphics context to alternate between this graphics context's current color and the new specified color.
String	toString()	Returns a String object representing the Graphics object's value.
abstract void	translate(int x, int y)	Translates the origin of the graphics context to the point (x, y) in the current coordinate system.

Vector-drawing Methods

Several methods of the Graphics class allow us to draw straight and curved lines on a graphics object. For example, to draw a filled oval, you can use the fillOval() method, which draws a solid ellipse or circle, as follows:

```
g.fillOval    (50, 60, 200, 100);
              -- -- --- ---
              |  |  |   |__ height of bounding rectangle
              |  |  |_____ width of bounding rectangle
              |  |_____ y of upper left corner
              |_____ x of upper left corner
```

Where:

50 = x of upper left corner

60 = y of upper left corner

200 = width of bounding rectangle

100 = x of upper left corner

Other methods that take similar parameters are the following:

```
fillPolygon()
fillRect()
fillRoundRect()
```

Methods that start with the word "draw" do not fill the interior of figures. For example:

```
drawRect()
drawOval()
```

The drawLine() method allows us to draw a straight line its end points define. The line attributes are defined in the device context. For example:

```
drawLine(int x1, int y1, int x2, int y2)
               --------------  ---------------
               |                  |___ x/y of end point
               |_____ x/y of start point
```

Where:

```
int x1, int y1   =   x/y of start point
int x2, int y2   =   x/y of end point
```

Some vector-drawing methods of the Graphics class take arrays of coordinates as a parameter. For example:

```
int[] xCoords = {350, 500, 500, 350};
int[] yCoords = {50, 150, 50, 150};
...
g.drawPolygon(xCoords, yCoords, 4);
               -------  -------  --
               |        |        |__ number of points
               |        |_____ array of y coordinates
               |_____ array of x coordinates
```

Where:

```
xCoords   =   array of x coordinates
yCoords   =   array of y coordinates
4         =   number of pointers
```

Other methods that take similar parameters are the following:

```
drawPolyline()
fillPolygon()
```

We use the `drawArc()` method to draw an arc of an ellipse, as follows:

```
g.drawArc( 50,          // x of start point
           280,         // y of start point
           150,         // width
           100,         // height
           45,          // start angle
           180);        // arc angle
```

All line-drawing methods use lines that are one pixel thick. This is a great limitation of the AWT that Java programmers are supposed to fix in later versions.

Geometrical Transformations

**10 Min.
To Go**

One of the most powerful features of vector graphics is the possibility of transforming an image by manipulating its coordinate points. Suppose there is a rectangular-shaped polygon the x- and y-coordinates of its four screen points define. If we add a constant value to each of the x-coordinates, the amount we add to each coordinate translates the rectangle along the x-axis of the monitor. By the same token, we can translate a vector image to any screen location by adding or subtracting a constant value to each of its x-and y-coordinates. Figure 27-2 shows the translation of a rectangular polygon by adding a constant to its x- and y-coordinates.

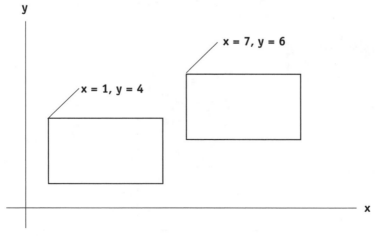

Figure 27-2
Translation of a vector-based polygon

In Figure 27-2, we manipulate the coordinate parts of the rectangle in solid lines to translate it to the position of the rectangle in dashed lines. In this case, we add a value of 6 to each x-coordinate and a value of 2 to each y-coordinate.

Other geometrical transformations we can perform on vector images are *scaling* and *rotation*. In scaling, we multiply each coordinate point by a scaling factor, which can be different for each coordinate plane. In the rotation transformation, the vector-based object moves along a circular arc when we apply a trigonometric function to each coordinate point.

Geometrical transformation is one of the most interesting topics of computer graphics. By applying translation, scaling, and rotation transformation, we can make objects appear larger or smaller, stretched, shrunk, and even animated. For example, we can make the vector-based arms of a graphical clock move by applying a series of rotation transformations. We can make an object move diagonally on the screen by consecutively applying a translation transformation. In either case, the graphics application must follow a cycle of drawing, transforming, erasing, and redrawing each image.

The program VectorGraphics.java shows some of the fundamental manipulations in Java vector graphics. The source file is found in the Session 27 directory on the book's CD-ROM.

Figure 27-3 is a screen snapshot of the **VectorGraphics.java** program.

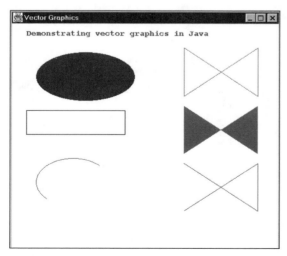

Figure 27-3
Screen snapshot of the VectorGraphics program

Raster Graphics in Java

Raster (bitmap) graphics are not based on geometrical figures but on images stored dot-by-dot. In this case, a rectangle of colored dots forms the image. We can store photographs and other raster images in GIF or JPEG format and can display them in Java programs. We must store the image file in the directory in the Java `classpath`.

Creating the Image Object

To display an image stored in a Java-compatible file, the application must first create an Image object. We accomplish this by retrieving the default Java AWT toolkit and using the `getImage()` method of the `Toolkit` class. For example, if you want to display an image stored in a file named **stars.gif,** start by creating the Image object, as follows:

```
Image hstImage =
         Toolkit.getDefaultToolkit().getImage("stars.gif");
```

Displaying the Bitmap Image

We can display the object `hstImage` (of the class `Image`) on screen by using the `drawImage()` method of the `Graphics` class, as follows:

```
g.drawImage(hstImage, 120, 350, 200, 200, this);
          --------- -------- --------  ----
                |        |        |       |___ image observer
                |        |        |_____ scaling rectangle
                |        |_____ x/y location
                |_____ image object
```

Where:

`hstImage`	=	image object
`120, 350`	=	x/y location
`200, 200`	=	scaling
`this`	=	image observers

The fifth parameter in the call to drawImage() is an ImageObserver interface. When the call to drawImage() takes place, Java starts a new program thread to load the requested image. When Java acquires the image data, the thread notifies the image observer. Because the Component class implements the ImageObserver interface, we can use the "this" operator as an image observer in the call to drawImage().

The program RasterGraphics.java demonstrates the display of a bitmap file in Java. The source file is found in the Session 27 directory on the book's CD-ROM.

Figure 27-4 is a screen snapshot of the **RasterGraphics.java** program.

Done!

Figure 27-4
Screen Snapshot of the RasterGraphics Program

REVIEW

Vector and raster graphics are the principal technologies we use to generate and display images on the graphics screen. Vector graphics describes images mathematically. We can manipulate vector-based objects by transforming the values that represent the object's coordinate points. Raster graphics consists of defining an image in terms of the individual screen dots that form it. The dots are in rows and columns, and each dot is associated with a color attribute.

Java places the drawing origin at the top-left corner of the program frame. It is usually convenient to move this point to the top-left corner of the client area. We accomplish this by means of the `translate()` method of the `Graphics` class. We define colors by means of standardized symbolic names or by the red, green, and blue components. We call this method the RGB color format.

The `Graphics` class provides methods to draw onto graphics devices and off-screen images. Vector-drawing methods allow us to draw lines, rectangles, polygons, and ovals. Some drawing methods draw the outline of geometrical figures, and other methods also fill the interior. We can use the geometrical transformations of translation, scaling, and rotation to manipulate vector images on screen. Java supports the manipulation and display of raster-based images in GIF and JPEG formats.

QUIZ YOURSELF

1. Explain the difference between vector and raster graphics. (See "Session Checklist.")

2. Write a Java statement that translates the frame origin from the frame to the client area. (See "Translating the Frame Origin.")

3. Write an expression in RGB format that produces a light-gray shade. (See "Color in Java Graphics.")

4. List three vector graphics methods in the Java Graphics class. (See "Vector-drawing Methods.")

5. Write a Java expression to draw a straight line from coordinates x = 50, y = 75, to coordinates x = 200, y = 250. (See "Vector-drawing Methods.")

Engineering the Java Application

Session Checklist

✔ Software engineering: the programmer as an artist

✔ Software characteristics and qualities

✔ Principles of software engineering

**30 Min.
To Go**

Developing a software application requires more than knowing how to code in a particular programming language. In fact, many developers consider coding one of the simplest phases in the software development process. We need to analyze and design programs before we can code them. In addition, we must test, correct, and install software. In this session, we discuss technologies that facilitate software development.

Software Engineering

Software engineering is an effort to facilitate the often frustrating task of designing and developing computer programs. Around this time, the computer community became increasingly worried about the fact that software projects were typically over budget and behind schedule. The term *software crisis* came to mean that software development was the bottleneck of computing.

During the first years of computing, software developers incurred grave fallacies by applying rules that originated in other fields of human endeavor or that derived from common sense. For example, developers assumed that if a certain task took a single programmer one year to code, four programmers could accomplish it in approximately three months. They also assumed that if a single programmer was able to produce a software product with a quality value of 25, four programmers could create a product with a quality value of approximately 100. In general, because engineering technologies worked when developing organizational tools, theories, and techniques for building bridges and airplanes, these technologies should also be capable of developing a straightforward scientific methodology for developing software products.

Unfortunately, solving these problems was not as easy as it first seemed. In the first place, computer programming, unlike ditch digging or apple harvesting, is not a task we can easily partition into isolated functions or can perform independently. The different parts of a computer program interact with each other often in complicated and hard-to-predict ways. Considerable planning must precede partitioning a program into individual tasks. Then it turns out that the quality of a software product is difficult to ensure and even to measure. Conventionally engineered products have qualities that persist beyond their defects. We can still use a dishwasher that fails to dry perfectly. We can still drive a car to work that is difficult to park. However, a word-processor program that hyphenates incorrectly or that occasionally destroys the source file is useless even if it has some other good qualities. When a computer program fails catastrophically, it is difficult for us to appreciate any residual usefulness in the software product.

The Programmer as an Artist

Donald Knuth has written a series of books titled *The Art of Computer Programming*. In the preface, he states the following:

"The process of preparing programs for a digital computer is especially attractive, not only because it can be economically and scientifically rewarding, but also because it can be an aesthetic experience much like composing poetry or music."

If computer programming is an art, any effort to reduce programming to follow a strict and scientifically defined set of rules is likely to fail. However, this fact does not preclude the use of engineering and scientific principles in pursuing this art. Software engineering is not an attempt to reduce programming to a mechanical process; it is a study of those elements of programming we can approach technically and of the mechanisms we can use to make programming less difficult.

Software Characteristics

From an engineering viewpoint, a software system is a product that serves a function. However, one unique attribute makes a computer program much different from a bridge or an airplane: programs are easier to change. The malleability of software is both an advantage and a danger. It's an advantage because often we can correct an error in a program much more easily than we can fix a defect in an airplane or an automobile. It's a danger because, when we modify a program, we can introduce unanticipated side effects that may impair the functionality of the components that execute correctly before the change.

Another unique characteristic of programs is the type of resources necessary for their creation. A software product is basically an intellectual commodity. The principal resource necessary for producing software is human intelligence. The actual manufacturing of a program is simple and inexpensive in comparison to its design, coding, testing, and documenting. Software contrasts with many other engineered products in which the resources used in producing them are a substantial part of the product's cost. For example, a considerable portion of the price of a new automobile represents the cost of manufacturing it, but a less significant portion pays the engineering costs of design and development. In the case of a typical computer program, these proportions are reversed.

Software Qualities

Usually, we associate an engineered product with qualities that define its usability. For example, a bridge supports a predetermined weight and withstands a given wind force. An airplane is capable of transporting a specific load at a certain speed and altitude. The principal goals of software engineering are to define, specify, and measure software qualities and to describe the principles we can apply to achieve these software qualities.

We can base the classification of software qualities on their relation with the software product. In this sense, we can speak of qualities desirable to the user, to the developer, or to the manager. Table 28-1 lists some qualities according to this classification.

Table 28-1
Software Qualities

USER	DEVELOPER	MANAGER
reliable	verifiable	productive
easy to use	maintainable	controllable
efficient	extensible	lucrative
	portable	

We can also talk about software qualities that are internal and external to the product. Internal qualities are visible to developers and managers, and external qualities are visible to the user. It is easy to see that reliability from the user's viewpoint implies verifiability from the developer's viewpoint. On the other hand, this distinction is often not well defined. The following are some of the most important qualities we associate with software products.

Correctness

Correctness means that a program behaves as we expect. More technically, we can say that a program is correct if it behaves according to its functional specifications (described later in this session). We can verify correctness experimentally or analytically. Certain programming tools and practices tend to improve correctness, and others tend to diminish it.

Reliability

Reliability means that a program is trustworthy or dependable. More technically, we can define reliability as the statistical probability that a program will continue to perform as we expect over a period of time. We can say that reliability is a measure of correctness.

Robustness

Robustness attempts to measure program behavior in circumstances that exceed formal requirements. In other words, it is a measure of the program's reaction to unexpected circumstances. For example, a mathematical program can assume that a user will not enter a negative value to the square root function because this operation is undefined. A more robust program recovers from this error by posting an error message and requesting a new input; a less robust program may crash.

Efficiency

Efficiency is a measure of how economically a system uses available resources. An efficient system is one that makes good use of resources. In software engineering, we equate efficiency with performance. A slow application or one that uses too much disk space reduces productivity and increases operational cost. Often, software efficiency is difficult and costly to evaluate. Conventional methods of evaluation rely on measurement, analysis, and simulation.

Verifiability

Verifiability refers to our ability to ascertain the properties of a software product through analytical methods or testing. Often, verifiability is an internal quality of interest, mainly to developers. At other times, the user needs to determine that software performs as expected, as with program security. Some programming practices foster verifiability, but others do not.

Maintainability

Maintainability refers to the ease with which we can maintain a program. Programmers discover rather early in their careers that a software product is never finished. Some extremists state that a finished program is an oxymoron. Programs evolve throughout their life span because of changes that correct newly detected defects or modifications that implement new functionalities. In this sense, we refer to software maintenance as a program-upkeep operation. The easier a program is to maintain, the greater its maintainability.

User Friendliness

User friendliness is measurement of usability and is perhaps the least tangible software property. The main problem is that different users may consider the same program feature to have various degrees of friendliness. Software engineers often consider the user interface the most important element in a program's user friendliness, but user preferences often vary according to previous levels of expertise. Several other attributes affect a program's user friendliness. For example, we can hardly consider a program that performs poorly with low levels of correctness and reliability user friendly.

Reusability

Reusability characterizes the maturity of an engineering field. For example, we can use to power a washing machine the same electric motor we use in a furnace fan and a reciprocating wood saw. However, notice that in the case of the electric motor, reusability is possible because of a high degree of standardization. For instance, different types of belts and pulleys are available off-the-shelf for adapting the motor to various devices. Also, the electric power is standardized so that the motor generates the same power and the same number of revolutions per minute in various applications.

The most important reason for promoting software reusability is that it reduces the cost of production. On the other hand, reusability of software components is often difficult to achieve because of a lack of standardization. For example, the search engine for a word processor may not be directly usable in another program because of variations in the data structures used for storing and formatting the text file. Also, a mathematical routine that calculates square root may not be reusable in another program because of variations in required precision or in numeric data formats.

Portability

Portability is related to the word *port*, which is a computer connection to the outside world. We say software is portable if we can transmit it through a port, usually to another machine. More generally, a program or part thereof is portable if it can execute in different hardware and software environments. Portability is an important economic issue because we need often to transfer programs to other machines and software environments. Java's portability makes it a popular programming language.

Measuring Software Qualities

One of the greatest challenges of software engineering is the measurement of the software attributes. It is relatively easy to state that a program must be robust and reliable and another matter to measure its robustness and reliability in predetermined units. If we have no exact way of measuring a particular software quality, it is difficult to determine if this quality is achieved in a particular case or to what degree this quality is present. Furthermore, to measure a quality precisely, we must first be able to accurately define it, which is not always an easy task.

Most engineering fields have standard metrics for measuring product quality. For example, we can compare the quality of two car batteries by means of the cold-cranking amps they are capable of delivering. On the other hand, nonengineered products typically lack quality measurements. In this sense, we cannot determine from the label on a videocassette the entertainment value of the movie it contains, nor are units of information specified in the jacket of a technical book. Software is also a field in which there are no universal quality metrics, although substantial work in this direction is in progress. The verification of program correctness directly relates to software quality metrics.

**20 Min.
To Go**

Principles of Software Engineering

We start this session on the assumption that software development is a creative activity and that programming is not an exact science. From this point of view, we may even consider the term software engineering unsuitable because we can speak of software development technique, which does not imply the rigor of a formal engineering approach.

Software engineering is the conventional name that groups the technical and scientific aspects of program development. In this sense, we must distinguish among *principles*, *techniques*, and *tools* of software engineering.

- Principles are general guidelines applicable at any stage of the program production process. They are abstract statements that describe desirable properties but are of little use in practical software development. For example, the principle that encourages program reliability does not tell us how to make a program reliable.
- Techniques, or methods, refer to a particular approach to solving a problem. Techniques help ensure that a product has desirable properties.
- Tools are specific resources used in implementing a technique.

We can state as a principle that floating-point numbers are a desirable format for representing decimals in a digital machine. Also, we can state that the floating-point techniques described in the ANSI standard 754 are suitable for our application and that we should be follow them. Finally, we can state that a particular library of floating-point routines, which complies with ANSI 754, is an adequate tool for implementing the mathematical functions our application requires. Figure 28-1 shows the relationship among principles, techniques, and tools of software engineering.

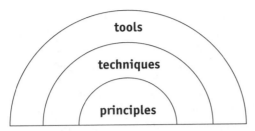

Figure 28-1
Relationship among principles, techniques, and tools

Over the years, we have identified several principles of software engineering. The most notable principles are rigor; separation of concerns; modularization; abstraction; malleability; maximum generalization; incremental development; and concurrent documentation.

Rigor

One of the drawbacks when we consider a program an art form is that we place emphasis on inspiration rather than on accuracy and precision; programming, however, is an applied art rather than a pure art. We may find it charming that Michelangelo planned his statue of David rather carelessly and ended up with insufficient marble for sculpturing the feet. To the contrary, a client may not be willing to forgive an artistic-minded programmer who does not find inspiration to implement hyphenation when developing a word processor program.

It is possible to distinguish several degrees of rigor. The highest degree, called formality or formal specifications, requires that we develop programs according to laws of mathematics and logic. A logical formalism allows the precise specification of software. Mathematical expressions, usually based on predicate calculus, allow representation of complete programs, or of program fragments, in symbolic expressions we can manipulate according to mathematical laws.

In programming practice, we must often settle for a degree of rigor that falls short of formal specifications. This approach, sometimes called semiformal specifications, is a methodology for program development based on following a sequence of well-defined steps. In this book, we use invariants to define abstract data types. We can consider invariants a form of semiformal specifications.

Separation of Concerns

When dealing with complex issues, we must analyze each facet. Because software development is an inherently complex activity, separation of concerns becomes a practical necessity. In any construction project, we immediately see three concerns or levels of activity: technical, managerial, and financial. Technical concerns refer to the technological and scientific part of the project; managerial concerns refer to project administration; financial concerns refer to monetary and fiscal activities.

We must realize that separation of concerns is a convenience for viewing the different aspects of a project. It is an analytical tool that does not necessarily imply a division in decision authority. Separation of concerns relates to separation of responsibilities and to specialization of labor.

Modularization

Modularization is a general-purpose mechanism for reducing complexity; it transcends programming languages and environments. Conceptualize modules as units of program division not necessarily equated to subroutines, subprograms, or disk files.

Modularization is an effective organizational tool. Usually, we identify two methods of modularization: the first, *top down,* decomposes a problem into subproblems we can tackle independently. The second, *bottom up,* builds a system starting with elementary components. The main advantage of modularization is that it makes the system understandable. However, we usually achieve understandability in stages during program development.

Modular cohesion refers to the relationship among the elements of a module. For example, a module in which the processing routines, procedures, and data structures are strongly related has high cohesion. Plugging into a module some unrelated function just because we can find no better place for it reduces the module's cohesion. M*odular coupling* refers to the relationship among modules in the same program. For example, if one module is heavily dependent on the procedures or data in another module, the modules are tightly coupled. Modules that have tight coupling are difficult to understand, analyze, and reuse separately; therefore, we usually consider tight coupling an undesirable property. A general principle is that a good modular structure has high cohesion and loose coupling.

Abstraction

A unique property of the mind is that it can reduce a problem's complexity by concentrating on a certain subset of its features while disregarding some of the details. For example, we can depict an automobile by observing its component parts: motor, transmission, chassis, body, and wheels. This functional abstraction, based on the tasks each component performs, ignores the details of other parts in the abstraction.

Malleability

We should not envision a program as a finished product but as a stage or phase in a never-ending development process. We can speak of a program as satisfying a certain set of requirements or as being ready for the market. To a software developer, a "finished program" does not exist. For a program to be finished, we must assume that it has no defects, that all present or future user requirements are perfectly satisfied, and that no improvements or modifications are necessary. Because we can never be sure of any of these conditions, we can never consider a program finished.

The fact that software products are fragile encourages the notion that we must design malleable software, which means that we must anticipate change. Change comes from two possible causes: program repair and evolution. A naive software developer does not know that program defects will be detected after the program's release or cannot anticipate that new requirements will be identified and that former requirements will change. Perhaps this inherent fragility distinguishes software from many other industrial products.

**10 Min.
To Go**

Maximum Generalization

The more generalized a software product, the larger the audience to which it appeals. The more generalized a program routine or procedure, the greater its possibilities for reusability. This implies the convenience of maximum generalization at the level of the application's design and the convenience of the routines, procedures, or modules. In these cases, the maximum generalization approach is based on trying to discover a more general problem equivalent to the current problem or a more general solution.

Incremental Development

Regarding software, incremental development refers to the creation of product subsets we can deliver to the customer for early evaluation and feedback. In reality, we can define very few software projects at the starting point. Therefore, it is often reasonable to divide program specification into progressive stages, perhaps associating each stage with a test version of the final product. One advantage of this method is that the customer gets to examine and evaluate several prototypes.

However, the incremental development method introduces new management and organizational problems because we define the project itself "on the fly." One issue we must address is the management of the documentation for each of the development stages as well as for the corresponding prototypes. A badly managed incremental development project can easily turn into disorder and anarchy.

Concurrent Documentation

One of the most important lessons of software engineering refers to the need for adequate and rigorous project documentation. The most notable difference between a correctly engineered development project and a haphazard effort is in documentation. Too often, programmers tend to consider program documentation a secondary problem, one that can be addressed once the project is finished. This tendency is probably traceable to the same human fallacy that makes some programmers believe they can insert comments into the code after programming concludes. As writing comments is part of the chore of programming, documentation is part of the task of program development. Comments and documentation cannot be approached as afterthoughts.

We can identify the following types of documentation:

- Written reports that mark the conclusion of a phase of the development cycle. We sometimes call these documents *deliverables* because we often present them to the client as each development phase concludes. Typical deliverables are the feasibility study, the analysis and requirements document, and the detailed design document.

- User manuals and training guides, which we can print or access online.

- Operations documents, more often in large computer environments, such as run-time schedules; input and output forms and media; delivery, routing, and distribution charts; data file specifications; update schedules; recovery procedures; and security controls.

- The project scrapbook, which we use to collect memos, schedules, meeting minutes, and other communications generated during the project.

The most important principle of project documentation is concurrency. Documentation must be a substantial part of the development effort and must take place with each development phase. However, documentation is often the development activity most easily postponed or even sacrificed by programmers and developers. When time is running short, it is tempting to defer documentation. At this point, the project manager must be aware that when documentation loses its concurrency, it also loses a great portion of its usefulness.

Done!

REVIEW

Software engineering is an attempt to solve the software crisis by providing a scientific method for program development. Although often we consider programming an art, we can develop programs by following a rigorous methodology. Software qualities can be internal or external. These qualities are correctness; reliability; efficiency; verifiability; maintainability; user friendliness; reusability; and portability.

We identify several solid principles of software engineering. These principles are rigor; separation of concerns; modularization; abstraction; malleability; maximum generalization; incremental development; and concurrent documentation.

QUIZ YOURSELF

1. List two fallacies that often result from adopting a conventional approach to software development. (See "Software Engineering.")

2. What are some of the advantages and disadvantages that result from the malleability of software? (See "Software Characteristics.")

3. Describe four software qualities. (See "Software Qualities.")

4. What is the difference among the principles, techniques, and tools we use in software engineering? (See "Principles of Software Engineering.")

5. What are the ideal cohesion and coupling in a program module? (See "Modularization.")

Application Development Techniques

Session Checklist

✔ Object-oriented analysis

✔ Modeling the problem domain and system responsibilities

✔ Managing complexity

✔ Class and object decomposition

✔ Searching for objects

✔ Neat and dirty classes

**30 Min.
To Go**

In Session 11, we discuss the fundamentals of object orientation and develop modeling tools for classes and objects. Armed with these tools, a basic knowledge of the Java programming language, and the fundamentals of software engineering, we now attempt to put everything together in the design of a Java application. Be warned that the task is not a trivial one. Object-oriented analysis is a complex specialty field of object-oriented programming. It is possible to devote your entire career to this specialty. The presentation here is merely a tour of the fundamentals.

Object-Oriented Analysis

Both major programming paradigms (structured programming and object orientation) started with the development of programming languages. Later, these models were extended to software design and finally to analysis. This implies that the maturity of a programming model coincides with the advent of a system-analysis methodology. In regard to object-oriented systems, full-featured programming languages were already available in the late '70s and early '80s. System design discussions started at about that time, although the object-oriented analysis methodologies are a product of the late '80s and early '90s.

Object-oriented analysis provides a practical methodology for project modeling during the analysis phase. At this stage, the system analyst starts by critically evaluating whether a project gains from using an object-oriented approach. It is generally accepted that the greatest benefits of object-orientation result when the methodology permeates the entire development process; in other words, we achieve the best results when we analyze and design the application by using object-oriented tools and then code the application in an object-oriented language. A decision to use object-oriented analysis implies that we also follow object orientation in the design phase and that we code the program in an object-oriented programming language. Paradigm mixing, although theoretically possible, is usually not a good idea.

Modeling the Problem-Domain

Object orientation's main justification is that it provides a reasonable way of modeling the problem-domain. Other advantages of object orientation are that it makes modeling complex systems possible, facilitates building systems that are more flexible and adaptable, and promotes reusability. Object-oriented analysis is a problem-set modeling tool.

One of the predicaments of software development is that the programmer must become an expert in the domain field. Someone contracted to develop an air-traffic control system has to learn about radar, air-to-ground communications, emergency response systems, a flight scheduling, and a multitude of other technical and business topics related to the activity at hand. How much knowledge the analyst must acquire and to what technical level this knowledge must extend is difficult to determine. Many projects fail because developers do not grasp important details of the problem set. The urge to "get on with the coding" often works against us at this stage.

A tool that facilitates the learning stage of a software development project is indeed a valuable one. Once analysts grasp the necessary knowledge, they can transmit this information to other members of the development team. At the end, analysts must present the model of the proposed solution-set to clients, users, or higher-level managers for their validation and feedback. A model that facilitates this communication among clients and developers is an additional asset.

System Responsibilities

Usually, we begin object-oriented analysis by defining the system's responsibilities. The analysis of an air-traffic control system starts with determining what functions and operations are within the system's burden. Does the air-traffic control system have the obligation of informing commercial airlines of delays in arrivals or departures of aircraft? How does the air-traffic control system interface with the emergency response mechanisms at the airport? At what point does the tracking of an aircraft become the responsibility of a particular air-traffic control system, and when does this responsibility cease? A system's responsibilities refer to what a system should do. Answering this question is one of the fundamental tasks of object-oriented analysis. Questions related to how a system operates are left for the design and coding phases.

Managing Complexity

The analysis phase is necessary because natural systems are often elaborate and complicated, which means that they are difficult to understand or manage. Object-oriented analysis provides a toolset for managing complexity. This toolset is based on topics with which you are already familiar: abstraction, encapsulation, inheritance, and message passing. We now briefly review these concepts.

Abstraction

Abstraction consists of eliminating what is superfluous or trivial and concentrating on what is fundamental. A definition is an exercise in abstraction. We make an abstraction when we say that a fountain pen is a hand-held writing instrument that uses liquid ink, an ink discharge mechanism, and a fine tracing point. The description attempts to collect the fundamental attributes of a fountain pen that distinguish it from a typewriter, a ball-point pen, and a pencil. However, it ignores the less important features such as the pen's color, the color of the ink, the instrument's exact dimensions, and its design or style.

In object-oriented analysis, abstraction refers to the class mechanism that simultaneously provides procedural and data abstraction. In other words, the object-oriented notion of a class is an abstraction that represents both processing operations and the data elements of the problem set.

Encapsulation

In the object-oriented approach, we relate encapsulation to the notion of attributes and methods we package together by means of the class construct. The methods visible outside the class are its interface. The principal purpose of encapsulation is hiding the implementation details yet stressing the interface.

Inheritance

Inheritance relates to the possibility of one class accessing the public members of a super class. Class inheritance promotes the highest level of abstraction, reduces code size, and simplifies programming. The result is a class hierarchy that goes from the most general to the most specific. Typically, a derived class incorporates all the features of its parent classes and adds unique features.

Message passing

Object-oriented systems access processing functions by means of a mechanism called message passing. One of the disadvantages of hard-coded program structures such as jump tables, cascaded if statements, or case constructs is that we must update them with every program modification or change. The message passing mechanism, on the other hand, automatically directs execution to the appropriate member function. This functionality brings about two major advantages: First, we avoid introducing new defects into code we have tested and debugged. Second, we can expand a system by supplying relatively small modules that contain the new functions.

**20 Min.
To Go**

Class and Object Decomposition

Becoming an object-oriented analyst starts by learning to think in terms of classes and objects. We must free our minds of concern about algorithms, programming structures, or any other implementation issues. Our task during analysis is to model the problem-domain and to define the system's responsibilities. We accomplish both purposes by means of class and object decomposition.

Consider an object an abstraction of a discrete element in the problem domain. An object is characterized by an identity the system can preserve. Therefore, each object must have a uniqueness that allows its identification. Every object belongs to a class of objects.

A class is a description of a set of unique attributes and methods associated with an object type. In this sense, an object is an instance of a class. An abstract class is a description of an interface that lacks implementation. Its fundamental purpose is to define an inheritance path. We cannot instantiate objects from an abstract class.

In the modeling process, do we start by thinking of objects or classes? It is a matter of semantics, but, strictly speaking, an object is a run-time construct, and a class is an abstraction that groups common attributes and methods for an object type. Therefore, it appears that we should think of object types or classes rather than of possible instantiations. On the other hand, the concept of a class of objects requires that we visualize a typical object. Suppose we are attempting to model a system that uses a window to display text messages. To define the text message window type, we must first imagine what the object looks like. Figure 29-1 shows what may be our initial visualization of a text window object.

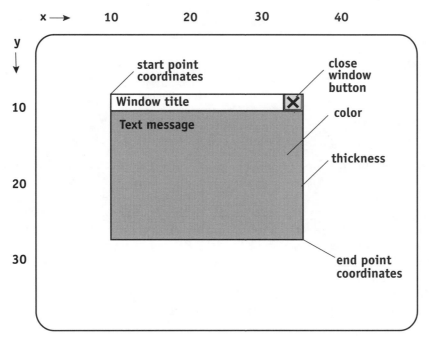

Figure 29-1
Visualizing a text window object

Once we vizualize the object, we can deduce the attributes and methods of the object itself and the class that represents it. For example, start and end coordinates define screen location and object size. The object also has border thickness and a color. Its text attributes are the window's title and its text. A control button on the top right corner enables us to destroy the text message window. We can associate three methods with this object: one to display the window, one to report its current status, and one to destroy it. Using class diagrams, we can represent the object type TextWindow to any degree of detail. The left-hand diagram in Figure 29-2 merely states an object class named TextWindow, although its attributes and methods are undefined. The diagram on the right shows the specific attributes and methods.

TextWindow

TextWindow
startX
startY
endX
endY
color
thickness
windowTitle
textMessage
status
drawWindow()
returnStatus()
destroyWindow()

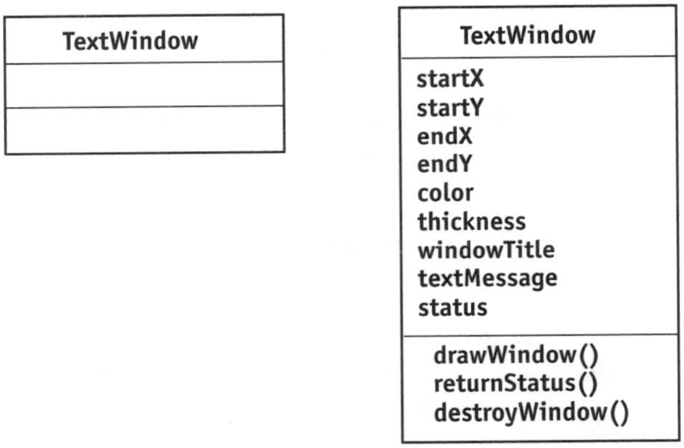

Figure 29-2
Class diagrams for a text window object

It is common practice to make the class name a singular noun or an adjective followed by a noun. It is also a good idea to use the client's standard vocabulary when naming classes. During the analysis phase, we can enter the class name by using any reasonable style of spacing and capitalization. However, if our class names are not compatible with the syntax we use in the design and coding phases, we must modify these names at a later date. Because any modification can be a source of errors, it is better to name classes, attributes, and methods by using a style consistent with the programming environment.

Simplified class diagrams, in which attributes and methods are not explicitly listed, are useful when we show class relations and inheritance structures, such as a system with two types of window objects: one representing windows that contain nothing but text and a second that includes a bitmap (graphic). We can designate the first type as a TextWindow and the second as a GraphicWindow. We can depict the class structure in the class diagram in Figure 29-3.

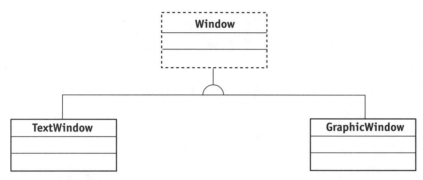

Figure 29-3
Inheritance diagram for window-type classes

In Figure 29-3, TextWindow is a subclass of Window, as is GraphicWindow. Window is an abstract class. We can instantiate objects of type TextWindow or of type GraphicWindow; but Window objects cannot exist because the abstract nature of the base class precludes this possibility. A more detailed diagram of the classes is in Figure 29-4.

We use italics to identify abstract methods in Figure 29-4. This is consistent with the Coad/Yourdon notation.

In Figure 29-4, a GraphicWindow class is a subclass of Window that adds functionality to the base class. The new functionality is in the form of three new attributes that locate the bitmap on the viewport and a new method to draw the bitmap. The programmer defines the basic coordinates and characteristics of the window itself in the base class because these attributes apply to any Window object.

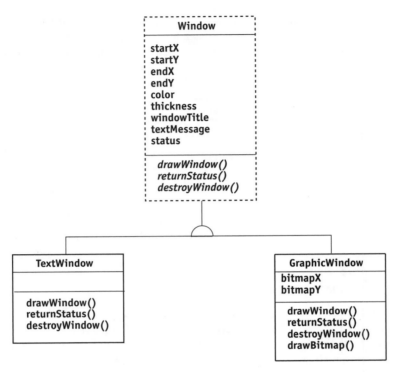

Figure 29-4
Refined diagram for window-type classes

**10 Min.
To Go**

Searching for Objects

The search for objects should not begin until we gain familiarity with the problem domain. It is futile to attempt to identify objects and classes in an unfamiliar technology. The following are the main sources of information about a problem domain:

- Published materials and the Internet
- Firsthand observation
- Consultation with domain experts
- Client documents

Firsthand observation consists of familiarizing ourselves with a system by participating in its operation. For example, to analyze an air-traffic control system, we may begin by sitting in the air-traffic control tower for several days while observing air-traffic controllers in action. Domain experts are often the source of valuable and unique information. Many systems are totally or partially unpublished, part of trade or government secret, or confidential. In these cases, published materials may be of little use. Our only option is to locate individuals with knowledge and expertise and to have them describe or explain the system to us. Client documentation can also be a valuable source of information.

Neat and Dirty Classes

Sometimes classification is a clear and neat process, but not always. When conceptual objects correspond to real-world objects, the classification process is often simple and straightforward. For example, to define a mini CAD program, the classification can be relatively uncomplicated. In such a case, the screen objects give rise to classes, such as drawings composed of lines, curves, geometrical figures, and text. On the other hand, classification may be somewhat less clear when the task is to design an editor or word processing program. In this case, we may start thinking of program operations as objects. But is it reasonable to consider operations such as inserting, replacing, and deleting text physical objects? What about the user's text file? Other projects may be even more difficult to classify. For example, consider the task of designing and coding a virus-detection utility. Can we consider the viruses objects? Does this mean that if we find no viruses the program executes without instantiation? Is the search itself an object? In many cases, any classification we develop is probably unsatisfactory, and the classes themselves are probably untidy and unreal. We may better handle this type of case outside of object orientation.

Done!

REVIEW

Object-oriented analysis is a modeling tool we use in the development of major software applications. The process usually begins by defining the system's responsibilities. Analysis manages complexity by means of abstraction, encapsulation, inheritance, and message passing.

The analyst's main task is to locate the classes and objects in the problem domain. The first step is usually to gain familiarity with the problem domain by using the following resources: published materials, firsthand observation, consulting with domain experts, and information in the client's documents. Finding classes and objects usually consists of searching the following options: class associations;

mechanisms and devices; related systems; preserved data; roles played; sites; organizational units.

Once we define a model, it is a good idea to test its validity by making sure of the following conditions: there is information to remember about the object; the class provides processing operations; there are several associated attributes; more than one object instantiates from the class; the attributes and methods are always applicable; the objects relate to the problem domain; the processing is not a simple calculation or derivation. Subsystems serve to manage extreme complexity in major projects. It is often possible to equate a subsystem with a program module.

Quiz Yourself

1. When do we derive the greatest benefits from object-oriented analysis? (See "Object-Oriented Analysis.")
2. What is one of the programmer's greatest predicaments? (See "Modeling the Problem Domain.")
3. What are the system's responsibilities? (See "System Responsibilities.")
4. List three topics related to managing complexity. (See "Managing Complexity.")
5. List three sources of information about the problem domain. (See "Searching for Objects.")

Program Testing and Debugging

Session Checklist

✔ The art of software testing: formal approaches

✔ Testing techniques: designing the test cases; black box and white box methods

✔ Debugging Java programs and console-based programs

✔ The JDB debugger and JDB commands

✔ Sample debugging session

30 Min.
To Go

Unfortunately, the one certain fact about any computer program is that, at some time or another, it fails. In spite of the inherent fragility of software, very often we underestimate the importance of solid verification, correction, and maintenance methods. In the PC field, program verification and testing often become an afterthought in the development process, which means that programs are distributed by their vendors with less than optimal quality and reliability. In this session, we briefly discuss software quality assurance methods and the debugging tools and techniques available in Java.

The Art of Software Testing

Ascertaining and proving program correctness is one of the core topics of software engineering. Software quality is the result of using reliable development techniques in the analysis, design, coding, and testing phases of program development; it is also the result of adopting a development methodology in which software quality assurance plays a central role. We cannot take software quality for granted. To ensure quality, development methodology must include the following elements:

- The application of technical reviews at critical points in the development process.
- Multitiered testing strategies in which different channels use various testing procedures to check the program's features.
- A rigorous approach to software documentation that includes keeping detailed records of program changes and corrections.
- The adoption of reliable methods of program development.

To summarize, we ensure software quality by using reliable development methods and techniques and by ensuring that the product is sufficiently tested before we deploy it. The two golden rules of software quality assurance are:

- It is easier to prevent a software defect than to remove it.
- It is cheaper to fix a defect during program development than after we release it.

Formal Approaches

Several formal approaches to software quality assurance have been proposed in the literature. The defenders of formal specification methods argue that a program is a mathematical object, that the semantics and syntax of a programming language make it possible to rigorously specify program functions. Once we formally specify a program, we can mathematically prove its correctness.

Another formal approach to software quality is based on statistics. In this approach, the program development organization first collects and categorizes information about software defects in its products. The organization then traces each defect to its underlying cause (for example, design error, noncompliance with standards, or specification defect). Once the organization identifies the most important causes of defects, called the *vital few*, it applies the necessary corrective measures to the development methodology so that these defects do not occur in future products.

Formal specification and verification methods and the statistical approach to software quality assurance are combined by some authors, in what we call the *cleanroom process*. In this model, developers use mathematical proofs of correctness in place of program debugging. They determine software quality statistically and identify the cause of errors. They repeat the process until they reduce the number of defects to an acceptable limit.

Testing Techniques

The principal tool for ensuring software quality is program testing. Most beginning programmers underestimate the importance of program testing as well as the time expenditure involved. It is not unusual in a commercial software project to spend 40 percent of total project time on testing and verification. In some critical or potentially dangerous applications, testing and verification can consume three to five times as much time and resources as all other development phases combined.

An often overlooked element in software testing relates to the developer's psychology. Programmers are creative people; discovering a defect in their software product is a way of destroying their creation. Therefore, it is instinctive to avoid testing. When programmers do test their own software, they usually test it in a way that minimizes the possibility of finding errors. Because finding program defects is precisely what testing is about, testing your own software is often a self-defeating proposition. Of all the possible testers for a software product, the programmer or programmers who create it are usually the least suitable.

In designing a program-testing strategy, keep in mind that the purpose of testing is uncovering unidentified program defects. A successful test is not one in which we uncover no defects but one in which we discover a maximum number of errors with minimal effort and time expenditure. We should design tests according to program specifications since their principal purpose is to demonstrate that software conforms to its specifications. A common process usually follows a spiral pattern, as follows:

- We design and apply tests.
- We correct defects and evaluate program quality. Testing then resumes at step 1.
- If we detect no further defects, the program's quality and reliability are acceptable, or the tests are inadequate.

Designing the Test Cases

The most important consideration in designing test cases is to follow a systematic approach that makes no assumptions regarding program correctness. It is dangerous to assume that a program function or execution path, because of its simplicity or straightforwardness, does not require testing. We can develop test cases according to two approaches: *black box* and *white box* testing. In most cases, both methods are required.

Black Box Testing

In black box testing, we develop the test cases taking into account the functions that the program is designed to perform. The term "black box" refers to the fact that in this testing mode the program internals are completely ignored in the test. The black box testing protocol is usually based on the program's specifications and on the details of the user interface. Access to the source code is not necessary in black box testing.

The test cases in black box testing are the set of input conditions that exercise all program functions and test all of its functional requirements. The black box tests usually reveal the following type of errors:

- Incorrectly implemented or missing program functions.
- Errors in the user interface.
- Errors in data management, data structures, or data storage functions.
- Performance errors.
- Errors in initialization or termination functions.
- Typographical errors in coding.

Typically, we apply black box testing at the latter stages of program development.

White Box Testing

White box testing is based on the internal workings of the software product. In this case, we derive the testing protocol by observing the program's operation and by following the source code. Software testers design test cases to ensure the following optimal conditions:

1. We have exercised all execution paths at least once.
2. We have tested all logical decisions for their true and false options.

3. We have executed all loops at their operational bounds.

4. We have validated all internal data structures.

In theory, white box testing should lead to programs that are 100 percent correct. If we exercise all possible logical paths of execution of a program and evaluate the results as correct, program logic is flawless. In reality, even in simple processing routines, it is practically impossible to test all possible options. Pressman, in his *book Software Engineering: A Practitioner's Approach,* shows a simple processing routine with five decisions in a loop that performs no more than 20 iterations. The result is a number of paths that take 3170 years to test even if we can evaluate each processing option in one millisecond.

On the other hand, white box testing reveals defects that black box methods often miss. Black box tests are taken from the program's mainstream; however, program errors often creep in while processing unusual or unanticipated cases. Program flow is not always intuitive. Unconscious black box assumptions often lead to untested paths that can hide catastrophic errors.

Debugging Java Programs

It has been often related in the literature that in the early days of computing, Grace Hopper was attempting to find a program defect and found a moth caught between the contacts of an electromechanical relay. Since then, we have used the word "bug" to refer to a computer software or hardware error. For the same reason, we call finding and correcting bugs *debugging*, and a *debugger* is a software tool that helps locate program defects.

Debugging is an art that every successful programmer must master sooner rather than later because program bugs often appear almost as soon as coding starts. In the simple programs we have developed so far in this book, we can often accomplish successful debugging by critically reading the source code. Many bugs are the result of simple typographical errors, and we can correct them as soon as we detect them. In addition, the Java compiler detects syntax errors in the code. We can use the compiler error messages to correct these errors. Furthermore, a well-designed program should contain exception handlers to catch common error conditions during input and output, as well as to catch fundamental processing problems. In this sense, the exception handler routines debug our code.

This discussion does not deal with simple program errors such as typos, elementary programming mistakes the compiler detects, or elementary error conditions our exception handlers report. Real debugging takes place when the program error is beyond these basic causes. In many cases, a program that compiles correctly and raises no exceptions can still produce incorrect results. Often, we can run over each line of code many times and still not see the reason for the malfunction. Here debugging tools and techniques must earn their worth.

Debugging Console Applications

Often, we can debug programs that output to the console by using the time-honored method of including print statements to display the values of local variables or class fields. The method is a simple as it is useful. For example, a program manipulates the variables x, y, and z in performing a calculation. We can inspect the value of these variables at any place in the code by inserting the following statements:

```
System.out.println("x = " + x);
System.out.println("y = " + y);
System.out.println("z = " + z);
```

We can use similar code to display the values of entire arrays or all the data fields of a class. The main objections to this debugging method are that we must continually make changes to the source and that we must remove print statements or comment them out when we finish debugging. Furthermore, private fields are only visible inside the class that contains them, which forces us to place print statements accordingly.

**10 Min.
To Go**

The JDB Debugger

Debugging based on print statements to display the value of local variables and class fields is not suitable for graphics applications. Furthermore, we can simplify debugging console-based applications by using tools that facilitate inspecting the values of variables, stopping program execution at any point in the code (called a breakpoint), and executing java code line-by-line (called single-stepping). These are the fundamental functions a commercial debugger performs.

Java includes a debugger program named the JDB. The JDB is dual-purpose. In the first place, it is a debugging tool that allows us to inspect variables, set breakpoints, and run programs in single-step mode, among other debugging functions. Additionally, the **sun.tools.debug** package of the JDB includes classes for developing customized debugger programs. In this session, we discuss the JDB debugger tool only. Writing your own debugger programs is beyond the scope of this book.

Using JDB

JDB is a command-line debugger modeled after the DBX debugger popular in UNIX systems. The JDB is an application that we execute from the MS DOS command line. We must compile applications we debug with the JDB with the -g option. For example, to compile the **VectorGraphics.java** program, developed in Session 27, so we can debug it with JDB, enter the following command:

```
javac -g VectorGraphics.java
```

The resulting class file contains information visible to the JDB debugger. Now you can launch the debugger and specify the **VectorGraphics.java** program as a debugging target, or you can launch the JDB debugger and later load the class file. In the first case, enter the following command:

```
jdb VectorGraphics
```

In the JDB, a breakpoint is a location in the source code where we can suspend program execution. Breakpoints are a powerful debugging tool because they allow us to examine variables at critical points in the code. Single-stepping is executing a program, or a portion of a program, line-by-line. This allows progressing through the code one statement at a time to locate problems.

JDB Commands

The current version of JDB has 33 commands we can enter from the MS DOS prompt. Table 30-1 lists a few of these commands.

 We exclude the thread-related JDB command because we do not cover threads in this book.

Table 30-1
Most Used JDB Commands

Command	Function
help (or ?)	Displays the documented commands JDB supports.
exit (or quit)	Terminates a debugging session.

Continued

Table 30-1 *Continued*

Command	Function
memory	Displays the amount of free and used memory in the remote Java Virtual Machine.
!!	Repeats the last command.
load	Loads a class into the debugger.
run	Starts execution of a loaded class.
use	Displays or changes the source path.
classes	Lists classes currently known to JDB.
dump	Displays all information for a thread, variable, class, field, or argument.
list	Displays source lines.
locals	Prints all current local variables.
print	Displays information for a thread, variable, class, field, or argument.
methods	Lists the class' methods.
stop in class.method	Sets a breakpoint at the first bytecode of a method.
stop at class:line	Sets a breakpoint at a line in the source code of the class.
clear	Removes all existing breakpoints.
clear class:line	Clears a specific breakpoint.
where	Displays the call stack.
step	Executes the current line.
next	Executes the next line. Method calls are not single-stepped.
cont	Continues execution from breakpoint.
gc	Collects garbage and frees unused objects.

A Sample Debugging Session

A preliminary consideration in debugging is using an editor program that displays line- number information. This facilitates finding specific lines in the source code. The Shareware editor on this book's CD-ROM greatly simplifies finding the program line. Line numbers start with the first line in the source file as number 1. All program lines are numbered, including those that are comments. The line the editor program displays is usually the line on which we place the editor's cursor.

Most debugging sessions open several command windows simultaneously. One window usually contains the editor program, loaded with the source code of the file we are debugging. A second window contains the JDB debugger. During debugging, we must execute the offending program. This creates a third program window on the desktop. Working with multiple windows in a debugging session is an easy skill to master.

A more advanced debugging technique consists of running the JDB in one window and the class file in another window. We accomplish this by using the -debug **option when we execute the Java Virtual Machine (JVM).**

The first step in preparing a program for debugging is compiling it with the -g switch. This option creates a file the JDB program uses that includes variable names and line number information.

Once we prepare the class file for debugging, the next step is executing JDB. You can reference the class file as a command tail, or you can execute the debugger and later use the load command described in Table 30-1. Figure 30-1 is a screen snapshot of the commands we use to create a debugging session.

Figure 30-1
Screen Snapshot of a JDB Debugging Session

The most common debugging technique consists of placing a breakpoint in a source line where we want to investigate the state of variables or the visual appearance of the output screen. To set a breakpoint, we must first start a JDB session with the class file under investigation. We must place the breakpoint in a code line. Placing a breakpoint in a line that contains a comment results in a JDB error message.

For example, if we are debugging the **VectorGraphics.java** program developed in Session 27, we can set a breakpoint on line 56. A portion of the **VectorGraphics.java** source file that contains source line 56 is as follows:

```
. . .
// Create and set a shade of blue
Color aBlue = new Color(0, 0, 255);
g.setColor(aBlue);
// Draw a filled oval
g.fillOval(50, 60, 200, 100);

// Draw a black-border rectangle
Color aBlack = new Color(0, 0, 0);
g.setColor(aBlack);                    // <= code line 56
g.drawRect(30, 180, 200, 50);

// Draw a green polygon
Color aGreen = new Color(0, 180,0);
g.setColor(aGreen);
g.drawPolygon(xCoords, yCoords, 4);

// Translate the image by adding 120 to the
// y coordinates of the polygon
for(int x = 0; x < 4; x++)
    yCoords[x] = yCoords[x] + 120;

// Fill the translated polygon
g.fillPolygon(xCoords, yCoords, 4);
. . .
```

The command for setting the breakpoint on line 56 is as follows:

```
stop at VectorGraphics:56
```

To which the JDB responds:

```
Breakpoint set at VectorGraphics:56
```

Once we set the breakpoint, the debugger executes the program until it reaches the marked source line. We accomplish this with the run command, as follows:

```
run VectorGraphics
```

The debugger executes the VectorGraphics class file until it reaches the breakpoint line. At this point, the program's thread stops and execution returns to the debugging session. We can now use debugger commands to inspect variables or other data elements, and we can check the displayed program to make sure that output is as we expect. For example, to see the value of the color object named aBlue, we can type:

```
print aBlue
```

The JDB responds by listing the value associated with the object at this point in the code, which in this case is as follows:

```
aBlue = java.awt.Color[r=0,g=0,b=255]
```

We can also use the print command to display the value of a local or global variable. For example, to inspect the current value of index number 1 in the global array xCoords[],we can type the following:

```
print xCoords[1]
```

To which the JDB responds:

```
xCoords[1] = 500
```

Done!

We can use the locals commands to display the value of all local variables simultaneously.

REVIEW

One of the most important phases of software development is making certain the application performs correctly and executes all the functions in its specifications. Software engineering shows it is easier to prevent program defects than to correct them, and it is better to fix problems during development than after we release the application. Formal approaches to software quality assurance assume that a program is a mathematical object we can rigorously specify. If so, we can logically prove program correctness. The statistical approach is based on finding the most common causes for program defects and applying the necessary corrections. Formal methods and the statistical approach are combined in the *cleanroom* process.

Testing techniques require developing a testing strategy and designing the test cases we use. In *black box* testing, we select the test cases taking into account the program's design and specifications. In this case, access to the source code is not required. *White box* testing is based on making sure that the program routines and algorithms execute as we expect. White box testing requires access to the source code. A good testing strategy usually combines both black box and white box techniques.

Effective debugging is a skill every programmer must master. Sometimes, we can debug Java console-based applications by introducing `print` statements in the source code. These statements display the values of local variables and objects, thus allowing the detection and correction of program defects. We cannot easily debug graphical programs with this method. JDB is a command-line debugger available in the Java JDK. We can use JDB to execute an application under the debugger's control. It allows us to insert breakpoints and inspect program data.

Quiz Yourself

1. List three elements that ensure software quality. (See "The Art of Software Testing.")

2. What are the golden rules of software quality assurance? (See "The Art of Software Testing.")

3. What is the main advantage of the formal specifications method of software quality assurance? (See "Formal Approaches.")

4. Describe the difference between white box and black box testing methods. (See "Testing Techniques.")

5.   List three optimal conditions that white box testing cases should ensure. (See "White Box Testing.")

PART

VI

Sunday Afternoon
Part Review

1. Explain one difference between vector and raster graphics.
2. Write a Java statement that translates the frame origin from the frame to the client area.
3. Write an expression in RGB format that produces a light-gray shade.
4. List three vector graphics methods in the Java Graphics class.
5. Write a Java expression to draw a straight line from coordinates x = 50, y = 75 to coordinates x = 200, y = 250.
6. List two fallacies that often result from adopting a conventional approach to software development.
7. What are some of the advantages and disadvantages that result from the malleability of software?
8. Describe four software qualities.
9. What are the differences among the principles, techniques, and tools we use in software engineering?
10. What are the ideal cohesion and coupling in a program module?
11. When do we derive the greatest benefits from object-oriented analysis?
12. What is one of the programmer's greatest predicaments?
13. What are the system's responsibilities?
14. List three topics related to managing software complexity.
15. List three sources of information about the problem domain.
16. List three elements that ensure software quality.

17. What are the golden rules of software quality assurance?

18. What is the main advantage of the formal-specifications method of software- quality assurance?

19. Describe one difference between white box and black box testing methods.

20. List three optimal conditions that white box testing cases should ensure.

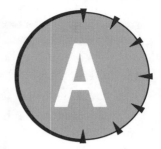

Answers to Part Reviews

Friday Evening Review Answers

1. Because of its timeliness and portability.

2. That applications would be machine-independent.

3. **a.** Both languages use similar syntax.

   b. Both languages are strongly-typed.

4. Answer can vary.

5. Answer can vary.

6. Answer can vary.

7. Answer can vary.

8. Answer can vary.

9. Answer can vary.

10. Yes.

11. In general, Java ignores white space characters.

12. **a.** Grouping : { }/

    b. Comment: //, /*, and */

13. Answer can vary.

14. Each column of digits has a specific weight.

15. **a.** 11001111 = CF hexadecimal

    b. 00111100 = 3C hexadecimal

    c. 00001101 = 0D hexadecimal

16. **a.** Eight.

    b. Two.

    c. 1024.

17. There are two encodings for zero, and machine arithmetic is complicated.

18. **a.** 12.3344 = 1.23344 E1

    b. .0000456 = 4.56 E-5

    c. 12345 = 1.2345 E4

19. The ; symbol.

20. The program name, the name of the author or authors, and the date of program creation.

Saturday Morning Review Answers

1. int, short, long, byte, float, double, char, and boolean.

2. Identifiers are case sensitive, must start with a letter, cannot contain symbols (except $ and _), and cannot contain spaces.

3. Numeric, character, and boolean types.

4. ```
   double decNumber = 1.2233;
       int wholeValue = (int) decNumber;
   ```

5. See the program Exercise6-1.java on the book's CD-ROM.

6. See the program Exercise6-1.java on the book's CD-ROM.

7. See the program Exercise6-3.java on the book's CD-ROM.

8. Assigns the value of the expression to the right of the = sign to the variable to the left of the = sign.

9. Only a variable name.

10. The operators are +, -, *, /, and %. The remainder operator returns the remainder of an integer division.

11. The + operator.

12. x++;
   ```

13. A computer can make simple decisions.

14.   `if(age > 12 && age < 20)`
         `System.out.println("is a teenager");`

15. By nesting the second `if` statement in the first one.

16. To provide a processing alternative in cases in which the `if` statement is false.

17. The do-while loop ensures that the loop routine executes at least once.

18. Float average(double a, double b, double c double d).

19. The modifier sets the properties for the method.

20. Yes.

Saturday Afternoon Review Answers

1. In the work of Nygaard and Dahl at the Norwegian Computing Center.

2. No.

3. The attributes.

4. Inheritance.

5. In the driving class.

6. By noting if the variable is declared outside methods. Variables declared outside all methods are field variables. Variables declared inside methods are method variables.

7. Numeric variables are set to zero, strings are set to null, and boolean variables are set to false.

8. Overloading produces static polymorphism, and overriding produces dynamic binding.

9. When two methods have the same name.

10. Abstract.

11. Yes.

12. **a.** A class can access the public members of another class.

    b. An object can be a member of a class.

    c. A class can instantiate an object of another class.

13. Is-a-kind-of relationship.

14. Yes.

15. Prolog, Pascal, and C.

16. The activation record.

17. `if y = 0 then x^y = 1`
    `    x^y = x + x^(y-1)`

18. No.

19. No Java operator creates a clone. You must use the clone() method of the Object class.

20. The rules that determine how the instance variables are managed.

Saturday Evening Review Answers

1. In a linked list, each element contains a reference to the next element in the list.

2. **a.** The integer variable data holds the node's data element.

   b. The link component is null for the last node in a list; otherwise, the link element references the next node.

3. Accessor methods to get the data and link elements, and mutator methods to change the data and the link elements.

4. **a.** IntNode head holds the address of the first node in the list. Mutator methods must always update this object.

   b. numNodes is a convenience counter so that code does not need to traverse the list to determine the number of elements.

5. Methods for traversing the list, for inserting an element into the list, and for deleting an element from the list.

6. PUSH and POP.

7. Last-In-First-Out.

8. **a.** IntNode top holds the address of the first node in the stack. Mutator methods must always update this variable.

   b. stackSize records the number of elements in the stack. Mutator methods must always update this variable.

9. If we store a node at offset [i], the left child (if it exists) is at offset [2i + 1], and the right child (if it exists) is at offset [2i + 2].

10. Hardware errors, software errors, and algorithmic errors.

11. Errors in binary-to-decimal conversions.

12. **a.** An error takes place.

    b. The error is detected, and an exception is raised.

    c. An exception handler provides and error response.

13. Throw, try, and catch.

14. Throws.

15. English, Spanish, French, and Italian.

16. Byte-based I/O relates to input and output streams. Character-based I/O relates to readers and writers.

17. Input stream and output stream.

18. To obtain a byte of data from the current input stream.

19. To write a byte to the current output stream.

20. Input, output, and error.

Sunday Morning Review Answers

1. To files and network connections.

2. **a.** Use only ASCII characters.

   b. Begin the filename with an alphanumeric character.

   c. Keep names to less than 32 characters.

3. .exe, .com, .txt, .c, bat. and .h.

4. Readers and writers are character based.

5. FileWriter, OutputStreamWriter, and PrintWriter.

6. Better performance.

7. They are easier to code, but they hide intermediate objects.

8. It is the number-formatting style a local culture, language, script, or social group uses.

9. Allows code to break a string into its blocked fields by using one or more separator tokens.

10. Graphical User Interface.

11. By means of operating-system services.

12. Buttons, scrollbars, sliders, menus.

13. Applets execute within a Web browser program. Applications are stand-alone programs the Java interpreter executes.

14. Graphics in a GUI environment.

15. The client area, the window's title bar, and the window's border.

16. No.

17. WindowAdapter and ActiveFrame classes.

18. An object of the Graphics class.

19. Yes.

20. By redefining the paint() method.

Sunday Afternoon Review Answers

1. In vector graphics, an image is described mathematically; in raster graphics, an image is described in terms of its individual dots.

2. `g.translate(getInsets().left, getInsets().top);`

3. `g.setColor(new Color(80, 80, 80);`

4. **a.** fillPolygon()

    b. drawRect()

    c. drawOval()

5. `drawLine(50, 75, 200, 250);`

6. **a.** A task that takes one programmer one year to code can be accomplished by four programmers in approximately three months.

    b. If a single programmer produces a software product with a quality value of 25, four programmers can create a product with a quality value of 100.

7. Errors are easier to fix, but modifying a program often introduces side effects you do not anticipate.

8. Correctness, reliability, robustness, and efficiency.

9. A principle is a general guideline; a technique is an approach to solving a problem; a tool is a specific resource.

10. A module should show high cohesion and low coupling.

11. When modeling a complex system that is to be coded in object-oriented language.

12. That programmers must become experts in the field.

13. What a system should do.

14. Abstraction, encapsulation, and inheritance.

15. Published materials, firsthand observation, consulting with domain experts.

16. **a.** Technical reviews at critical points in the development process.

    b. Multitiered testing strategies.

    c. A rigorous approach to documentation.

17. **a.** It is easier to prevent a defect than to correct it.

    b. It is cheaper to fix a defect during program development than after the product is released.

18. One a program has been formally specified, its correctness can be mathematically proved.

19. In black-box testing, the text cases are developed based on the functions that the program is designed to perform. White box testing is based on the product's internal workings.

20. **a.** That all execution paths have been exercised at least once.

    b. That all logical decisions have been tested for their true and false values.

    c. That all loops have been executed at their operational bounds.

What's on the CD-ROM

The CD-ROM that accompanies this book contains the following:

- The sample programs developed or discussed in the text.
- Several shareware editors suitable for Java programming.
- A self-assessment test to help you measure how much you have learned.

System Requirements

The following are the system requirements for running the CD-ROM:

- A PC with a 486/DX or faster CPU.
- Windows 95, Windows 98, Windows 2000, or Windows NT 4.0 installed.
- At least 32 MB of RAM.
- A minimum of 350 MB of disk storage space to install the JDK and the sample programs.
- A CD-ROM drive.
- A Windows-compatible monitor with at least 256 colors.

The software provided with this book is not compatible with the Mac OS, Linux, or other operating systems or non-PC hardware. However, the source files (extension .java) and the bytecode files (extension .class) should work in any Java implementation.

Installation Instructions

The sample programs are in the Samples directory on the CD-ROM. You may copy the entire directory to you hard disk drive or select individual subdirectories or programs and copy them as needed.

Please note: Files contained on a CD-ROM are usually tagged as read-only. This tag remains in effect when you copy directories or files to you hard drive. To edit or compile the Java source samples, proceed as follows:

- Using Windows Explorer, select the desired file or files by clicking the file-name. You can select more than one file by holding down the Ctrl key.
- Once you select the files, right click to display the dialog box. Then click the Properties button.
- De-select the Read-only attribute, and click the Apply button.

The directory named Self-Assessment Test contains the installation program Setup.exe. With the book's CD-ROM in the drive, open the Self-Assessment Test directory, and double-click the program icon for Setup to install the self-assessment software and to run the tests. The self-assessment software requires that the CD remain in the drive while the tests are running.

What You'll Find

The Samples directory contains subdirectories for each session with sample programs. These are:

Session 3

Session 6

Session 7

Session 8

Session 9

Session 10

Session 12

Session 13

Session 14

Session 15

Session 16

Session 17

Session 18

Session 19

Session 20

Session 21

Session 22

Session 23

Session 26

Session 27

Each directory is self-sufficient; each contains all software and support files necessary for executing the samples.

Directory names are chosen for clarity. However, DOS mangles filenames that contain spaces or more than eight characters. If you intend to work with these directories, it may be a good idea to rename them with shorter names. For example, you can rename the directory Session 10 Sess10 so that it is listed literally while in a DOS session.

The Self-Assessment Test directory contains test software and data files. Their purpose is to help you determine how much you have learned from this book and to help you identify sessions you may need to study more, as well those you can skip.

Index

Symbols and Numerics

Continued

IDG Books Worldwide, Inc.
End-User License Agreement

READ THIS. You should carefully read these terms and conditions before opening the software packet(s) included with this book ("Book"). This is a license agreement ("Agreement") between you and IDG Books Worldwide, Inc. ("IDGB"). By opening the accompanying software packet(s), you acknowledge that you have read and accept the following terms and conditions. If you do not agree and do not want to be bound by such terms and conditions, promptly return the Book and the unopened software packet(s) to the place you obtained them for a full refund.

1. **License Grant.** IDGB grants to you (either an individual or entity) a nonexclusive license to use one copy of the enclosed software program(s) (collectively, the "Software") solely for your own personal or business purposes on a single computer (whether a standard computer or a workstation component of a multiuser network). The Software is in use on a computer when it is loaded into temporary memory (RAM) or installed into permanent memory (hard disk, CD-ROM, or other storage device). IDGB reserves all rights not expressly granted herein.

2. **Ownership.** IDGB is the owner of all right, title, and interest, including copyright, in and to the compilation of the Software recorded on the disk(s) or CD-ROM ("Software Media"). Copyright to the individual programs recorded on the Software Media is owned by the author or other authorized copyright owner of each program. Ownership of the Software and all proprietary rights relating thereto remain with IDGB and its licensers.

3. **Restrictions On Use and Transfer.**

    (a) You may only (i) make one copy of the Software for backup or archival purposes, or (ii) transfer the Software to a single hard disk, provided that you keep the original for backup or archival purposes. You may not (i) rent or lease the Software, (ii) copy or reproduce the Software through a LAN or other network system or through any computer subscriber system or bulletin-board system, or (iii) modify, adapt, or create derivative works based on the Software.

    (b) You may not reverse engineer, decompile, or disassemble the Software. You may transfer the Software and user documentation on a permanent basis, provided that the transferee agrees to accept the terms and conditions of this Agreement and you retain no copies. If the

Software is an update or has been updated, any transfer must include the most recent update and all prior versions.

4. **Restrictions on Use of Individual Programs.** You must follow the individual requirements and restrictions detailed for each individual program in Appendix B of this Book. These limitations are also contained in the individual license agreements recorded on the Software Media. These limitations may include a requirement that after using the program for a specified period of time, the user must pay a registration fee or discontinue use. By opening the Software packet(s), you will be agreeing to abide by the licenses and restrictions for these individual programs that are detailed in Appendix B and on the Software Media. None of the material on this Software Media or listed in this Book may ever be redistributed, in original or modified form, for commercial purposes.

5. **Limited Warranty.**

   (a) IDGB warrants that the Software and Software Media are free from defects in materials and workmanship under normal use for a period of sixty (60) days from the date of purchase of this Book. If IDGB receives notification within the warranty period of defects in materials or workmanship, IDGB will replace the defective Software Media.

   (b) **IDGB AND THE AUTHORS OF THE BOOK DISCLAIM ALL OTHER WARRANTIES, EXPRESS OR IMPLIED, INCLUDING WITHOUT LIMITATION IMPLIED WARRANTIES OF MERCHANTABILITY AND FITNESS FOR A PARTICULAR PURPOSE, WITH RESPECT TO THE SOFTWARE, THE PROGRAMS, THE SOURCE CODE CONTAINED THEREIN, AND/OR THE TECHNIQUES DESCRIBED IN THIS BOOK. IDGB DOES NOT WARRANT THAT THE FUNCTIONS CONTAINED IN THE SOFTWARE WILL MEET YOUR REQUIREMENTS OR THAT THE OPERATION OF THE SOFTWARE WILL BE ERROR FREE.**

   (c) This limited warranty gives you specific legal rights, and you may have other rights that vary from jurisdiction to jurisdiction.

6. **Remedies.**

   (a) IDGB's entire liability and your exclusive remedy for defects in materials and workmanship shall be limited to replacement of the Software Media, which may be returned to IDGB with a copy of your receipt at the following address: Software Media Fulfillment Department, Attn.: *Java™ 2 Weekend Crash Course™*, IDG Books Worldwide, Inc., 10475 Crosspoint Blvd., Indianapolis, IN 46256, or call 1-800-762-2974. Please allow three to four weeks for delivery. This

Limited Warranty is void if failure of the Software Media has resulted from accident, abuse, or misapplication. Any replacement Software Media will be warranted for the remainder of the original warranty period or thirty (30) days, whichever is longer.

(b) In no event shall IDGB or the authors be liable for any damages whatsoever (including without limitation damages for loss of business profits, business interruption, loss of business information, or any other pecuniary loss) arising from the use of or inability to use the Book or the Software, even if IDGB has been advised of the possibility of such damages.

(c) Because some jurisdictions do not allow the exclusion or limitation of liability for consequential or incidental damages, the above limitation or exclusion may not apply to you.

7. **U.S. Government Restricted Rights.** Use, duplication, or disclosure of the Software by the U.S. Government is subject to restrictions stated in paragraph (c)(1)(ii) of the Rights in Technical Data and Computer Software clause of DFARS 252.227-7013, and in subparagraphs (a) through (d) of the Commercial Computer — Restricted Rights clause at FAR 52.227-19, and in similar clauses in the NASA FAR supplement, when applicable.

8. **General.** This Agreement constitutes the entire understanding of the parties and revokes and supersedes all prior agreements, oral or written, between them and may not be modified or amended except in a writing signed by both parties hereto that specifically refers to this Agreement. This Agreement shall take precedence over any other documents that may be in conflict herewith. If any one or more provisions contained in this Agreement are held by any court or tribunal to be invalid, illegal, or otherwise unenforceable, each and every other provision shall remain in full force and effect.

my2cents.idgbooks.com

Register This Book — And Win!

Visit **http://my2cents.idgbooks.com** to register this book and we'll automatically enter you in our fantastic monthly prize giveaway. It's also your opportunity to give us feedback: let us know what you thought of this book and how you would like to see other topics covered.

Discover IDG Books Online!

The IDG Books Online Web site is your online resource for tackling technology — at home and at the office. Frequently updated, the IDG Books Online Web site features exclusive software, insider information, online books, and live events!

10 Productive & Career-Enhancing Things You Can Do at www.idgbooks.com

- Nab source code for your own programming projects.

- Download software.

- Read Web exclusives: special articles and book excerpts by IDG Books Worldwide authors.

- Take advantage of resources to help you advance your career as a Novell or Microsoft professional.

- Buy IDG Books Worldwide titles or find a convenient bookstore that carries them.

- Register your book and win a prize.

- Chat live online with authors.

- Sign up for regular e-mail updates about our latest books.

- Suggest a book you'd like to read or write.

- Give us your 2¢ about our books and about our Web site.

You say you're not on the Web yet? It's easy to get started with IDG Books' *Discover the Internet,* available at local retailers everywhere.

CD-ROM Installation Instructions

The sample programs are contained in the Samples directory in the CD-ROM. You may copy the entire directory onto you hard disk drive or select individual sub-directories or programs and copy them as needed.

The directory named Self-Assessment Test contains the installation program Setup_st.exe. With the book's CD-ROM in the drive, open the Self-Assessment Test directory and double-yclick on the program icon for Setup_st to install the self-assessment software and run the tests. The self-assessment software requires that the CD-ROM remain in the drive while the tests are running.